School of American Research
Advanced Seminar Series

DOUGLAS W. SCHWARTZ, GENERAL EDITOR

SCHOOL OF AMERICAN RESEARCH
ADVANCED SEMINAR SERIES

Reconstructing Prehistoric Pueblo Societies
EDITED BY WILLIAM A. LONGACRE

New Perspectives on the Pueblos
EDITED BY ALFONSO ORTIZ

Structure and Process in Latin America
EDITED BY ARNOLD STRICKON AND SIDNEY M. GREENFIELD

The Classic Maya Collapse
EDITED BY T. PATRICK CULBERT

Methods and Theories of Anthropological Genetics
EDITED BY M. H. CRAWFORD AND P. L. WORKMAN

Sixteenth-Century Mexico
EDITED BY MUNRO S. EDMONSON

Ancient Civilization and Trade
EDITED BY JEREMY A. SABLOFF AND C. C. LAMBERG-KARLOVSKY

Photography in Archaeological Research
EDITED BY ELMER HARP, JR.

Meaning in Anthropology
EDITED BY KEITH H. BASSO AND HENRY A. SELBY

Meaning in Anthropology

Advanced Seminars are made possible
by a gift in recognition of

PHILIP L. SHULTZ

for his efforts on behalf of
the School of American Research

MEANING
IN ANTHROPOLOGY

EDITED BY

KEITH H. BASSO

AND

HENRY A. SELBY

A SCHOOL OF AMERICAN RESEARCH BOOK

UNIVERSITY OF NEW MEXICO PRESS · Albuquerque

A0173

Foreword

The symbolic character of cultural phenomena is of greater interest today than at any other time in the history of anthropology. It is appropriate, therefore, that the seminar from which this volume developed explored meaning and its relationship to cultural symbols, theories of language, belief systems, thinking, the concept of culture, and the "native's point of view" and its manifestations in speech and social learning and kinship. As Keith Basso says in his thorough introduction, "the idea of meaning provides . . . an effective conceptual rallying point for much that is new and exciting in anthropology." These papers, written prior to the seminar and revised following exhaustive discussion, are unique in the intensity with which they approach this topic of critical current interest.

Beginning with Michael Silverstein's "pragmatic" model for speech analysis and the importance of recognizing a plurality of sign functions for the understanding of meaning, the book proceeds to consider from various perspectives the types of messages that can be and are relayed by a variety of behavioral acts and cultural symbols. Harold W. Scheffler argues for the merits of the distinctive feature model of lexical meaning, and, with it, critically evaluates David M. Schneider's work on American kinship. Basso, analyzing Western Apache metaphors, discusses the inadequacies of transformational grammars in their failure to explain the production and interpretation of figurative speech and presents his views on how the study of metaphors can provide a deeper appreciation of linguistic creativity.

Susan Ervin-Tripp, focusing on the social function of the "alternative ways to say the same thing" in English, sees one of the important functions of symbolic diversity as providing continuous information to participants regarding their interacting roles. Roy G. D'Andrade, through the examination of middle-class American beliefs about illness and disease, considers the use of cultural knowledge in the production of inferences and decisions. Fadwa El Guindi and Henry A. Selby examine Zapotec symbols of personal identity occurring in opposition and provide an entree into the conceptual foundation of the culture of these residents of the Valley of Oaxaca. David Schneider looks at "meaning-in-action" from an integrated theory of culture and behavior. Finally, in a delightfully written overview of the "senses of selfhood" with reference to the Balinese, Javanese, and Moroccans, Clifford Geertz considers the anthropologist's approach to the native's versions of reality.

In his chapter on Western Apache "wise words" Basso says that the use of these metaphors is associated with "adult men and women who have gained a reputation for balanced thinking, critical acumen, and extensive cultural knowledge." This description also could be applied to the contributors to this volume, who have used existing structures of thought on meaning and cultural symbols and have creatively forged new ones.

Douglas W. Schwartz

School of American Research

Preface

This volume is the result of a conference held on the days of March 18–22, 1974 at the School of American Research in Santa Fe, New Mexico. The conference was designed to bring together anthropologists whose interest in the study of meaning and cultural symbols was well established, but whose ideas on the subject were sufficiently different to preclude redundancy and guarantee discussion and debate. Each participant was invited to present a paper that described his or her views, illustrating them, where appropriate, with analyses of ethnographic data. In this way, we hoped to see more clearly what our differences were, and how, if at all, they could be usefully reconciled. Simultaneously, we hoped to identify fresh theoretical strategies for future research. Our expectations were not disappointed.

Ten scholars attended the conference: Michael Silverstein (University of Chicago); Harold W. Scheffler (Yale University); Keith H. Basso (University of Arizona); Susan Ervin-Tripp (University of California, Berkeley); Roy G. D'Andrade (University of California, San Diego); Henry A. Selby (Temple University); David M. Schneider (University of Chicago); Clifford Geertz (The Institute for Advanced Study, Princeton); Elli Kongas Maranda (University of British Columbia); and Ira R. Buchler (University of Texas). All the participants have contributed papers to this anthology except for Maranda and Buchler, whose essays, regrettably, were too lengthy to be included.

The conference at Santa Fe, as well as this book, would never have materialized without the generosity and cooperation of Douglas W. Schwartz, Director of the School of American Research. From start to finish, Dr. Schwartz provided support, encouragement, and substantial amounts of helpful advice. His hospitality, as consistently warm as it was apparently boundless, brightened our days in Santa Fe and made us feel completely at home. We are truly indebted to him and offer him our sincerest thanks. We are also grateful to members of the staff at the School of American Research: Harry King, David Noble, and especially Ella Schroeder, whose graciousness and unfailing good cheer added immeasurably to the pleasantness of our stay. The School of American Research affords an ideal setting for the exchange of ideas, and we responded to it by talking . . . and talking . . . and talking.

At the University of Arizona, where the manuscript was prepared for publication, Carrie Zwerg performed a heroic job of typing and Cherie Scheik did yeoman service in pursuing elusive bibliographic references and attending to other details. In other ways, equally important but somewhat less tangible, we were aided and assisted by Ellen B. Basso, Hermann K. Bleibtreu, and Raymond H. Thompson. At the University of New Mexico Press, Elizabeth Heist brought the book to its final form with skill, precision, and sensitivity. To all, our gratitude and appreciation.

Finally, and here we speak just for ourselves, we thank our colleagues who joined us in New Mexico. Had it not been for their interest and enthusiasm our own would have gone for naught.

Keith H. Basso
Henry A. Selby

Contents

Figures

Tables

1
Introduction

KEITH H. BASSO
University of Arizona
HENRY A. SELBY
Temple University

The reader familiar with recent developments in cultural anthropology will probably see that the title of this volume is open to at least two interpretations. And he or she, having also noticed that those interpretations conflict with one another, might suspect that a deliberate attempt was being made to highlight a paradox. The suspicion would be correct.

On the one hand, our title implies that a concern with the analysis of meaning, or, more exactly, with cultural symbols and how and what they signify, has come to occupy a prominent place within the discipline —prominent enough, at least, to be distinguishable from other concerns, to be recognized as the motivating force behind a number of influential studies and ideas, and, perhaps most obvious of all, to be representative of "current anthropological interests" in a genuine and nontrivial sense. All this is true. At no time in the history of anthropology has interest in the symbolic character of cultural phenomena been more clearly pronounced than during the last two decades; and at no time has it been pursued more skillfully or with such provocative results. So fundamental, in fact, has the concern with meaning become that it now underlies whole conceptions of culture, conceptions which are explicitly grounded in the premise that the semiotic dimension of human affairs—the full array of signs and concepts men use to communicate with each other and to interpret themselves and the world around them—should be the central object of description and analysis.

On the other hand, our title could be taken to mean that anthropologists have developed a uniform approach to the study of meaning, an "official paradigm," so to speak, that serves by unanimous consent as the guiding framework for all investigations of symbolic forms. This is not true. Such a paradigm has not been formulated and for this reason a unitary "Anthropological Study of Meaning" does not yet exist. What we have instead is a variety of approaches—"partial paradigms" they might be called—that have proven useful in illuminating certain aspects of meaning systems but have not been successfully fitted together to form a logically articulated whole. Consequently, one cannot point to an all-embracing "Anthropological Theory of Meaning"; at present there are only theories of meaning that have been proposed and applied by anthropologists. The paradox alluded to earlier should now be clear: whereas the analysis of meaning has become an integral part of modern anthropology, modern anthropologists have still to fashion an integrated set of analytical principles that all agree upon and accept as necessary and satisfactory.

The concept of meaning is nothing if not encompassing, and, as the essays in this volume illustrate, it lends itself easily to different interpretations at different levels of specificity and abstraction. Consequently, it can be—and is—used to pose a variety of questions. What, for example, is the relationship of meaning to language? Is it the meaning of words in isolation we want to understand, or the meanings of whole sentences, or the messages conveyed by the way words and sentences are used in conversation? What is the relationship of meaning to thought? In other words, how do the conceptual categories labeled by cultural symbols get organized in the mind, and what can such organizations tell us about principles of human cognition? Nonverbal actions are immensely symbolic—but how? What is signified by the way the members of a society arrange themselves in space, or hold themselves while dancing, or sit down to eat in the presence of a mother-in-law? And

Introduction

why should man's habitat be neglected? Complex meanings are attached to colors, sounds, odors, and innumerable physical and nonphysical objects. What is the relationship of meaning to environment? Matters become more complicated when we consider activities involving large numbers of people and dozens of separate symbols. Yet surely we can talk about the meaning of a Hopi kachina dance, a Bach fugue, or a heavyweight championship bout. We can even talk about the meaning of Watergate, abstract expressionism, and the Weimar Republic.

In the face of such an impossibly large universe, the reader may wonder what sort of intellectual fabric holds studies of meaning in anthropology together. In what sense can these studies be said to share what one philosopher has called a "shaping comomn denominator"? The answer to this question—or at least the most obvious answer—lies in a set of assumptions about the nature of culture and the aims of ethnography.

For in the broadest sense, where does ethnography begin if not in a disciplined attempt to discover and describe the symbolic resources with which the members of a society conceptualize and interpret their experience? And why else, if not in an effort to gain access to these conceptualizations and interpretations, to grasp, however obliquely, the "native point of view," do we struggle with difficult languages, describe events we do not at first (and sometimes never) fully comprehend, and spend countless hours questioning native consultants about everything from plural suffixes to ancestor worship? Why indeed, if not to construct a theory of the way in which a particular version of being human—a particular culture—a particular system of symbols—confers order, coherence, and significance upon a people, their surroundings, and the workings of their universe. Constructing such a theory is not all there is to good ethnography, but it is certainly an important part. And it leads to an inescapable conclusion: The study of culture necessarily entails the study of meaning.

This view of culture and cultural analysis does not imply, as some critics have charged, that ethnographers are uninterested in what takes place in the realm of observable behavior. On the contrary, an understanding of behavior is essential. The critical question is, What is necessary to understand it? If we assume that behavior is a form of symbolic action and therefore that it is unfailingly communicative, it stands to reason that some kind of theory is required to inform us *how* it is communicative. In very simple terms, what is needed is a theory of what kinds of messages are—and can be—conveyed by what kinds of behavioral acts. Such a theory is fundamental because without it we have no principled basis for assigning meaning to acts of behavior or determining their significance. A theory of culture provides such a basis by making explicit the information necessary to construct "readings" of behavior which, assuming they are good ones, our native consultants can recognize as being rooted in appropriate interpretations of symbolic phenomena that they themselves consider important. And how can the appropriateness of our readings be assessed—and the validity of our theory be tested—if we do not pay careful attention to behavior, the very thing we are trying to read? To repeat: Ethnographers concerned with the symbolic content of culture do not ignore behavior; they try as best they can to formulate theories of what behavior means.

It is important to understand that the theories formulated by ethnographers are inevitably their own and not those of native consultants. This point has sometimes been misunderstood, and a brief word of clarification may be helpful. As previously stated, a theory of a culture necessarily involves an attempt to explain how some set of things have —or can have—meaning for the members of a society. As such it is not to be confused either with the meanings of the things or the things that have meaning. This much is obvious. But neither is it to be confused with how these things and meanings are *represented* by our consultants —how they are produced, identified, enacted, depicted, portrayed, described, or even written down. No matter how closely the ethnographer's theory follows upon native representations (and for certain purposes one can argue the closer the better), it is not isomorphic with them; it is not native reality. For at some point—actually at many, many points —the ethnographer must step back, turn analyst, and, using concepts and principles alien to the culture he is studying, perform an act of interpretation. In so doing, he translates a collection of native representations from one system of meaning (theirs) into another (his own), thereby transforming them into a new and wholly distinct representation. This representation—the ethnographer's theory—is inevitably a second-order representation; it is a representation of representations.

Although models for the analysis of meaning have become fairly plentiful in recent years, none have been applied more extensively than those derived from the study of language. This was not always the case. As late as 1952 no less an authority than Roman Jakobson (1971:556) was compelled to remind an audience of eminent linguists and anthropologists that ". . . the basic, the primary, the most important semiotic system is language: language really is the foundation of culture." More significantly, Jakobson took this same occasion to issue an emphatic call for intensive work in semantics, an area of linguistics which up to that point had been seriously neglected:

> Linguists [have done] their utmost to exclude meaning and any appeal to meaning from linguistics. Thus, meaning remains a no man's land. This game of give-away must end. For years and decades we have fought for the annexation of speech sounds to linguistics, and thereby established phonemics. Now we face a second front—the task of incorporating meaning into the science of language (1971:567).

There is no need to recount all that has happened in linguistics and cultural anthropology since 1952; suffice it to say that in both disciplines the game of giveaway has come to an end and semantics is a no-man's-land no more. One could hardly ask for better evidence of this than the essay by Michael Silverstein that opens the present collection. Dedicated to Roman Jakobson and pursuant upon lines of inquiry that Jakobson initiated, Silverstein's paper proceeds from the premise that a satisfactory understanding of meaning in speech depends upon the recognition of a plurality of sign functions or "modes of signification." By means of a detailed analysis of these functions, especially shifters and indexes, Silverstein develops a "pragmatic" model for speech analysis that contrasts in important ways with other current approaches. The significance of Silverstein's work extends well beyond language per se for, as he himself points out, a systematic pragmatics could have far-reaching implications for a clearer conceptualization of the linkage between language and culture.

The distinctive-feature model of lexical meaning has been the subject of considerable debate in recent years, and few have defended it more persistently—or applied it to a larger number of actual cases—than Harold W. Scheffler. In his contribution to this volume Scheffler argues the merits of the model once again, simultaneously providing a detailed and sweeping critique of David Schneider's work on American kinship. Scheffler and Schneider differ on a number of points, but the major one

5

concerns a question of structural and analytical priorities. Scheffler's position is that distinctive features (which in the case of kinship categories are genealogical components) are structurally prior to nondistinctive features, and therefore that the former define primary meanings. Schneider's position is that distinctive and nondistinctive features exist on a structural par, and that neither set can be assigned priority except in terms of some specified social context. For Schneider it is context that determines which meanings are primary, not the logical relationships among kinship categories.

In an essay centering upon an analysis of Western Apache metaphors Keith H. Basso finds that semantic theories currently employed by transformational grammarians are inadequate to explain the ability of human beings to produce and interpret figurative speech. After illustrating the premise that the successful interpretation of Apache metaphors entails the formation of at least one unitary concept of meaning, Basso goes on to show that these concepts are not lexically coded in the Western Apache language. On the basis of this finding, together with evidence drawn from other sources, he argues that the discovery of meaning in metaphor rests on the exercise of a genuinely creative skill—the ability to form novel semantic categories. Such an ability is not accounted for in transformational models of language, and Basso concludes by discussing the implications of this deficiency for the revision of key concepts in linguistics and the construction of an adequate theory of communicative competence.

Susan Ervin-Tripp is also concerned with communicative competence, particularly as it manifests itself in what she has termed "systems of alternations." These systems are identified from the fact that the same communicative intent (for example, giving an order) can be realized in speech in very different ways—so different, in fact, that the variants may exhibit no syntactic or lexical similarity at all. Why should such diversity exist, how can it be explained, and above all, what functions does it serve? Ervin-Tripp answers these questions through a careful study of how speakers of American English accomplish directives. She discovers that selections from this system are made according to the social attributes of participants in speech events, and therefore that the meaning of any particular directive consists in part of the information it conveys about the relationship of speaker to hearer. The primary functions of alternation systems, Ervin-Tripp suggests, are to remind participants continuously of their relationships to one another, while also providing an instructional milieu in which children, by seeking explanations for linguistic variation, can learn the major features of adult social structures.

Ervin-Tripp's interest in the acquisition of sociolinguistic rules reflects the view of many ethnographers that culture is essentially a learned phenomenon and, as such, embodies a complex cognitive dimension that warrants careful study. A good example of this approach and where it has led is provided by Roy G. D'Andrade's chapter on middle-class American beliefs about illness and disease. The main purpose of D'Andrade's contribution is to compare two types of models that have been used to represent and analyze cognitive systems. One type is based on the techniques of multidimensional scaling and corresponds to a quantified version of the distinctive feature model mentioned earlier; the other type, which D'Andrade demonstrates to be the more versatile, is based on a propositional analysis of subset-superset relations. D'Andrade discusses his findings in terms of their relevance to recent work in ethnographic semantics which, he believes, has focused too much on problems of classification and not enough on how cultural knowledge is used to make inferences and decisions.

In a chapter dealing with Zapotec symbols of personal identity, social relationships, and moral categories, Fadwa El Guindi and Henry A. Selby take an approach that draws upon recent work in dialectics. Their interpretation, which places primary emphasis upon the process of mediation, yields a conception in which the meanings of cultural symbols are seen to be "located in," and thus to be discoverable through analyses of, their relationships in dialectical series. After discussing the identifying characteristics of mediating categories, El Guindi and Selby go on to consider the vital role such categories play in providing belief systems with the openness and flexibility necessary to accommodate novel and/or anomalous events. Ultimately, then, El Guindi and Selby are concerned with productivity in systems of belief and the adaptive functions served by the process of mediation.

The subject of David M. Schneider's chapter—an integrated theory of culture and behavior—will come as no surprise to anthropologists who have followed the development of his ideas during the last decade. Schneider's position is that a culture, which he defines simply as a system of symbols and meanings, can and should be studied *sui generis*.

However, he is keenly aware that unless such a view is modified it precludes analysis of behavioral data. Consequently, he distinguishes sharply between culture and norms, the latter being defined as shared moral propositions that operate as templates or patterns for social action. Having separated culture from norms, Schneider proceeds to show that the two are inextricably related and that analysis of one presupposes and requires analysis of the other. This involves him in a discussion of "cultural units," the organization of symbols into clusters or "galaxies," and finally the principles by means of which symbols are realized—through norms—in social action. Since social action is also symbolic action, the circle is complete, and the foundations are laid for a unified ethnographic description.

If there is one endeavor that underlies all the contributions to this volume it is the ethnographer's unceasing search for better methods with which to capture and describe the "native's point of view." In the final chapter, Clifford Geertz addresses himself to this issue, illustrating the principles he believes should guide the search with a comparative analysis of the concept of self as formulated and expressed in the cultures of Java, Bali, and Morocco. Geertz explains that since the ethnographer can never experience the native's point of view directly, the best he can do is learn as much as possible about what the natives perceive "with"— the full inventory of forms, concepts, and meanings that inform their version of reality. For Geertz, interpreting this reality involves a relentless yet delicate pitting of minute ethnographic details against the backdrop of whole civilizations and historical epochs, a thorough yet subtle exegesis of the dialogue between particular systems of cultural symbols and the universal existential conditions to which they impart significance. Geertz's approach, which, he emphasizes, owes much to Dilthey's conception of the hermeneutic circle, is similar to styles of interpretation found in philosophy, psychoanalysis, and the arts, and it is the aspect of his work—its catholic scope and far-flung complementarity—that has accounted for much of its appeal both within and outside anthropology.

The foregoing remarks, which are as unfortunately condensed as they are necessarily brief, may give the impression that the most notable aspect of the essays published here is their diversity. And diversity there certainly is. None of the chapters, nor the volume as a whole, purports to an overarching synthesis that solves all problems or joins all points

8

of view. But diversity need not be a sign of confusion, and neither need it signal the absence of shared concerns, those "shaping common denominators" we talked about before. This was confirmed again and again during our conference at the School of American Research. For there, comfortable, relaxed, and stimulated by the opportunity to engage in unfettered talk, our differences, though openly acknowledged and freely debated, frequently got lost in lively discussions of particular problems and issues. Happily, a number of these—reference, polysemy, productivity, metaphor, symbol use and symbol function, and, above all, cultural description—are discussed in several of the papers, thereby linking them and providing the collection with a real measure of integration.

But finally the book is about meaning. We have not tried to define meaning, nor did we attempt at the School of American Research to construct an adequate logico-deductive system in which meaning plays a central role equivalent to that of "energy" in classical physics. This analogy is not misplaced. For had physicists waited until an appropriate mathematics was available for the exploration of electromagnetic forces, then physical knowledge would have stayed its hand for many decades. Similarly, if we were to wait until a qualitative mathematics is devised for the full and proper axiomatization of a general theory of meaning, a great deal of necessary work would not get done. It may appear strange that one of our most central notions is not fully defined, but, as Alfred North Whitehead remarked, the last thing a science understands is what it is about.

The idea of meaning provides an apposite focus, an effective conceptual rallying point for much that is new and exciting in anthropology. For the idea of meaning is wide enough, yet pointed enough as well, to capture both the spirit and the major objectives of an entire conception of culture and cultural analysis. And if that conception is not yet fully developed, if at times it seems diffuse and a bit too widely ramified, it is nevertheless a richly productive one that has already demonstrated considerable utility. The prospect of making it better is a compelling one indeed. We believe the paradox can be resolved.

2

Shifters, Linguistic Categories, and Cultural Description[1]

MICHAEL SILVERSTEIN
University of Chicago

For Roman Jakobson

INTRODUCTION

This chapter will try to develop consequences of the statement that speech is meaningful social behavior. In itself, this statement is one of those set phrases of pidgin science that are used to ensure minimal trade relations in the contact community of linguists and social anthropologists. It gives us no analytic or descriptive power. What I wish to do here is demonstrate that we do, in fact, already have a full, subtle "language" with which to describe the elaborate meaning structures of speech behavior. It is a language that speaks of the "function" of signs, their modes of signification, distinguishing from among the types of sign functions *shifters* or *indexes*. The meaning of this functional sign mode always involves some aspect of the context in which the sign occurs. In making the nature of this involvement clearer, I hope to demonstrate that this "pragmatic" analysis of speech behavior—in the tradition extending from Peirce to Jakobson—allows us to describe the real linkage of language to culture, and perhaps the most important aspect of the "meaning" of speech.

At one level, language has long served anthropologists as a kind of exemplar for the nature of things cultural. It seems to display these "cultural" properties with clarity in the tangible medium of articulate phonetic speech. Thus, and at another level, could the analytic lessons of linguistics be transferred analogically to other social behavior, giving a kind of structuralized anthropology, or, more remarkably, could the actual linguistic (especially lexicographic) structures of language be called culture. I will be developing the argument that this received point of view is essentially wrong. That aspect of language which has traditionally been analyzed by linguists, and has served as model, is just the part that is functionally unique among the phenomena of culture. Hence the structural characteristics of language in this traditional view cannot really serve as a model for other aspects of culture, nor can the method of analysis. Further, linguistic (or lexicographical) structures that emerge from the traditional grammatical analysis must of necessity bear a problematic, rather than isomorphic, relationship to the structure of culture.

LINGUISTIC AND OTHER COMMUNICATION

To say of social behavior that it is meaningful implies necessarily that it is communicative, that is, that the behavior is a complex of signs (sign vehicles) that signal, or stand for, something in some respect. Such behavioral signs are significant to some persons, participants in a communicative event, and such behavior is purposive, that is, goal oriented in the sense of accomplishing (or in failing to accomplish) certain ends of communication, for example, indicating one's social rank, reporting an occurrence, effecting a cure for a disease, and so forth. In general, then, we can say that people are constituted as a society with a certain *culture* to the extent that they share the same means of social communication.

Language as a system of communication has the same characteristics as the rest of culture. So in order to distinguish analytic subparts of culture, such as language, we have traditionally distinguished among types of communicative events on the basis of the signaling medium. In the case of language, the signaling medium is articulate speech, and events can be isolated on this basis.

Speech Events

By such analysis, a *speech event,* endowed with an overt goal in a socially shared system of such purposive functions, consists of some sequence of speech behaviors in which some speaker or speakers signal to some hearer or hearers by means of a system of phonetic sign vehicles called speech messages or utterances. The utterances are organized into a system for the participants by virtue of their knowledge of a linguistic code, or grammar. The speech event takes place with the participants in given positions, or loci, and over a certain span of time. The roles of speaker and hearer may be taken by different individuals during the course of such an event. Many other characteristics of such speech events must also be taken into consideration, among them the other sociological aspects of the individuals in the roles of speaker and hearer, which are frequently salient in defining the event, the prior speech events (if any), the gestural or kinesic communication that invariably accompanies spoken language, the distinction between roles of hearer and audience, and so forth. A description of the speech event must minimally take into account these fundamental defining variables.

Speech events so defined, moreover, are cooccurrent with events based on distinct signaling media, and these together make up large-scale cultural routines. Descriptively, the simplest speech events would be those which themselves constituted the entire goal-directed social behavior. It is doubtful that such events exist. In our own culture, reading a scholarly paper can come close to being a speech event pure and simple, the purpose of which is expressible in terms of informative discourse among social categories of scholars. The possibility of distinct forms of symbolism that can be involved in these events is not at issue. I am dealing here only with the purposive nature of the speech event in a system of social action. The more embedded speech events are those which are part of such large-scale cultural enterprises as complex rituals including speech, song, dance, dress, etc., where the meaning of the speech behavior in the speech events is usually integrally linked to the presence of these other signaling media. Analytically, the problem of trying to give the meanings of signals in such a situation is very complex.

Referential Speech Events

But the ultimate justification for the segmentation of speech from other signaling media lies in one of the purposive uses that seems to distinguish speech behavior from all other communicative events, the function of *pure reference*, or, in terms more culturally bound than philosophical, the function of description or "telling about." The referential function of speech can be characterized as communication by propositions—predications descriptive of states of affairs—subject to verification in some cases of objects and events, taken as representations of truth in others. Reference so characterized is a communicative event, and the utterances of referential discourse are made up of sign units in grammatical arrangements, the meaning of the whole being a descriptive or referring proposition. It is this referential function of speech, and its characteristic sign mode, the semantico-referential sign, that has formed the basis for linguistic theory and linguistic analysis in the Western tradition.

Referential Linguistic Categories

All linguistic analysis of the traditional sort proceeds on the basis of the contribution of elements of utterances to the referential or denotative value of the whole. And it is on this basis that the traditional segmentation, description, and definition of all *linguistic categories* is made. Our standard ideas about the significant segmentation of utterances all rest on sameness or difference of utterances in terms of referring or describing propositions, coded in speech. Plural vs. singular "number," for example, as a pure referential linguistic category, can be analyzed by the contribution of such markers to propositions describing more-than-one vs. not-more-than-one entity. In English, this is illustrated by *The boys run* vs. *The boy runs*, where noun suffixed with -s and unsuffixed verb signal the category of plural-number subject, and unsuffixed noun and verb suffixed with -s signal the category of singular-number subject. Thus we segment $-s]_N$ $-\emptyset]_V$: $-\emptyset]_N$ $-s]_V$. Durative or progressive vs. punctual "aspect" as a pure referential category contributes to propositions describing events as continuous or ongoing (where they are not necessarily so) vs. momentaneous or complete. In English, this is illustrated by *The boy was jumping* vs. *The boy jumped*, with segmentation *be(-ed)* -*ing*]$_V$: Ø   (-*ed*)]$_V$, *be + ed* represented by *was*.

Any form of grammatical analysis in this referential mode, from Greco-Roman to transformational-generative, defines the signs, the categories, and their rules of combination and arrangement in this fashion. All of our analytic techniques and formal descriptive machinery have been designed for referential signs, which contribute to referential utterances in referential speech events. (We shall see below that certain among the referential categories cause difficulties with this whole approach.) When we speak of linguistic categories, we mean categories of this referential kind; hence one of the principal reasons social functions of speech have not been built into our analyses of language: the sign modes of most of what goes on in the majority of speech events are not referential.

Semantics and Linguistic Analysis

The study of the "meaning" of linguistic signs is usually called semantics. It is clear from the way I have characterized traditional linguistic investigation, however, that the actual object of study of semantics has been the referential meanings of utterances, of the words and categories and arrangements in terms of which we can analyze them. For the purposes of this chapter, the term will be restricted in this way, so that semantics is the study of pure referential meaning, embodied in propositions coded by speech. This property of speech, abstract reference or description, can be called its *semanticity*.

From an operational point of view, all grammatical analysis of the traditional sort depends on this semanticity. To be able to analyze linguistic categories, we must be able to give evidence about the semantic relations of parts of sentences. We must ultimately be able to say, in other words, whether or not a certain stretch of language is semantically equivalent, within the grammar, to some other stretch of language. By determining such equivalence relations, we can build up a notion of defining, or *glossing*, certain grammatical stretches of a language in terms of others. But glossing is itself a referential speech event.

Metasemantics

Glossing speech events take language itself, in particular the semantics of language, as the referent, or object of description. These events use language to describe the semantics of language, and are thus *metasemantic* referential speech events. Such metasemantic speech events are the basis of all grammatical analysis and description, and hence of all semantic description as well. They are the basic activity of the traditional linguistics, which may be seen as the discovery of the glosses of a language, of the class of all possible metasemantic speech events in the language. Leonard Bloomfield's (1933) "fundamental postulate" is essentially one about the semantic and formal equivalence of certain sentences that underlie utterances within a speech community. Similarly, such semantic equivalence at the level of phrases and sentences has become the stock-in-trade of the transformational grammarian, who postulates a common "underlying" structure for semantically equivalent "surface" syntactic arrangements.

But it is interesting that metasemantic speech events are a natural occurrence in everyday speech, a culturally learned speech function. In our society, parents are constantly glossing words for children by using grammatically complex but semantically equivalent expressions, expressions that make the same contribution to reference of utterances as the glossed items.

The metasemantic property of language, the property that makes semantic analysis (and hence semantically based grammar) possible, is the one that is unique to language, and upon which rests the speech function of pure reference. It is what makes language unique among all the cultural codes for social communication. Anthropologists have long analyzed ritual, myth, or other media of social behavior as making symbolic statements about categories of social structure. But of what medium other than referential speech can we say that the behavioral signs can describe the meanings of the signs themselves? There are no naturally occurring "metamythic" events in the same way that there are metalinguistic ones, nor "metaritualistic" events with the same functional possibilities. It is in other functional properties of language, which can be exploited in speech events, that the commonalty of language and many other cultural media lies.

Simultaneous Nonreferential Functions

Speech events that do not have referential functions accomplish socially constituted ends comparable to those of nonspeech events. For example, it is frequently through speech that we set social boundaries on an interaction, rather than through the physical separation of participants. To characterize such behavior abstractly, we note that we can choose the language in which we speak so as to preclude comprehension on the part of some individuals present; we can use a language all understand, but with pronominal markers that make the intended boundaries of participation clear; we can use phraseology only some can understand; we can spell out the written representations of words in the presence of those illiterate in some written language; and so forth. This purposive privacy function of the speech behavior is simultaneous with, but analytically distinct from, whatever referential function there is in the event for speaker and intended hearer(s), for only they participate in those roles in the referential communication.

One of the most interesting aspects of speech behavior, in fact, is this multifunctionality of what appear to be utterances in sequence, the traditionally recognized referential nature of some parts of utterances seeming to have intercalated many other functional elements simultaneously. From the point of view of the traditional semantico-referential linguistics, these other functional modes of language use seem to be "riding on" descriptive propositions. But this is a rather limited point of view. For it takes considerable analysis of the use of such speech itself to characterize what is going on in such cases as those given above. The only behavioral data are the speech signals themselves. To say, for example, that the speaker is using a different "language," just in the semantico-referential sense, presupposes a grammatical description of each of the distinct referential media, and hence presupposes the isolation of the referential function of speech in two distinct systems of semantic signals. So the functional analysis of a given use of speech behavior requires that we can contrast signs, all other things remaining the same. From the point of view of functional analysis, then, we must make sophisticated hypotheses of *isofunctionality*, or comparability of function of the signaling media, before any structural description is justifiable.

Reference and "Performative" Speech

Just like reference, however, other uses of speech get some socially constituted "work" done; they accomplish or "perform" something, whether achieving privacy, as in the example above, or marking the social status of the participants, or making a command for someone to do something, or effecting a permanent change in social status, for example, marrying two people or knighting someone.

Much recent analysis has been focused on this performative aspect of language use, in what I have here termed purposive or functional speech events. Following upon the work of Austin, some have distinguished between "performative" aspects of speech and the "semantic" content (the term not rigorously circumscribed as it is here). Others, particularly the philosopher Searle (1969), have distinguished "speech acts" represented by utterances as distinct from their propositional content. (It is somewhat unfortunate, by the way, that "speech act" has been used as a term for the level of purposive functional speech events, since I will be using it in another sense below.)

All these approaches, in other words, start with a basically semantico-referential linguistic analysis from which the linguistic categories, the grammatical arrangements, etc., emerge in the traditional way. They tack onto this analysis a description of how these semantico-referential categories can be "used" performatively. This approach entirely misses the point that referential speech events are, a fortiori, speech events, endowed with the same kind of purposefulness as other speech events. Reference is one kind of linguistic performance among many. The linguistic categories that emerge from analysis of speech in the semantico-referential modes are not necessarily the same as those that emerge from other functional modes, and it is presumptuous to speak of arrangements of a basically propositional nature being "used" in other ways.

The physical signals of distinct functional modes of speech may be partially alike, since they seem to be superimposed in the same formal utterances, but the meanings, in this larger sense of functional cultural meanings, are different, and hence we have distinct signs. The priority of reference in establishing linguistic categories and structure rests

18

squarely on the manipulability of this mode by the metalinguistic property. But reference itself is just one, perhaps actually a minor one, among the "performative" or "speech act" functions of speech. We do not use basically "descriptive" linguistic structure to accomplish other communicative goals; description happens to be one of those goals, one that overlaps in formal structure of signals with other functional ends.

Abbreviatory Extensions

In certain cases, of course, the extension of descriptive referential language to other performative uses is patent. One such class of events is conversational abbreviations used as requests. A statement to another person in a room with an open window such as "I'm cold" or "It's cold in here" could lead to a discussion until the interlocutor is asked to close the window and does so. Or, more naturally for sophisticated persons in our society, we can abbreviate, the statement itself leading to the accomplishment of the action.

Several subtypes of statements require such experience and deduction based on full forms of linguistic sequences. But such seemingly descriptive utterances used as abbreviatory request events are very circumscribed and constitute a level of delicacy of manipulatory signaling highly susceptible to failure. In general, the point holds that descriptive reference is one among the speech functions, not the basis for all others.

Pragmatic Meanings of Linguistic Signs

The linguistic signs that underlie utterances, then, appear in speech that serves many socially constituted functions. The *meanings* of such signs, as they emerge from grammatical analysis, are traditionally described in terms of their contribution to referring propositional speech, of necessity a partial description. The problem set for us when we consider the actual broader uses of language is to describe the total meaning of constituent linguistic signs, only part of which is semantic in our narrowed terminology. We must begin with the facts of purposive utterances in speech events, and isolate their several functions. The linguistic signs have distinct kinds of meanings which depend on their contribution to the several kinds of functional speech events we can isolate.

We can see in this way that while some linguistic signs have semantic meanings, contributing to reference, others have nonsemantic meanings, contributing to other distinct speech functions. In general, we can call the study of the meanings of linguistic signs relative to their communicative functions *pragmatics,* and these more broadly conceived meanings are then *pragmatic meanings.* Semantic meaning is, of course, in one sense a special form of pragmatic meaning, the mode of signification of signs that contributes to pure referential function. This fits exactly with the discovery that grammatical analysis of the traditional sort is equivalent to discovering the class of all possible metalinguistic or glossing referential speech events.

Pragmatic Categories

General pragmatic meaning of signs and more particular semantic meaning are largely superimposed in the formal signals of speech. In fact, there is a class of signs called *referential indexes,* to be characterized below, in which the two modes are linked in the same categories, segmentable and isolable simultaneously in at least two functional modes, one referential, one not. By examining only those categories that unite at least two functional modes in the same isolable speech fraction, for example an English deictic *this* or *that,* we might get the mistaken idea that the superimposition is always of discrete referential categories intercalated with otherwise functional ones. If speech consisted only of pure referential categories (which traditional linguistic theory postulates) and referential indexes, then all isolable segments would have semantic meanings, and some residual segments would have an additional pragmatic mode. This is false, as we shall see, since utterances include nonreferential and hence nonsemantic formal features.

It is thus possible to have entirely distinct analyses of the same overt speech material from different functional points of view. The linguistic signs that have various pragmatic meanings are only apparently represented at the "surface" of speech in continuous utterances. We may recall Victor Hugo's couplet, "Gal, amant de la Reine, alla (tour magnanime!) /Gallamment de l'arène à la Tour Magne à Nîmes." Analysis in general leads to this kind of superimposed structural heterogeneity, depending on the functional mode of the pragmatic meanings of utterances. Once we realize that distinct pragmatic meanings yield distinct analyses of utterances, we can sever our dependence on reference as the

controlling functional mode of speech, dictating our traditional seg-
mentations and recognition of categories. We can then concentrate on
the manifold social pragmatics that are common to language and every
other form of socially constituted communication in society.

THE NATURE OF LINGUISTIC SIGNS

Having discussed the framework of function in terms of which all
meaning is constituted, I shall turn now to an examination of the nature of the modes of signification of linguistic signs in utterances. By
means of the analysis of propositional content in the referential mode,
we will be able to see the limitations in principle of pure semantic grammatical approaches, and use the critical overlapping of functions in
referring indexes to motivate a separation of three principal classes of
sign modes. In particular, we can elaborate on the class of indexes,
which appear to give the key to the pragmatic description of language.

Utterance and Sentence, Message and Code

For purposes of semantico-referential description, all *utterances*, or
messages, in speech events are analyzed as instances of *sentences*. Such
sentences are constructed from a finite repertoire of elements according
to rules of arrangement, and express referential propositions. These constituents and the rules together constitute a *code* or *grammar* for the
language. We separate here, then, the several individual instances or
tokens occurring in actual speech from the semantico-grammatical *types*
or elements of sentences in a language, which these instances are said to
represent in speech.

In a given speech event, an utterance or message occurs in context.
The traditional grammatical analysis of such utterances, however, depends upon the hypotheses of sameness and difference of segments of
underlying sentences in the code, other tokens of which are manipulable
in glossing speech events by the metalinguistic property of the medium.
In other words, semantico-grammatical analysis can function only if sign
tokens preserve their reference in all the speech events in which they
occur, including the crucial glossing event or its equivalent. We explain
this sameness of reference by postulating the underlying sign type, with
a semantico-referential meaning. We must always be able to distinguish

sentence-bound, context-independent types from utterance-bound, contextualized tokens in this pure semantico-referential analysis of language. Where this property of speech signals is not found, the traditional form of grammatical analysis breaks down.

Propositional Analysis

Using the traditional grammatical approach, we can analyze any sentence the signs of which are purely referential, that is, where tokens in metalinguistic usage can be said to represent precisely the same underlying type. We can analyze as distinct sentence elements a great number of the nouns of a language, such as English *table, chair, man* (in several "senses"); a great number of verbs, such as *stand, run, eat*; and a number of apparent grammatical categories, such as 'number' and 'aspect', which I discussed above. So predications of timeless truths coded by sentences with such elements are readily analyzable as such, e.g., *Unicorns drink ambrosia*. (The verb here is "tenseless"; that is, does not refer to the present but to all time.)

This example has a plural noun-phrase subject and a transitive predicate with verb and mass object noun, and it codes the universal proposition that all unicorns drink ambrosia. We might represent this proposition, in a kind of rough-and-ready way, without logical quantification, as 'drink(unicorns, ambrosia)', showing that 'drink' is a "transitive" predicate of two places that makes a claim about an "agent" (represented by the subject in grammatical construction) and a "patient" (represented by the object). For each of the sign types that make up the constituents of the sentence, we can gloss another token of the form with a paraphrase—*A unicorn is* . . . , *Ambrosia is* . . . , *To drink is to* . . .—under hypotheses about the grammatical categories they represent. (It would require a treatise in grammatical analysis to give the heuristics of discovery. Language in the semantico-referential mode being a loose system, much of the analysis must be completed to justify a particular hypothesis.) For the residual grammatical categories, such as [mass] : [count] nouns, and subject-of-verb-representing-agent, object-of-verb-representing-patient, we can show the proportionality of meanings under transformational manipulation, as our (post-)Saussurean principles demand.

Referential Indexes in Propositional Speech

However, the situation becomes more complex for propositional analysis of sentences that include referential indexes, such as signs for 'tense'. I specified above that the verb *drink* in the example was "tenseless." But consider on the other hand an utterance such as that represented by the common example *The boy hit the ball*. By a similar sort of grammatical analysis, we can say that a sentence of English is represented here with agent and patient and transitive verb. The noun phrases *the boy* and *the ball* are both "definite" (a term the analysis of which I do not wish to take up here). But when such an utterance is made with "past tense" verb token, how are we to give the meaning (and hence analyze) the underlying categorial types?

Clearly, the form *hit* is to be segmented as $hit]_v$ + Past (: $hit]_v$ + Present : : $walk]_v$ + Past : $walk]_v$ + Present). Under such an analysis, we can gloss the stem *hit* and give its "senses" as grammatically complex paraphrases. But what of the morphological segment Past that we wish to attribute to the sentence underlying the utterance? While it is perfectly feasible to segment such a category as a residual of the grammatical analysis, as we can see in the proportion just above, to give a semantico-referential meaning in terms of glossing is impossible; and yet there is clearly a contribution to reference not explicable by grammatical arrangement. The category of past tense, in other words, is not represented in utterances by pure referential sign tokens, and hence a strict semantico-referential analysis is powerless to describe this obvious category of language. (That this fact has not hindered the description of languages merely attests the truth that the natives' theories do not always tell us what the natives are really doing, nor do they prevent obvious solutions that are strictly out of theoretical bounds.)

Indexical Presupposition of Reference

In order to describe the meaning of this kind of category, we have to make certain observations about the class of tokens of "tense" in utterances. These contribute to propositions by describing the time of an event; that is, the whole proposition makes some claim to be verifiable for a particular time. In this sense such sign tokens are referential. But more specifically, the past tense tokens refer to a time t_r that is assertedly prior to the time t_{sp} at which the utterance containing them is spoken. In other words, temporal categories, and past tense in particular, compare the time for which the proposition of a referential speech event is asserting something with the time of the referential speech event itself. So the referential meaning of any categorial type 'tense' to which we want to assign the several tokens depends upon a comparison of the time referred to with the time of utterance in each speech event incorporating the token.

The proper utterance or interpretation of each token of the past tense category, then, presupposes the knowledge of the time at which the speech event takes place. A tense category takes the time of the speech event as the fixed point of comparison in referring to another time, t_r. It assumes cognitive "existence" of t_{sp}, just as t_{sp} demands cognitive "existence" only when such a tense category, or its equivalent occurs.

Double-Mode Linguistic Categories

This kind of referential index has also been called a *shifter*, because the reference "shifts" regularly, depending on the factors of the speech situation. It is very interesting that these presupposing, referential indexes, or shifters, are what Jakobson (1957) calls "duplex signs," operating at the levels of code and message simultaneously. The segmentation of sentences in the semantico-referential mode leads to the recognition of this semantic residue, unanalyzable by the methods depending on the metalinguistic property, but constituting a distinct kind of superimposed linguistic type that fits tongue-in-groove with pure semantic categories. Such categories as tense unite in a single segmentable sign vehicle a referential or quasi-semantic meaning and an indexical or pragmatic one. The referential value of a shifter, moreover, depends on the presupposition of its pragmatic value.

All languages incorporate these duplex signs, referential indexes. They are pervasive categories, which anchor, as it were, the semantico-referential mode of signs, those which represent pure propositional capabilities of language, in the actual speech event of reference, by making the propositional reference dependent on the suitable indexing of the speech situation. Not only is tense such a duplex category, but also *status*, which, following Whorf, indicates the truth value for the speaker in a referential event of the proposition encoded by the semantico-grammatical elements; *deixis*, which indicates the spatio-temporal relations of some presupposed referent in the speech event to speaker, hearer, or other referent; and so forth. A very large part of the Whorfian oeuvre (1956), in fact, can now be seen as a first attempt to draw out the Boasian implications of how pure referential (semantic) categories and duplex (referential-indexical) ones combine differently from language to language to accomplish ultimately isofunctional referential speech events. What one language accomplishes in utterances with a single referential index (for example, tense), another accomplishes with a combination of semantic category plus referential index (for example, aspect + status). Whorf himself lacked the theoretical terminology with which to make this clear, and his writings have had the sad fate of being misrepresented in the "popular" anthropological literature for a generation, under the guise of some vague "relativity" taken literally, rather than as the metaphorical idiom of the then-beginning atomic age.

Rules of Use

A consideration of such duplex signs brings up the question of how the indexical mode of such segmentable elements of utterances is to be described, that is, to be given a systematic account in terms of sign types and meanings. We have seen that the particularly indexical aspect of the meaning of such shifters involves a presupposition of the "existence" of, or cognitive focus on, some specific value in the domain of variables of the speech situation. On the one hand, the referential contribution of a shifter depends on the specific value of one or more of the variables being realized; on the other hand, the specific value being realized during some specific utterance permits the category to occur as a shifter of that specific sort.

We can summarize these converse properties of implication between contextual variable and indexical token by a general function we can call a *rule of use* or *rule of indexicality*. We can say that a rule of use is a general constraint on the class of actual shifter tokens occurring in the class of actual speech contexts. In this sense, the specifically indexical aspect of a shifter token can be said to represent some indexical type, that is, some underlying general sign that stands in the same relation to its tokens—permitting us to analyze them as "the same"—as the usual sort of general semantico-referential sign. It is clear that the senses in which we have sign types in these two modes are quite different, a fact not always easy to grasp, for the one depends on rules of use for definition of the type, the other on the metalinguistic operations of glossing speech events or the equivalent.

Formal Description of Indexicality

A rule of use is a general function that describes the relationship between speech context, given as a set of variables, some of which must have specific values, and some portion of the utterance, some message fraction. Recalling the minimal description of the speech event given at the outset, we can say that speaker x speaks to hearer y about referent z, using message fraction θ_n (message itself θ), analyzable in terms of semantico-referential grammar G, at time t, in spatial configuration $l_x, l_y, (l_z)$—the referent need not be present independent of its creation by the speech event itself—plus other factors. Some of the variables will be present in a description as such, while for others we will have to specify particular values in order to characterize the appropriate use of the shifter.

Thus, for English past 'tense', where we refer in the speech event to a time before the time of the utterance, we can describe the indexical aspect of this shifter by the schema:

$$sp(x,y,t_r < t_{sp}, \{-ed\}, G_E, t_{sp}, l, \ldots) \rightarrow \text{Past tense}$$

where t_r is the specific value of the referent z, and t_{sp} is the specific value of the time of utterance. For assertive 'status', where the speaker asserts the truth of the proposition being uttered, in English we use a heavily stressed inflected verb, such as auxiliary or modal, in the general case. We can describe this by:

$$sp(x,y,T(f(z_1, \ldots, z_n)), [A\dot{u}\dot{x}], G_E, t, l, \ldots) \rightarrow \text{Assertive}$$

where the proposition $f(z_1, \ldots, z_n)$ may take several arguments and $T(f)$ is the truth-value indicator.

Such rules of use for shifters are necessary to describe their indexical mode of meaning, much as rules of a grammar G are necessary to describe their semantico-referential meaning. In these cases, where two modes are united in the same category, we have a fortunate illustra-

26

tive case. But in both modes of a shifter, the description can proceed only by defining sign types for occurring tokens. In the referential mode, this is accomplished through traditional referentially based linguistic analysis, which leaves shifters as residuals. In the indexical mode, it is accomplished through the constitution of general rules of use.

Peirce's Trichotomy of Signs

These two modes of signification combined in the classical shifter illustrate 2 of the 3 elementary sign types given by one semiotic analysis of C. S. Peirce (1932). Altogether, he presented three trichotomies of signs, each one classified on a distinct basis. The first was based on the nature of the sign vehicle, the second on the nature of the entity signaled, and the third, the most important, on the nature of the relationship between entity signaled and signaling entity, that is, on the nature of the meaning that is communicated. (Of the 27 logically possible sign types, only 10 occur, though I will not develop this Peircean deduction here.)

The three sign types, each characterized by its own type of meaning for the users, are icon, index, and symbol. *Icons* are those signs where the perceivable properties of the sign vehicle itself have isomorphism to (up to identity with) those of the entity signaled. That is, the entities are "likenesses" in some sense. *Indexes* are those signs where the occurrence of a sign vehicle token bears a connection of understood spatiotemporal contiguity to the occurrence of the entity signaled. That is, the presence of some entity is perceived to be signaled in the context of communication incorporating the sign vehicle. *Symbols* are the residual class of signs, where neither physical similarity nor contextual contiguity hold between sign vehicle and entity signaled. They form the class of "arbitrary" signs traditionally spoken of as the fundamental kind of linguistic entity. Sign vehicle and entity signaled are related through the bond of a semantico-referential meaning in the sense elaborated earlier.

Every linguistic sign token is an icon of the linguistic sign type, and in this sense every linguistic sign trivially incorporates an iconic mode. Further, every symbol token is an index of the symbol type, since its use in context depends upon cognitive "existence" of that part of the semantico-referential grammar which explains its referential value. In this sense, as Peirce noted, there is exemplified the progressive relationship of inclusion of the three sign modes.

Icons

I do not deal here extensively with iconism in language, since, interesting though the subject be, it is largely peripheral to our concern with the cultural contextualization of language. At the formal level of single units, however, all languages are seen to contain *onomatopoeias*, which duplicate the thing signaled in the physical medium of sound. Thus, *bzzz*, to a speaker of English, is an onomatopoeia that means 'noise that sounds like the sign vehicle', used particularly to describe bees' flight, high-speed saws cutting through wood, and so forth. It is usually assimilated as a lexical item to the phonemic pattern of the language. Since monosyllables in English require a vowel, it is written out as *buzz*, pronounced [bʌz(:)] or [bəz:]. This assimilation is frequently found for onomatopoeias, giving a remarkable variety to those in different languages said to represent the same noise. But this should not obscure the fact that, to the users, the iconic mode of meaning is the one that gives the sign significance in speech.

There are many kinds of icons in languages, ranging from *replicas* and *images*, where the physical properties of signal and thing signaled are indistinguishable or totally alike, through *diagrams*, where the perceived parts are structurally isomorphic. Many diagrams are speech-internal. Universal laws of sequencing of morphemes, for example, are frequently direct or inverse diagrams of syntactic units, and so forth.

Symbols

In the symbolic mode of sign mechanism, language is most "language-like" in the traditional sense. From the negative characterization of no necessary physical or contextual connection between sign vehicle token and entity signaled, the symbolic mode of communication depends entirely on an abstract connection, motivated through semantico-grammatical sign types and their rules of combination. This kind of pure reference forms the closed system of classical discussions of language semantics. The referential value of sign tokens in any given event depends only upon the general propositional contributions of the sign types in certain arrangements that underlie the tokens. This propositional value of the signs in terms of equivalence relations can be analyzed by metasemantic manipulation. Such symbols, then, are what we described in the section above on propositional analysis.

Symbols vs. Shifters

It is to be observed that the symbolic mode of signs is one mechanism for achieving reference in actual referential speech events. The implementation of the symbols by tokens depends on—presupposes—the knowledge of the grammar G in a pure referential event. In contrast, the shifters, referential indexes, are a mechanism in which there is no abstract system of propositional equivalence relations, but only the rules of use which specify the relationship of actual referent of the sign token to the other variables of the context, among them the sign vehicle. The referential value of a shifter is constituted by the speech event itself; shifters may presuppose any variables of the speech event, including the semantically based grammar G (for example, anaphoric "switch reference"). So we must distinguish between semantically constituted symbols, the abstract propositional values of which are implemented in actual referential events, and the shifters, or referential indexes, the propositional values of which are linked to the unfolding of the speech event itself. These are two distinct types that merge in the apparent structure of utterances but are analytically separable.

Indexes

We have seen indexical reference exemplified in shifters. But it remains to observe that *indexicality*, the property of sign vehicle signaling contextual "existence" of an entity, is itself a sign mode independent of the other two. In the duplex categories illustrated above, the referential value depended upon the indexical value. Of course, then, it is possible to conceive of indexical signs of language which do not overlap with referential categories, that is, do not contribute to achieving reference. Such *nonreferential indexes*, or "pure" indexes, are features of speech which, independent of any referential speech events that may be occurring, signal some particular value of one or more contextual variables.

From the point of view of pragmatic analysis, we have to recognize such nonreferential indexical contributions of speech behavior, regardless of the dominant speech event occurring. These various indexical elements of language go into constituting distinct speech events. They are functionally discrete, but behaviorally they potentially overlap with referential speech in multifunctional utterances, as we noted above. Pure indexical features of utterances are describable with rules of use, just as are referential indexes. But the rules of use do not specify a referent independent of those created by other elements of the utterance, for these indexes are not referential. The "meaning" of these indexes is purely pragmatic and does not intersect with semantico-referential meaning exemplified in symbols.

Nonreferential Indexes

Such indexes as do not contribute to the referential speech event signal the structure of the speech context. Some of the most interesting of these indexes, certainly for the social anthropologist, are those that index features of the personae of the speech event. For example, *sex indexes* for some languages are formally systematic categories or other obvious features. In the Muskogean languages of the southeastern United States, such as Koasati (Haas 1944), there was a suffix -*s* (or its etymological equivalent) that appeared (with characteristic phonological alternations in shapes) on the inflected verb forms of every non-quotative utterance spoken by a socially female individual. In direct quotation, as we might expect, the sex of the original speaker is indexically preserved. It is important to see that the referential value of the utterance, and of the verb especially, is exactly the same, whether or not the form has the suffix. The suffix makes no referential contribution, but rather its presence or absence provides the categorial information about the sociological sex of the speaker. Not only "first person" forms of verbs, in utterances referring to speaker, but verb forms of all "persons" take this suffix, and the referential content of the speech in both suffix-bearing and suffixless forms is unaffected.

A more complex case is reported by Sapir (1929) for Yana, a language of California, in which there is one form of all major words in utterances spoken by sociological male to sociological male, and another form for all other combinations. The two forms are typically related by the operation of phonological changes in the one form and not in the other. And these pairs of related forms can function referentially in exactly the same way; the only difference in utterances containing them is in the pragmatic suitability for certain classes of speaker and hearer. These essentially morphological and phonological mechanisms of sex indexing must be functionally abstracted from utterances and described by rules of use, for example, Koasati sp($♀$(x),y,z,V]+s,G_K,t,l, . . .); I will take up the characterization of the Yana case further below, in discussing rule mechanisms.

Exactly the same sort of nonreferential indexical mode is found in *deference indexes*, where speech signals inequalities of status, rank, age, sex, and the like. For example, we may take those of Jaɣanese, reported by Geertz (1960) and more lucidly by Uhlenbeck (1970) and Horne (1967; 1973), where one of the modes of contrast is between a vocabulary set and certain grammatical restrictions (the variety called krɔmɔ) used basically by lower-to-higher or high-to-high on these scales, while other, "unmarked" vocabulary items and all constructions (ŋɔkɔ) are used in the opposite cases. It is interesting that most vocabulary items and virtually all constructions do not have these alternate forms, yet the power of the alternation was apparently very great in traditional Javanese society. Here again, the propositional content of the utterances with corresponding krɔmɔ/ŋɔkɔ vocabulary is just the same, while the deference they index between speaker and hearer differs. The rules of use based on the parameters for deference are always of the form sp(H(x),L(y), . . .), sp(L(x),H(y), . . .) and so on.

These deference indexes frequently and especially intersect with the referential indexes called "first and second person pronouns" in the standard literature, giving, as for example in Thai and Burmese (Cooke 1970), upwards of a score of sets of segmentable "pronouns" for use as referential personal index plus pure deference index combined into one apparent surface category. In many languages (see Brown and Gilman 1960), functionally analogous marking of social deference in pronominal indexes is accomplished by skewing otherwise referential categories of 'person' and 'number'. These special effects, *pragmatic metaphors* (to be dealt with below), are to be distinguished from a distinct indexical expression of social deference with unique formal signals.

A distinct nonreferential bifurcation of lexical items into complementary indexical sets was widespread in Australian Aboriginal speech communities. As described by Dixon (1971; 1972) for Dyirbal, a language of the Cairns Rain Forest in Northern Queensland, there is an "everyday" set of lexical items, and a "mother-in-law" set, which had to be used by a speaker only in the presence of his classificatory mother-in-law or equivalent affine. In other words, the mother-in-law vocabulary, totally distinct from the everyday one, indexes the specified affinal relation between speaker (x) and some "audience"—not the socially defined addressee (y)—in the speech situation. As such, the switch in vocabulary serves as an *affinal taboo index* in the speech situation, maintaining and creating sociological distance.

It is interesting that the grammatical structure in the traditional sense remains exactly the same in these two kinds of situations. What changes is the entire set of nongrammatical lexical items. Moreover, since the ratio of everyday to mother-in-law vocabulary is approximately 4:1, the strictly semantic content of propositions coded in everyday vocabulary will require more elaborate grammatical constructions and many more lexical items to code in mother-in-law vocabulary. Semantic content was apparently severely reduced in actual communication. Further, the glossing possibilities back and forth, under the same grammar, can be exploited, as was done by Dixon, to justify semantic description. But the principle of this being a pure indexical device, independent of the semantico-referential content, makes the general form of the rule of use $sp([\imath x][Af(x,y')],y,z,\{L_2\}, \ldots)$, where $Af(x,y')$ expresses the relationship between speaker and "audience" and $L_2(:L_1)$ represents the disjunct set of lexical items.

So there is a distinction between referential indexes, such as tense, and nonreferential ones, such as the disjunct sets of forms to code sociological relations of personae in the speech situation. Some phenomena, however, appear to be interesting borderline cases between shifters and pure indexes. In Javanese, where the basic distinction of vocabulary into krɔmɔ and ŋɔkɔ sets is a pure deference index, there is another, less pervasive distinction between a set of lexical forms (krɔmɔ iŋgyel) showing deference of speaker to some exalted human referent. This set of forms, coded in stems having to do with parts of the body, personal activities, and so forth, occurs in both krɔmɔ and ŋɔkɔ styles. It constitutes an independent axis of lexical choice, but one which intersects with the speaker-hearer deference when the hearer is also the focused referent (that is, sp(x,y,y, . . .)). Since the lexical alternants have the same basic propositional value in krɔmɔ iŋgyel or plain styles, under strict semantic analysis we should want to describe this speaker-referent deference switch as a pure indexical one. But especially in the case of speaking about the addressee, where the reference is perforce of an indexical sort, the two systems krɔmɔ : ŋɔkɔ, krɔmɔ iŋgyel : [plain] seem to merge. The actual facts of any given instance probably rest ultimately on the distinction between indexically presupposed and indexically created referent, another axis of classification.

Indexical Presupposition

In all cases of indexes, we have constructed indexical sign types by rules of use. These rules of use state the relationship of mutually implied existence of sign vehicle token and certain aspects of the context of discourse. For all of the shifters we examined in the section on referential indexes, we could furthermore say that the aspect of the speech situation was *presupposed* by the sign token. That is, a given shifter token is uninterpretable referentially without the knowledge of some aspect of the situation.

A particularly clear case of such presupposition is the operation of deictics, in English, for example, *this* and *that* in the singular. When we use a token of the full noun phrase *this table* or *that table* (with stressed full vowel in both words), pointing out thereby some particular object, the referent of the token of *table* must be identifiable, must "exist" cognitively, for the deictic itself to be interpretable. The proper use of the token of the deictic presupposes the physical existence of an actual object which can properly be referred to by *table*, or it presupposes a prior segment of referential discourse which has specified such a referent. Otherwise the use of the deictic token is inappropriate; it is uninterpretable and confusing. (There is a related noun phrase incorporating reduced-vowel "deictic" form, with reduced stress and distinct intonation pattern, used for nondeictic definite reference, no presupposition of referent being involved, and no prior discourse necessary.) If we use the wrong deictic for the referent, or use the deictic with the wrong lexical noun (one that does not properly describe an object in correct position for the deictic), again confusion results, or correction by the interlocutor: "Oh, you mean that other table!" or "This is not a table, it's a chair!"

The use of the deictic, then, is maximally presupposing, in that the contextual conditions are required in some appropriate configuration for proper indexical reference with a deictic token. The general pattern of all the shifters is similar. Some aspect of the context spelled out in the rule of use is fixed and presupposed, in order for the referential contribution to be made. And in this sense, reference itself is once more seen to be an act of creation, of changing the contextual basis for further speech events. Recall that one of the ways in which the presupposition of the deictic can be satisfied is to have referred to the entity in question.

Indexical Creativity

But there is a general *creative* or *performative* aspect to the use of pure indexical tokens of certain kinds, which can be said not so much to change the context, as to make explicit and overt the parameters of structure of the ongoing events. By the very use of an indexical token, which derives its indexical value from the rules of use setting up the indexical types, we have brought into sharp cognitive relief part of the context of speech. In some cases, the occurrence of the speech signal is the only overt sign of the contextual parameter, verifiable, perhaps, by other, cooccurring behaviors in other media, but nevertheless the most salient index of the specific value. Under these circumstances, the indexical token in speech performs its greatest apparent work, seeming to be the very medium through which the relevant aspect of the context is made to "exist." Certainly, the English indexical pronouns *I/we* and *you* (vs. *he/she/it/they*) perform this creative function in bounding off the personae of the speech event itself; in those languages, such as Chinook (Columbia River, North America) with 'inclusive' and 'exclusive' pronominal indexes, the boundary function becomes even more finely drawn. Social indexes such as deference vocabularies and constructions, mentioned above, are examples of maximally creative or performative devices, which, by their very use, make the social parameters of speaker and hearer explicit. Adherence to the norms specified by rules of use reinforces the perceived social relations of speaker and hearer; violations constitute a powerful rebuff or insult, or go into the creation of irony and humor.

Classification of Index Types/Tokens

Indexical tokens range on a sliding scale of creativity or performative value from the extreme of presupposition displayed by deictics to the extreme of creativity displayed by subtle social indexes. The particular placement of any given indexical token depends to a great extent on the factors of the individual context of its use: how many events are simultaneously occurring; how many independent media are signaling the factors of the context; what prior events have taken place; how many cooccurrent indexes of a given functional sort are occurring in speech. As we have seen, the different kinds of indexical types have inherent ranges on the functional scale of presupposition. Underlying all these specific usages, however, are the rules of use, *norms* as it were, for the relationship of mutual existence between contextual variables and speech signals.

The referential vs. nonreferential nature of indexes, a measure of the independence of indexes from the semantico-referential mode of communication, is one axis of classification, of indexical types. The presuppositional vs. creative nature of indexes, a measure of the independence of indexes from every other signaling medium and mode in speech events, is another axis of classification, of indexical tokens. Because the two classifications interact, borderline cases exist. The speaker-referent deference vocabulary of Javanese, for example, seems to be used referentially or nonreferentially in a way that depends upon the presuppositional or performative nature of the given token in context. This discourse reference, the actual unfolding referential speech event, is once more seen to be distinct from abstract (semantic) propositional reference, implemented in discourse. The former type, characteristic of referential indexes and described with rules of use, responds to such indexical properties as presupposition/performance, while the latter, based on semantico-grammatical analysis, does not.

A kind of four-cell array is thus generated by these *functional characteristics* of indexes, in which we can place the examples discussed, and provide for further examples:

35

	presupposing	creative (performative)
referential	locative deictics, tense first person pronominals	second person pronominals
nonreferential	Dyirbal "mo-in-law" lexicon social sex markers	deference indexes of speaker- hearer relations

Referential, presupposing indexes contribute to propositional description in discourse, but only by taking as a starting point the value of some contextual variable, as for the computation of time reference in tense categories. Nonreferential presupposing indexes reflect in speech the existence of some specific values of contextual variables, such as the presence of affine audience in mother-in-law lexical items. Referential, relatively performative indexes contribute to propositional description in discourse, and in addition function as the signal for the existence of speech-event features, as in the choice of pronominals, which assign the event roles of speaker, hearer, audience, and referent to certain individuals in the maximal case. Finally, nonreferential, relatively performative indexes serve as independent speech signals establishing the parameters of the interaction themselves, as in deference forms, which in effect establish overtly the social relations of the individuals in the roles of speaker and hearer, speaker and audience, or speaker and referent.

Functional Aggregation in Indexical Forms

The Thai example cited above in which social deference indexes are united with pronominal referential indexes points up the fact that even indexical categories can be pragmatically multifunctional. On the one hand, the pronominals have discourse-referential values that contribute to description, and on the other hand, they have nonreferential values that structure the factors of the speech situation. The first indexical aspect contributes to the propositional mode of speech, while the second constitutes part of the social mode of marking equality or inequality. By analysis of the surface categories of speech, we might segment the pronominals as semantico-grammatical residuals, and then attempt to specify the pragmatic meaning of the forms. But inasmuch as two modes are united here in one surface category, it would take considerably more analysis to see that two distinct rules of use are involved, based on two distinct functions of the forms. At a functional level, then, there are *two* indexes which happen to be represented by the same surface indexical category, one a shifter, one not. This functional and hence analytic distinctness of the two modes must always be the starting point for the isolation of the pragmatic categories in language, and must rest ultimately on a sensitive analysis of the speech-event function of utterances, a task which is essentially social anthropological.

Referential Analogy in Discourse

The situation is even more interesting in the case of pragmatic metaphors connected with pronominal shifters referring to the hearer $(sp(x,y,y, \ldots))$, a phenomenon found in many languages. Instead of distinct forms indexing the quality of speaker-hearer social relations, the "second person" pronouns incorporate skewing of otherwise semantic categories (see Benveniste 1950; 1956). To analyze these data, we have to distinguish two kinds of extension or analogy of referential categories in discourse.

The so-called pronouns frequently seem to incorporate categories of 'person' and 'number', so that we tend to speak of "first and second person singular and plural" for pronominal forms. "Third person" pronouns can be true substitutes, *anaphoric devices* that obviate the need for repetition of a full, lexically complex referring noun phrase (thus, *The man sat down. He* ...). In the referential mode, they act as *negative indexes* in never indexing speaker or hearer participants in speech events. But "first and second person" forms are referential indexes, the contribution to discourse reference of which comes about by functionally distinct rules of use; such forms have no anaphoric properties.

37

When we use a "third person" pronoun, the singular or plural number is derived by the rules of anaphora from the semantic 'number' specification of the noun phrase it replaces. In this pure semantic mode, plural 'number' signals more-than-one of whatever entity is referred to by the lexical stems of the noun in question. But some occurrences of plural number category derive secondarily only at the level of discourse reference by a kind of summing up of individual semantically established entities (thus, English, *Jack and Jill went up a hill. They* . . .). It is at this second level of reference that the first and second person pronominal indexes get their apparent "singular" and "plural" forms. For English 'we' $\neq$ 'I' + 'I'; the form *we* is an index that refers to and presupposes a speaker and at least one other individual in the referential speech event, $sp(x,y,x\&w,we, G_E,t,l, \dots)$. Similarly, second person plural refers to and indexes hearer and at least one other persona, for example, Russian $sp(x,y,y\&v,vy,G_R,t,l, \dots)$. Only by the summation of the individual referents in discourse, which are referentially indexed by such pronominals, does their 'singular' or 'plural' referential value emerge.

With this analysis of the distinction between anaphoric and non-anaphoric pronominal indexes ("person"), and of semantically based (cardinal "number") vs. discourse-based (summed "number") reference to quantity, it is possible to see the nature of the skewings in so-called "honorific second person pronouns."

Pragmatic Metaphors of Grammatical Categories

For some languages, Russian for example, or French, we can index the same kind of speaker-hearer deference that is indicated elsewhere by vocabulary switch (see Friedrich 1966; Ervin-Tripp 1971), when addressing a single addressee, by using the "second person plural" (*vy, vous*) rather than the "singular" (*ty, tu*). In other words, the semantic cardinal number category, in its summed discourse use, either refers to plural addressees or refers to a single addressee, concomitantly indexing the deference of speaker to hearer. In some languages, for example Italian, the deferential second person index uses what is otherwise the "third singular (feminine)" pronominal form for combined referential indexing and social indexing. In other words, third singular feminine anaphoric, or nonpersonal pronoun, either replaces a third singular feminine semantic noun or refers to and indexes a singular addressee while indexing deference of speaker to hearer. Some languages, such as German and Worora (Northern Kimberley, Western Australia), switch both person ($2 \rightarrow 3$) and number (sg. $\rightarrow$ pl.) to express this deference. In those languages with a 'dual' number category, more highly marked than 'plural', deference is indicated along the axis of number by switch to dual-number addressee index. This occurs, for example, in Yokuts of south central California (Newman 1944) and Nyangumata of northern West Australia (O'Grady 1964). (Curiously, in both these languages, the deference must be accorded to a genealogically specified persona, mother-in-law and equivalent in the first, mother's brother and equivalent in the second.)

What unites all of these seemingly isofunctional usages is the unidirectionality, in every case, of switch from "second person pronoun" to "third," from expected "singular number" to "plural" (or "dual"), or both concomitantly. There is a kind of metaphor based on the discourse-referential value of the categories, it would seem. In the one case, it is shift out of the realm of second person address, where an individual is indexed in the speech situation face-to-face, to the realm of anaphora, where an already established entity is understood as the referent of the substitute. This makes the addressee larger than life by taking away the individual personhood implied by the face-to-face address. In the second case, it is a shift out of the realm of the singular, where an individual is referred to, and into the realm of nonsingular, where, as it were, the summed number of individuals referred to is greater than one. This makes the addressee count for more than one social individual; to his persona accrues the social weight of many, as compared with the speaker. (The "royal 'we'" does the inverse, we should note.)

Such universals in expression, examples of isofunctional indexing with seeming metaphorical plays upon semantic categories, are an important demonstration of the interplay between the semantic mode of language and the pragmatic constitution of social categories through speech. The semantically based analysis of categories, even with "fudges" to permit incorporation of the analytic residue of shifters, does not capture these generalizations. The perspective must be one that frees us from dependence on semantic categories, or even referential ones, as the defining segmentation of speech requiring analysis.

Functional and Formal Analogues

In each of these cases, I have been claiming a kind of functional comparability of the parallel formations. Rules of use are norms between the contextual variables and some formal feature of the message. To be *functionally analogous*, then, indexes must be described by rules of use that specify analogous contexts under analogous speech events. (Obviously, the utterance fractions in different languages can hardly be expected to be alike.) When indexes seem to be accomplishing analogous socially constituted tasks, we can speak of cross-linguistic comparability. So the claim of functional analogy from a heuristic point of view makes hypotheses about the social parameters of speech events. From a theoretical point of view it depends upon the results of social anthropology for a framework of description of social categories, for the structural significance of the pattern of indexical speech norms in the given society. Universals of functional signification thus are the necessary means for creating a real science of language pragmatics—that is, for establishing the ethnography of speech—just as within the semantic mode, universal hypotheses about phonetics and reference are the necessary empirical correlates of semantico-grammatical analysis.

On the other hand, *formally analogous* indexicals depend upon cross-systemic specification of equivalence of message fractions. In the case of the pragmatic metaphors illustrated above, there is formal comparability in the expression of deference through the pronominal categories themselves, which can be isolated in the referential mode in every one of the languages in question. (Note how the formal analysis in one mode depends on isofunctionality in others, as was mentioned above.) The languages all use formally similar categorial substitutions, definable in the semantico-referential mode, to index deferential address. From a formal point of view, then, we seek some way of characterizing as structurally analogous the message fractions serving as indexes. But any such structural specification depends upon analysis of forms, which itself rests on finding some isofunctional basis for comparison. Ultimately, then, cross-linguistic formal analogy and functional analogy are, like phonetic and referential frameworks in the semantic mode, linked as hypotheses that serve to justify a particular analysis.

Formal Distinctions Signaling Functional Ones

The parallel formal-functional analogy of all the pragmatic metaphors for speaker-hearer deference is an exceptional case. Ordinarily, given some social parameters constituted on nonspeech grounds and indexed in some language, we might want to ask whether or not these are indexed in some other language and, if so, how. The sex indexes of several American Indian languages mentioned above are somewhat diverse functionally, but all formally overlap in apparent phonological changes at the ends of words, in particular of inflected verbs. The Thai pronominal system for first and second persons—independent words that index in complex ways the various inequalities resulting in deference—includes among the grounds of deference distinction of sociological sex. So the several American Indian systems seem to isolate the social variable of sex, indexing it with a unique formal set of changes. (The ethnographic record establishes the great salience of the distinction, at least in the societies speaking Muskogean languages, but its cultural position has not been established.) The Thai (and other Southeast Asian) systems assimilate the social variable of sex to the functional characterization of inequality more generally, making a pointed ethnographic statement on equivalences of stratification. It is always necessary, as this example demonstrates, to take the functional perspective in terms of rules of use to be able to see in what way such pragmatic items fit into systematic sociological patterns, of which linguistic ones are a major part.

Formal Characterization of Indexes

From the formal point of view, the sign vehicles that function in an indexical mode are extremely varied. As we noted when dealing with the privacy function of language, switch of semantico-referential grammar can itself serve as an index. We have seen vocabulary, affixes, phonological rules, and syncretistic pronominal categories serving indexical functions within utterances. Indexical devices such as anaphoric pronouns, mentioned above, which maintain discourse reference in certain surface structural configurations, are formally defined only over at least two noun phrases, frequently found in distinct semantico-referential sentences. Intonation patterns and stress shifts are further kinds of features that are characteristically indexes, though I have not dealt with them directly by example. And syntactic constructions, such as the distinction between "active" and "passive" forms of utterances, or the English "performative" construction I [V] *you* [X], are virtually always pragmatic units, formally isolable on functional grounds. In other words, the range of possible formal elements that can serve as speech indexes, according to our traditional semantico-grammatical understanding, includes the entire range of language-level indexing, discourse-sequence level, sentence level, word and affix level, and phonological alternations that can be characterized by rules, including intonation and other nonsegmental gradient devices.

The description of all these occurring pragmatic formal features of speech presents a vast problem for our traditional ideas of what a grammar (G) is. From the point of view of a semantico-referential grammar, it would appear that every pragmatic index is a kind of "structural idiom," where the constructions cannot be analyzed according to semantico-referential combinatory regularities. This would make by far the greater bulk of a description of speech into a list of such "idioms." The undesirability of such an alternative is manifest, given the kinds of regularities of pragmatic function exemplified above.

So some attempt to patch up traditional grammar cannot serve as a principled description of the pragmatics of language—a fact that most contemporary linguistic theorists have not yet appreciated. For the characterization of pragmatics as dependent on semantico-referential analysis—the "performative" approach discussed above—becomes totally hopeless once we consider that only a portion of the indexicals in speech are shifters, with connection to the semantically based grammar in the speech function of reference. The remainder of the indexes are just functionally independent of reference as such.

The question, then, becomes one of how to represent speech as the apparently continuous formal medium it is, while at the same time preserving the pragmatic distinction among (1) the pure referential function or semantic aspect of meaning, from which semantico-referential systems derive their analyzability, and on which one facet of referential speech acts rests; (2) the shifter function, or indexical-referential aspect of meaning, constituted by rules of use at the level of discourse reference; and (3) the pure indexical functions, serving other functional modes independent of reference, for which nonreferential rules of use are constituted. In (2) we have a point of overlap between (1) and (3)—hence their duplex nature. But a formal descriptive "pragmatic grammar" must integrate semantics, valid as a specialized mode, into an inclusive system.

PRAGMATICS AND CULTURAL DESCRIPTION

I have analytically separated functional modes of speech behavior, further showing the modes of meaning so constituted in linguistic signs. I want now to characterize briefly the integration of these modes in a systematic pragmatics of language, indicating how this purports to be a more adequate descriptive paradigm for speech and other communicative behavior. This will lead naturally to a consideration of the relationship of such pragmatic description to broader ethnographic or "cultural" description.

Functional Alternatives in Rules of Use

Rules of use for both shifters and other, nonreferential indexes show the existential relationship of contextual variables to some overt utterance fraction. The rules of use for shifters specify the referent (z) as well, consonant with the fact that such categories contribute to referential speech events. It would seem that formally, the third variable (corresponding to z) in nonreferential rules of use should be the functionally determined kind of entity which is being indexed, for example some sociological domain, such as kinship, sex, rank; some spatial configuration, such as the "proxemic" configuration of persons in the speech event; and so forth. In other words, not only referential speech events, but all other types as well have rules of use that specify the functional domain over which the particular pragmatic mode of meaning is being realized. So not only do we specify rules of use for $sp(x,y,z^r, \dots)$ where z^r is "referent," but also $sp(x,y,z^f, \dots)$ where z^f is a variable of functions more generally, defined by the range of speech events.

Under such a generalization, the "rules of use" we specify for shifters, the "duplex" categories, must be further analyzed into what are indeed two elementary functional modes. One such functional mode is referential, with variable z^r specified; another functional mode is non-referential, with some variable z^f to be specified, such as z^t "temporal parameter," z^p "privacy-boundary," and so forth. In shifters, an elementary referential function and a distinct elementary indexical function are united in the same surface speech category, but if we examine them carefully, we can see that the referent z^r is frequently of a different domain from the indexed z^f. Deictics, as we saw, presuppose the referent from previous discourse, for example, as well as the speaker or hearer location, and refer to the locus of the presupposed referent relative to that of speaker or hearer.

The Constitution of Speech Acts

We can call each one of these elementary functionally specific rules of use a *speech act*. We can note that such norms for pragmatic meaning relations depend upon the functional specification of speech at the level of speech events, for it is at this higher level of analysis that one can recognize various pragmatic modes, the socially constituted "tasks" which speech behavior accomplishes or "performs." Reference is one such pragmatic mode, and referential speech acts are of two kinds, which explain the nature of the referring utterance fraction. On the one hand, the shifters motivate elementary referential rules of use, where referent is specified with respect to some speech-event variable(s). On the other hand, the semantico-referential entities motivate rules of use which merely specify *variable* z^r and presuppose (index) the grammar G; that is, the referential value is determined by the semantico-grammatical rules implemented in a functionally referential speech event, no further specification being required. Other pragmatic modes define distinct kinds of speech acts, many of which, as we have seen, overlap in precisely the same, multifunctional surface indexes. For example Thai "pronouns" represent in utterances a bimodal shifter of personal referent, as well as a social index of deference. The widespread pragmatic metaphors for deference use otherwise referential categories in multiple functions expressing equality/inequality.

Speech acts are the elementary indexical formulae for specifying the pragmatic meaning or *function*₂ of speech signs. They operate within the framework of *purposive function*₁ of socially constituted behavior already discussed above. We can speak of the "referential function$_2$" of actual signs in the sense of the contribution they make to achieving a valid instance of function$_1$ of describing. Similarly, we can speak of the "socially seriating function$_2$" of actual signs in the sense of the contribution they make to the function$_1$ of defining hierarchies within social categories. Speech is multifunctional$_1$ in the sense that it can simultaneously be used to constitute distinct kinds of events. Speech is multifunctional$_2$ in the sense that apparent elements of surface form actually incorporate meanings of several distinct indexical types. This accords with our traditional notions of *grammatical function*, an instance of function$_2$, always ultimately specified in terms of the contribution of elements to the semantico-referential system.

The analysis of speech acts is thus a generalization of the analysis of semantico-referential systems, providing for meaning relations and language uses distinct from those of the traditionally analyzed sort. In a mathematical analogy, it is the more general structure of which the previously explored type turns out to be a special case. More particularly, the speech acts for semantico-referential signs function$_1$ exclusively in referential speech events—abbreviatory extensions and such aside—and are vacuously specified, with the exception of presupposing the grammar G.

The "Grammar" of Speech Acts

Such a characterization permits us to see at least the nature of a more inclusive kind of "grammar," which includes the traditional sort as a component. If grammar G, as in our present understanding, is a finite, recursive set of rules which relate semantico-referential representations to utterance types (or "sentences" in "surface form"), we can recall from the first part of this paper that the meanings within G are defined in terms of the function$_1$ of pure reference, and the sentences are segmentable into constituents on this basis. In pure referential sentences, the surface elements so functioning$_1$ form a continuous sequence.

To construct a *grammar* (*G'*) *of speech acts*, the analogous generalization is a set of rules which relate pragmatic meanings—functions$_2$ specified by functionally$_1$ indexed variables—to the "surface form" of utterances. Utterances are, we have several times remarked, continuous in nature. The great bulk of such utterances, moreover, give the appearance of formal integration in terms of phrase, word, and affix structure, especially for referential segments, the shifters and semantic elements. This would seem to indicate that the traditional grammatical rules (G) must be incorporated into pragmatics (G′), that is, that at least some speech acts consist of rules showing the contextual dependence of traditional grammatical rules for generating surface forms.

This is further confirmed by two pragmatic examples I have already mentioned. One is the switch of semantico-referential language, which can serve as an index. Here the whole set of rules of the traditional sort is a function of—indexes—the grammatical competence of speaker, hearer, and audience. So obviously our pragmatic description should show the selection of rules G^L, not just an infinite set of messages $\{\theta^L{}_i\}$, as a function of contextual variables. The second case is the Yana male vs. female indexing. Here phonological rules, which show the regularities of shape in pairs of forms for the majority of words in the language, characterize the context-sensitive indexing, rather than any affixation or other segmental material. We would want to characterize the indexing here as the dependence of the implementation of certain phonological rules upon the variables of speaker-hearer sociological sex. Any phonological indexes of this sort, such as those marking geographical *dialect* of the speaker, or class-affiliated *variety*, must be similarly treated.

So a grammar of speech acts G′ consists of rules of use that map the variables of speech events into rules generating utterances. With this characterization, we have moved from the heuristic device of directly relating contextual variables to "surface" utterance fractions—detailing, in other words, the definition of an index—to constructing a pragmatic system that explains the relation between apparent structural continuity of surface form and its multifunctional[1,2] nature. For any given utterance fraction, there may be many speech acts which motivate its presence in a speech event, that is, any utterance fraction may be a constituent of pragmatic structures in several modes, or a constituent in some mode and not a constituent in others. Reference, in particular, the function[1] which has heretofore motivated all our ideas about utterance constituency, motivates only one such pragmatic structure, at the core of which are essentially rules of use selecting G. The shifters require distinct functional[2] rules of G′, though they function[1] also in referential events.

46

Multifunctionality and Pragmatic Strategy

There is a structure to a pragmatic grammar so constituted, the details of which are now only partially clear. Speech acts are ordered, for example, a reflection of *pragmatic markedness relations* among functional$_2$ meanings of utterance fractions. For example, there is a hierarchical relation among all the kinds of sociological variables leading to deference indexes, which can be formally described by intrinsic ordering of the speech acts characterizing their use (see Ervin-Tripp 1971 for flow-chart characterization). And further, there are markedness relations of speech-event function$_1$ of utterance fractions, so that features of utterances contribute normally to some functional$_1$ mode, less appropriately, though possibly, to others. Pragmatic metaphors mentioned above are a case in point, basically semantic categories being extended, as it were, filling out "holes" in the pragmatic structure.

The multifunctionality of apparent utterances means that there is a kind of pragmatic indeterminacy of utterances taken out of context, and the possibility for strategic uses of language in the context of speech events. Out of context, we can only have recourse to the referential mode in determining the meaning of utterances, which, with certain exceptions for shifters, is essentially "context-free." Additionally, and especially in context where indexes are relatively creative or performative, there can be pragmatic indeterminacy in utterances that can be manipulated by the individuals in an interaction. This leads to such phenomena as *pragmatic contradiction,* or "double-bind" behaviors, which play upon two or more communicative media signaling contradictory indexical meanings to the receiver of the concurrent messages, or upon contradictory highly presupposing indexes within the same medium. Similarly, there is *residual semanticity,* the semantico-referential meaning which a speaker can claim after the fact for potentially highly pragmatically charged speech. Thus the characteristic speaker's denial of speech offensive to the hearer takes the form of "All I said was . . . " with a semantico-referential paraphrase or repetition of the referential content of the original utterance. A speaker can create a social persona for himself, playing upon the hearer's perspective of *imputed indexicality,* where the speaker has characteristics attributed to him on the basis of the rules of use for certain utterance fractions. Thus the phenomenon underlying the plot of *My Fair Lady.* Finally, *diplo-*

matic nonindexicality, on the analogy of diplomatic nonrecognition in foreign policy, allows the hearer to respond to speech as though it constituted a semantico-referential event, all the while understanding completely the distinct function$_2$ of the indexes which overlap in surface form.

Pragmatic contradiction and imputed indexicality are alike in depending on the unavoidably high functional$_2$ potential of utterances. Residual semanticity and diplomatic nonindexicality are alike in depending on the universal metasemantic awareness of people, whereby the semantico-referential function$_1$ of speech is the officially or overtly recognized one, the one to which actors may retreat with full social approval. (This point was made several times by Sapir.) But all of these *pragmatic strategies,* manipulation of pragmatic function$_2$ in actual behavior, depend in the last analysis upon the shared understanding of norms for indexical elements in speech acts. Obviously, some individuals are better at these pragmatic strategies than others, just as some individuals have a more explicit and accurate conception of the pragmatics of their own language. I wonder whether the two skills are related.

Metapragmatics

If strategy requires purposive manipulation of pragmatic rules, then it may also require an overt conceptualization of speech events and constituent speech acts. Such characterization of the pragmatic structure of language is *metapragmatics,* much as the characterization of semantico-grammatical structure is metasemantics. The distinction between these two realms is vast, however. While language as a pure referential medium serves as its own metalanguage in metasemantic referential speech events, there can be no metapragmatic speech events in which use of speech in a given functional mode explicates the pragmatic structure of that very functional mode. The metapragmatic characterization of speech must constitute a referential event, in which pragmatic norms are the objects of description. So obviously the extent to which a language has semantic lexical items which accurately refer to the indexed variables, to the constituents of speech, and to purposive function is one measure of the limits of metapragmatic discussion by a speaker of that language.

48

Shifters, Linguistic Categories, and Cultural Description

Limits to Metapragmatic Awareness

But more importantly, it would appear that the nature of the indexical elements themselves, along formal-functional$_1$ dimensions, limits metapragmatic awareness of language users. Indexes were characterized as segmental vs. nonsegmental, that is affix, word, phrase vs. some other feature of utterances; as referential vs. nonreferential, that is, shifter vs. nonshifter index; and as relatively presupposing vs. relatively creative or performative. It is very easy to obtain accurate pragmatic information in the form of metapragmatic referential speech for segmental, referential, relatively presupposing indexes. It is extremely difficult, if not impossible, to make a native speaker aware of nonsegmental, nonreferential, relatively creative formal features, which have no metapragmatic reality for him. Indexes of the first type, which are susceptible of accurate conscious characterization, are, of course, closest in their formal-functional$_1$ properties to semantico-referential segments, for which metasemantic manipulation is possible. Notice once again that metasemantic speech events (see above) are thus a special, equational sort of metapragmatic event. The extent to which signs have properties akin to those of strictly segmental, semantico-referential ones, in fact, is obviously a measure of the ease with which we can get accurate metapragmatic characterizations of them from native speakers. Investigation of the triply distinct formal-functional$_1$ elements of speech, on the other hand, requires interpretative observation in a functional$_1$ framework.

I think that every fieldworker has had such experiences, where a careful sorting out of kinds of pragmatic effects ultimately just cannot rely on the metapragmatic testimony of native participants. (That so-called generative semanticists insist on the validity of their own "intuitions" about pragmatics in *Gedankenforschungen* simply attests to the unfortunate naïveté and narrowness of most contemporary linguists on matters of speech observation and of systematic pragmatic theory.) In the course of investigating Wasco-Wishram (Chinookan), for example, I attempted to systematize with informants the diminutive-augmentative consonantisms which are ubiquitous in speech acts of endearment/repulsion felt by speakers toward referent, without referential contribution. They form a pragmatic metaphor on the more "physical" speaker estimation of size relative to a standard—the classic syncategorematic problem of small elephants and the like. These effects are entirely phonological, most consonants participating in pairs (or *n*-tuples) which alternate by phonological rules regardless of their position in lexical items. A lexical item thus appears in overt form with two or more sets of consonants, for example, the nominal adjectives for size, the paradigm elaborated example, *i- -qbaiλ* (super-augmentative), *i- -g(ʷ)aiλ* (augmentative), *i- -kʷaic* (quasi-diminutive), *i- -k'ʷaic'* (diminutive), *i- -k'ʷɛit'θ* (super-diminutive). Upon request for repetition of a lexical item with such effects that had occurred in discourse, informants invariably gave a lexically normal form—the pragmatically "unmarked" form. So requesting a repetition of *i-ǰa-muqbal* 'her belly [which I think is huge and repulsive, by the way]', one gets *i-ča-muqʷal.* "But you just said '-muqbal' didn't you; that means great big one, no?" "No, it's *ičamuqʷal.*" . . . "Well, how do you say 'her great big belly'?" *"Iagaiλ ičamuqʷal* ['It's large, her belly']." Notice that the last question is interpreted as a request for an interlinguistic metasemantic equation, the pragmatic marker of rules for augmentative consonantism being beyond studied manipulation.

Metapragmatic Lexical Items

A certain amount of reference to pragmatics at the level of speech events (purposive function$_1$) is accomplished in every language of which I am aware by quotation framing verbs, the equivalents of English phrases such as *he said (to him), he told (it) to him, he asked (of him), he ordered him,* and so forth. It is remarkable how many languages have only constructions expressing the first few of these, which serve to name the entire, undifferentiated set of speech events. Framed by such verbs, which describe certain speech events, and the inflections of which describe the participants, we find reported speech, the messages purportedly used. There is a whole range of devices for reporting speech events, from exact quotation through indirect quotation through pseudoquotation, paraphrase, and descriptive reference, the subtleties of which I cannot explore here.

Additionally, languages incorporate lexical items which in certain constructions refer to, that is, name, the speech event of which a token forms an utterance fraction. I have already adumbrated their description above (see *Reference and "Performative Speech,"* pp. 18–19 above). In English, for example, these items fit into the schema *I/we* [V] *you* [X], where the verb V is inflected for present, nonprogressive (punctual) tense-aspect. They actually name the socially constituted speech event of which they form an utterance fraction: *christen, dub, sentence,* and so forth, particularly socially salient routines which are primarily linguistic events behaviorally. They are referential, creative (or performative) indexes which are most important to ethnographic description, since they individualize certain ongoing functions₁ of speech as they are happening. They constitute a message about the function₁ of the medium, functionally₂ a pragmatic act. The cross-cultural investigation of these *metapragmatic shifters* is a very urgent and important anthropological desideratum.

Lexical Items in General

The metapragmatic content of certain lexical items brings up the complementary question of the pragmatic content of lexical items. As I have discussed above, metasemantic events that equate meanings of segmental, semantico-referential forms of language are the basis for grammatical analysis, and vice versa. Obviously, in the semantico-referential mode alone, the ideal language would consist of elementary referring grammatical categories and their rules of hierarchical combination. But, as many linguists, particularly Bloomfield (1933) and Chafe more recently (e.g., 1970) have seen, lexical items—the elements that enter into metasemantic equations—form a kind of irreducible set of "idioms" or "basic irregularities," the existence of which is really inexplicable on the basis of semantico-grammatical theory. True lexical items have that unpredictable quality of specialization or extension or multiple senses in their referential functions₁ which makes them what they are, referential primes of some sort.

But it is precisely at the level of pragmatics that the coding of seemingly arbitrary chunks of referential "reality" becomes clear. For *lexical items are* abbreviations for *semantic complexes* made up of semantico-referential primes in grammatical constructions (Weinreich 1966; Silverstein 1972 and refs. there), *together with* all of the *indexical modalities* of meaning that make the functional₁ result unexpected. In other words, traditional semantico-grammatical analysis can never hope to specify meanings for lexical items finer than the grammatical structure of implicit referential categories allows, for every lexical item includes a pragmatic residue—an indexical component motivated only at the level of speech acts, actual discourse reference being only one such mode. (Certain kinds of lexical content in the discourse-reference mode have been characterized by linguists as ad hoc "selectional" restrictions on the cooccurrence of lexical items.)

So such lexical items as so-called kinship terms or personal names in any society can hardly be characterized by a "semantic" analysis. It is the pragmatic component that makes them lexical items to begin with; it is the pragmatic functions$_2$ that make them anthropologically important, as Schneider, among others, have never ceased pointing out (see Schneider 1965; 1968; and chapter 8 in this volume). Further, so-called folk taxonomies of nominal lexical items, again "semantically" analyzed by a procedure of ostensive reference, essentially ripped from the context of speech, give us no cultural insight. For the whole pragmatic problem of why these lexical abbreviations form a cultural domain, rather than some other collection, why these lexical items occur at all, rather than some other semantic combinations, remains entirely to be explored. The so-called ethnoscientific structure of these vocabulary items turns out to be, from the point of view of a functional linguistics, a restatement of the fact that these semantico-referential abbreviations, rather than others, in fact occur.

Pragmatic Structure and Cultural Function

The linkage between the pragmatic grammar subsuming the traditional sort and the rest of "culture" is through the two types of function of speech. On the one hand, the cultural function$_1$ of speech comes from its goal-directed nature, which is to accomplish some kind of communicational work. Frequently, as we have seen, there are explicit lexical items which are shifters referring to such functions$_1$ in overtly recognized speech events. But these labels are not necessary for certain social functions$_1$ to be recognized. On the other hand, the cultural function$_2$ is the whole meaning structure described by the speech acts of a pragmatic grammar. As I have mentioned, all but a part of this function$_2$ is not susceptible, in general, to consciousness and accurate testimony by native participants, much as rules of semantico-grammatical systems are not. But these speech elements, which represent recurrences of behavior, have such indexical modes of meaning as presuppose and create the very categories of society which form the parameters of the speech event.

It is unreasonable, then, to take naïve native participant testimony, metabehavioral interpretation, as anything more than an *ethnosociology* which partially (and problematically) overlaps with a true *functional*[1, 2] *sociology* in terms of a pragmatic grammar based on indexical meaning. For the investigation of the latter must proceed with all the difficulties of interpretative hypotheses that are at once descriptive and comparative (see *Functional and Formal Analogues*, above pp. 40–41, and Goodenough 1970). And the interesting result is to see the ways in which societies use specifically linguistic means to constitute and maintain certain social categories, one society merging some of those given by comparative perspective, another society keeping them distinct. With a strictly linguistic focus, the pragmatic structures of speech give insight into the use of the same apparent "surface" material in distinct functional modes. And we can study the universal constraints on this rich patterning. From a broader anthropological perspective, the pragmatic system of speech *is* part of culture—in fact, perhaps the most significant part of culture—and a part the structure and function[1, 2] of which is probably the real model for the rest of culture, when the term is a construct for the meaning system of socialized behavior.

Cultural Meaning

Language is the systematic construct to explain the meaningfulness of speech behavior. We have seen that iconic, indexical, and uniquely symbolic modes of meaningfulness accrue to speech behavior. Thus any notion of language has to be inclusive enough to comprise these distinct modes, in particular, as I have stressed and elaborated, the indexical modes that link speech to the wider system of social life. The investigation here has claimed for language the uniqueness of a real symbolic mode, as that term can be justifiably used for pure semantic signs. I have linked this property to the possibility of the traditional semanticogrammatical analysis in terms of metasemantics, and have found the other linguistic modes to be categorically distinct. The pragmatic aspect

53

of language, for example, that which is constituted by its indexical mode, can similarly depend upon metapragmatic uses of speech itself in only very limited areas. Otherwise it depends upon sensitive observation and comparative illumination of functional$_{1, 2}$ speech acts and speech events for the indexical mode to be understood.

If language is unique in having a true symbolic mode, then obviously other cultural media must be more akin to the combined iconic and indexical modes of meaningfulness. In general, then, we can conclude that "cultural meaning" of behavior is so limited, except for speech, and see a *cultural description* as a massive, multiply pragmatic description of how the social categories of groups of people are constituted in a crisscrossing, frequently contradictory, ambiguous, and confusing set of pragmatic meanings of many kinds of behavior.

If there can be such apparent vagueness about pragmatic meaning, then one might be tempted to see in actual behavior the only level of integration, of orderliness, in culture. But for the social anthropologist, as for the linguist, regularities of pragmatic form and function$_2$ will ultimately define the orderliness and integration of such meaning systems. We need invoke "symbolism" for a certain modality of speech alone; the vast residue of language is culture, and culture is pragmatic.

Shake Well Before Using (L'envoi)

We must be careful how we use terms like "sign," "symbol," "semantic," "meaning," "function," and other lexical items referring to entities of semiotic theory. I have tried to be consistent in usage in this chapter, which necessitated, for example, using subscripts on certain terms. This intended careful semantico-referential function$_1$ of usage must be the sole criterion of judgment of the argument here that culture is, with the exception of a small part of language, but a congeries of iconic-indexical systems of meaningfulness of behavior.

Usage of the same terms by others should be similarly scrutinized for actual referential content, which may differ considerably in terms of the underlying theory. We must not be carried away by the rhetorical —that is, pragmatic—force of scientific argumentation, wherein, contradictorily enough, lies its sole power as natural communication, this chapter, alas, being another token of the type.

NOTE

1. This study replaces a longer one of the same title discussed at the School of American Research seminar "Meaning in Cultural Anthropology." That work was a draft for the opening sections of a larger work in progress on the anthropology of language. This work, narrowed in focus, refashions some of that, incorporating material from four lectures given during 1974 since the conference: "Pragmatic Functional Analogues in Language," University of New Mexico, March 25; "Metasemantics and Metapragmatics, Implications for Cognitive Research," University of Chicago, May 8; "The Meaning of Pragmatics and the Pragmatics of Meaning," University of Chicago, May 27, and Research School of Pacific Studies, Australian National University, September 18. For comments on the draft chapters, I would especially like to thank Carol Feldman, Paul Friedrich, and Norman McQuown, in addition to the participants at the School of American Research seminar. For particularly useful discussion of points raised in the lectures, aiding my attempts at clarification, I am indebted to Philip Bock, Carol Feldman, Marshall Sahlins, David Schneider, Milton Singer, James Talvitie, Anthony Forge, Roger Keesing, and Anna Wierzbicka. The final draft has been completed under the less-than-ideal conditions of fieldwork, and I beg the reader's indulgence of my bibliographic laxity. The galley proofs benefited from a careful reading of the manuscript graciously communicated by Rodney Huddleston.

3

The "Meaning" of Kinship in American Culture: Another View

HAROLD W. SCHEFFLER

Yale University

INTRODUCTION[1]

How do our respective orientations to the study of "meaning" and "cultural symbols" differ from one another, and how, if at all, can the differences be reconciled? Perhaps I can contribute to the clarification and understanding of these issues by critically evaluating and offering an alternative to some aspects of D. M. Schneider's interpretation of the meanings and relations among the meanings of American kinship terms and, more broadly, of "the meaning of kinship" in American culture.[2] In so doing, I offer an answer (though not the whole answer) to Schneider's (1972: 50) claim that "kinship," defined exclusively in terms of relations of genealogical connection, "does not correspond to any cultural category known to man." I hope to show that such a category does exist in American culture.

SCHNEIDER'S INTERPRETATION

Schneider (1970a: 88) claims to have shown that:

kinship is defined in three distinct but closely interrelated ways in American culture. It is first defined as a relationship of bio-genetic substance, second as a mode of interpersonal relationship governed by a code for conduct which demands enduring diffuse solidarity, and third as containing both of these elements at the same time, as in the case of the so-called "blood relatives."

The argument, in other words, is that two kinds of "relationship"—"by blood" ("in nature") and "in law"[3]—are distinctive features of kinship and of the several categories of "relative" in American culture. A person may be regarded as a "relative" or as a particular kind of "relative" if he or she is related to some ego or propositus in either or both of these ways (see table 1). According to Schneider (1968: 70, 93), relationships

TABLE 1

SCHNEIDER'S DISTINCTIVE FEATURES MODEL

	Kinds of Relative	Distinctive Features		Kinds of Father
		Nature	Law	
1.	In nature	+	−	Natural father
2.	In law	−	+	Father in law
3.	By blood	+	+	Real father

by blood (in nature) and in law are alternative necessary (as well as sufficient) conditions for designation as a *relative*[4] (or by some more specific kinship term). This, he argues, is demonstrated by the fact that it is acceptable for one person to assert of another that the other is *not* a "relative" if the two are related by blood but do not sustain a social relationship characterized by diffuse, enduring solidarity; or that the other *is* a "relative" if the two are not related by blood (or even by marriage) but do sustain such a social relationship. In Schneider's model, the three categories of "relative" are related paradigmatically; none is logically prior to, derived from, or contained in any other.

Schneider argues that the more specific kinship terms follow the same pattern. Thus, *father* also designates three categories (see table 1). One kind of "father" is the "natural father," a genitor who is not the mother's husband and who does not perform his duties or claim his rights as the genitor. Another kind of "father" consists of men, none of whom is ego's genitor, but with whom ego does sustain social relationships more or less like those normatively ascribed between genitors and their offspring. This class has no lexemic designation (simple or complex) but is divided into a number of subclasses designated *stepfather, foster father, adoptive father, father-in-law,* and so on. The third kind of "father" is that man to whom ego is related in both ways at once: ego's genitor, who is also ego's mother's husband, and who performs his duties and claims his rights as ego's genitor. According to Schneider, this category is designated *real father.* Schneider attempts to account for the fact that, in some churches, priests are designated as *Father* by arguing that a priest is a "father" of the second kind, a man who is not ego's genitor but with whom ego sustains a social relationship like that normatively ascribed between genitors and their offspring.

On the basis of this interpretation of the meanings and relations among the meanings of American kinship terms, Schneider argues that analyses such as that presented in Goodenough's "Yankee Kinship Terminology" (1965) are seriously misleading and distort ethnographic reality. They assume that kinship in American culture is genealogically defined—that relationship by genealogical connection and by marriage are the distinctive features of the categories designated by American kinship terms—and therefore do not take into account the social relationships referred to by the terms, except to note in passing that they are nondistinctive (that is, contingent) features of kin categories and irrelevant to the task at hand, which is to specify definitions for the kin categories themselves. But this assumption, Schneider argues, is quite false; genealogical and social relationships are alternative distinctive features of the categories designated by American kinship terms, and the definitions of these categories cannot be stated in genealogical terms alone. It follows, Schneider argues, that the definitions provided in an account like Goodenough's are at best incomplete and that the structure of the terminological system as a whole is seriously misrepresented by them.

According to Schneider (1972: 49), the American "kinship" system is by no means unique; the kinship systems, so-called, of many other cultures—he notes Yap, Apache, Zuni, Navajo, Nukuoro, Banaba, Bengali, Daribi, and Maue, "to mention only a few"—are not genealogically based, either. Indeed, Schneider argues, "kinship" defined exclusively in terms of genealogy "*does not correspond to any cultural category known to man*" (1972: 50; the emphasis is Schneider's).

Leaving aside the question of the validity of this sweeping generalization, we should note some of the difficulties for Schneider's argument about the American "kinship" system in particular. It is premised on certain alleged matters of ethnographic fact about which there is room for disagreement, and it is incomplete and internally inconsistent in some important respects.

SOME DIFFICULTIES FOR SCHNEIDER'S INTERPRETATION

If there is a single phrase that adequately summarizes Schneider's aim in *American Kinship* (1968), it is that he wishes to "discover the American cultural definition of what a relative is" (1968: 21, 22 n. 2). To do this, he insists, we "must take the natives' own categories and follow their definitions, their symbolic and meaningful divisions wherever they may lead" (1972: 51). This, however, is not what Schneider did.

We can "begin to discover what a relative is," Schneider says, "by considering those terms which are the names for the kinds of relatives—among other things—and which mark the scheme for their classification." He then argues that these terms "can be divided into two groups," basic and derivative terms, the latter "made up of a basic term plus a modifier" (1968: 21). The modifiers, he says, are of two kinds, "restrictive" and "unrestrictive." The restrictive modifiers are most relevant here. These modifiers, for example, *step* and *in-law*, Schneider says, "sharply divide blood relatives from those in comparable positions who are not blood relatives" (1968: 22). The phrase "in comparable positions" is not explained, but one plausible interpretation is that it refers to "social positions," and to the later argument that the "step" and "in-law" categories belong to an (implicit?) "in law" category whose distinctive feature is "relationship by a code for conduct which demands diffuse, enduring solidarity" in the absence of a blood relationship (1968: 76ff.). This is consistent with the claim (1968: 100) that the modifiers *den, house,* and *superior* "are all members of the same set" and have the same general semantic function as the modifiers *step* and *in-law*, which is to indicate that the denotatum is a person who "plays the role" signified by the term to which it is attached.

The underlying assumption here is that, in American culture, a bipartite distinction is made among all those individuals who are denoted by specific kinship terms in lexically unmarked or marked forms: (1)

those who are "blood relatives" and (2) those who are not "blood relatives" but who may or may not be regarded as "relatives" in some other sense of the term. This is a dubious assumption, however, for the fact of the matter is that some individuals who are denoted by specific kinship terms are not regarded (or regardable) as "relatives" in *any* sense of the term. While it is true, for example, that a step or adoptive mother may or may not be "counted as a relative," depending on which of the several senses of *relative* the speaker has in mind, a den mother or housemother is not a "relative" in any sense of the term. Also, as Schneider (1970a: 88) has noted, "There is no question but that the priest is *not* a relative," that is, a priest is not any kind of "relative." It follows that "mother, den mother, housemother" are *not* "a single set which consists in differentiated kinds of mother roles or mother relationships" (cf. Schneider 1970a: 88). What we have to deal with here are two sets: (1) those women who are "relatives" in some sense of the term and also "mothers" of one kind or another, and (2) those women who are not "relatives" of any kind but who are, even so, denotable by the expression *mother*, perhaps in some obligatorily marked form.

In other words, the distinction that must be recognized here—the distinction actually made in American culture—is between those individuals who are one's "relatives" and those individuals who are not one's "relatives," and, within the former category, the distinction between "blood relatives" and "relatives" of other kinds.

Specific kinship terms may be used to denote individuals who are not regarded as "relatives" of any kind. While Schneider notes this possibility, he does not consider it systematically and fails to account for it either formally or sociologically. He observes that "the person to whom the kinship term is applied may or may not be defined as a relative," and adds, apparently by way of explanation, "This follows from the fact that a person is the object which takes a kinship term; the kinship term is not the object itself" (1968: 100). This, however, is only a restatement of the previous observation, namely, that use of a kinship term to denote a person does not necessarily imply that the denotatum is regarded as a "relative" of one kind or another. In short, kinship terms may be used to denote nonrelatives.

The difficulty is that Schneider's distinctive features model does not allow for this possibility. The model posits the existence of three paradigmatically related categories of "relatives," one of which Schneider describes as *relatives by marriage* or *in laws*. The distinctive feature of this category is alleged to be "relationship according to a code for conduct which demands diffuse, enduring solidarity." According to Schneider, the existence of such a relationship between, for example, a woman and her Cub Scout charges is what accounts for her designation as a *den mother*. If, however, the existence of such a relationship between a man and his adoptive child is what accounts for his designation as the child's (adoptive) father as well as his designation as that child's *relative*, it must follow that a den mother also is a kind of "relative." Thus, Schneider's distinctive features model implies that all persons denoted by kinship terms should be denotable also as *relatives* in one or another sense of the term. The model leaves no room for the use of kinship terms as the "names" for any "things" other than "relatives" (cf. Schneider 1968: 21).

Another difficulty is that several of Schneider's observations about the relations among the meanings of American kinship terms are inconsistent with one another. As noted above, in Schneider's model the relationships posited among the several categories of "relative," such as "father," are paradigmatic and nonderivational. At one point, however, Schneider (1970b: 374) says, "relative by marriage is defined by reference to relative by blood in American culture." (And it is true that the "in-law" category is so defined; see below, pp. 69–70.) He does not explain, however, whether, in this context, *relative by blood* refers to "relative by blood alone" or "relative by blood and in law." It is difficult to see how it could be either, again because Schneider's definitions of the several classes of "relative" preclude any such relationships among them.

A key element in Schneider's argument is his claim that, in American culture, there is no category which includes the genitor alone and which is defined independently of whether or not the genitor sustains a particular kind of social relationship with ego; the category "natural father" contains the genitor, and the category "real father" contains the genitor who *does* perform his duties and claim his rights as genitor. If this is true, interaction according to "the code for conduct which demands enduring, diffuse solidarity" is a distinctive feature of one category ("real father") and its converse (not its absence or irrelevance) is a distinctive feature of the other category ("natural father").

To my knowledge, however, the expression *natural father* distinguishes genitors, who may or may not perform their duties and claim their rights as such, from other men who are not genitors but who have, either legally or morally, accepted the genitor's duties, or at least some of them. Further, to the best of my knowledge, *real father* may do the same. That is to say, these expressions do not designate different categories but are alternate expressions for one and the same category. This, of course, is not to claim that the expressions are wholly synonymous, for two expressions may designate the same category, and yet have quite different connotations[5] (as in the case of *dad* or *daddy* versus *father*; cf. Schneider 1970a: 88). Thus, it is true that *natural father* may be used to distinguish the genitor of a child from the man who is caring for it but who is not the child's genitor, and who, we may say, "is not its real or natural father but its step- (or adoptive or foster) father." People do prefer to say that an illegitimate genitor is "the child's natural father" rather than that he engendered the child out of wedlock. In this context, however, *natural father* is employed as a euphemism. *Natural father* is a suitable euphemism in this context only because it does not necessarily imply that the denotatum has engendered a child out of wedlock. The expression *real father* is not, I think, commonly used euphemistically to denote illegitimate genitors, and so its connotations are perhaps somewhat different from those of *natural father*, whose use in everyday discourse (but not in legal discourse) is largely restricted to contexts in which the euphemism is intended. Thus the difference between *natural father* and *real father* is in their respective connotations, not in the distinctive features of the kin categories they designate, which are the same.

Now just as there is no difference between "natural father" and "real father" as kin categories, there is, in general, no difference between the two broad categories of "relatives" to which Schneider claims these allegedly different classes of "father" belong, "relatives by blood alone" and "relatives by blood and in law." That these are one and the same category is indicated by the fact that the expression *blood relative* may be used to denote either a person to whom one is related by blood but with whom one sustains no social relations, or a person to whom one is related by blood and with whom one does sustain social relations characterized by diffuse, enduring solidarity (cf. Schneider 1968: 111).

As already noted, Schneider denies this apparent implication and argues that the expression *blood relatives* is polysemous, although he denies that the alleged two categories so designated are related in such a way that one may be said to be derived from the other.[6] Perhaps the key element in Schneider's argument on this point is his claim that it is acceptable to assert that a person to whom one is related by blood is not a relative, on the ground that the speaker and the person in question do not sustain a social relationship characterized by diffuse, enduring solidarity. In this connection, Schneider cites one woman who "asserted that her sister was not a relative because she had not seen or heard from her for some years now" (1968: 70). Schneider states that, because "this statement seemed in plain conflict with the fact (or with the statements of many other informants) that a blood relative always remains a relative," he "at first dismissed her statement as absurd." But this, he says, was the wrong thing to do; it was wrong because, he now sees, the woman was merely employing an alternative, culturally acceptable definition of "what a relative is," that is, a person to whom one is related by blood is not a "relative" unless one relates socially to that person.

Despite this argument, Schneider makes much of the fact that by and large his informants insisted that blood relationships are facts of nature which cannot be severed, lost, terminated, or changed, and that individuals who are related by blood always remain "relatives" even if they are unaware of each other's existence (Schneider 1968: 71; 1970b: 373). This plainly implies that a person is a "relative" (specifically a "blood relative") if and only if he or she is related by blood and that it is *irrelevant* whether or not one sustains a social relationship of any kind with that person. Equally plainly, this definition of what a "blood relative" is flatly contradicts the assertion that a person to whom one is related by blood is not a relative unless one relates socially to that person, since it cannot reasonably be argued that the two statements refer to or define two different categories.

The contradiction, however, is more apparent than real, not because it is somehow resolved (cf. Schneider 1968: 107–10)—for it is logically incapable of being resolved except by changing one of its terms—but because there is another and more plausible way to understand Schneider's informant's assertion that her sister is not a relative. It is to suppose that the statement is *figuratively* but not literally true. As Schneider himself notes, he "at first dismissed her statement as absurd," and most people, I think, would say that the assertion is false or absurd—if taken literally. Taken figuratively, however, it is readily understandable as an overstatement of (and as an elliptical reference to) what everyone knows to be true. We know that persons to whom we are related by blood but with whom we do not relate (that is, with whom we have little or nothing to do) are "relatives" nonetheless, but we know also that "they are not relatives in any meaningful sense"—which, again, is not to say that they are not "relatives" but only that the fact that they are is of no *immediate* social significance to us. One can easily overstate this argument by stating without qualification that the individuals in question are not "relatives," and the statement will be understood, though as a hyperbole rather than as an indication of one's understanding of the distinctive features of the category "relative."

Similarly, we know that people are often "closer" (socially) to non-relatives than they are to "relatives," so that nonrelatives may be "more like relatives" to us than some of our actual or real "relatives" are. Again, recognition of this can easily be overstated, but in this case by using *relative* metaphorically and by asserting that a person with whom one does not claim a relationship by blood or by marriage is a "relative." Thus, knowingly or not, another of Schneider's informants was speaking metaphorically when she "affirmed, and could not be dissuaded from the position, that her roommate was a relative even though she claimed no connection of blood or marriage between them" (1968: 70).

Schneider, as already noted, claims that these are not instances of figurative uses of kinship terms. This argument is premised on the assumption that interaction according to "the code for conduct which demands diffuse, enduring solidarity" is a distinctive feature of the categories designated by American kinship terms. The validity of this assumption is open to doubt because Schneider's argument in support of it suffers from at least two serious defects.

First, as Schneider has often noted, the social relationships in question are ascribed between individuals who are related by blood or by marriage; it is because they are so related that they are obliged to interact according to "the code for conduct which demands diffuse enduring solidarity." In other words, these social relationships are normative implications of membership in certain kin categories. They are contingent or nondistinctive features, rather than distinctive or defining features (cf. Schneider and Smith 1973: 71–72 on the "concomitant" features of "sex"). Schneider denies this and argues that interaction according to this "code for conduct" is one of the distinctive features of American kin categories. But, as we have already seen, this argument is false; the expressions *natural father* and *real father* refer to one and the same category (namely, the genitor who may or may not acknowledge his duties and claim his rights as genitor), and Schnieder's "relatives by blood alone" and "relatives by blood and in law" are also one and the same category.

The second difficulty concerns Schneider's category "relative by marriage" or "relative in law." Some of the persons who belong to this category are related to ego by marriage, but others are not; so Schneider argues that relationship by marriage is not a distinctive feature of the category. "To understand 'by marriage' and 'in law' as the names for this category," he argues, we must realize that *by marriage* is not to be taken literally (my phrasing, not his). The expression *by marriage*, he argues, here serves to symbolize "the order of law" (the order of "obedience to rules") in general, rather than marital relationships in particular, which are, however, the "in law" relationships par excellence within the domain of kinship (cf. Schneider 1968: 96; 1970b: 380).

The argument is not convincing. The fact of the matter is that *by marriage* and *in-law* are not the names of Schneider's category "relatives in law." According to Schneider, the step, foster, and adoptive relatives, as well as many nonrelatives such as den mothers, priests, and so on, are "relatives in law." None of these, however, are designatable as *in-laws*; some are not designatable as *relatives by marriage*; and others are not designatable as *relatives* in any sense of the term. Moreover, it is immaterial for designation as an in-law whether or not ego interacts at all with the person in question; a man's wife's mother is his mother-in-law and a kind of "relative" whether or not he has ever seen the woman; and a man may be regarded as someone's stepfather even if he systematically abuses that person and does not interact with him or her according to "the code for conduct which demands diffuse, enduring solidarity." Therefore, interaction according to "the code for conduct . . ." is not a distinctive feature of the category designated as *relative by marriage* or *in-law*.[7]

There is a problem, too, in Schneider's use of *par excellence*. When he says that marriage is the "in law" relationship par excellence (within the domain of "kinship") he appears to mean that it is singled out as a special case, somehow the most special case, of "in law" relationships in general; and because marriage is the most special case, the expression *by marriage* is made the designation for the class as a whole. We have already noted, however, that *relative by marriage* is not the designation for Schneider's "in law" class. Moreover, Schneider's analysis treats those who are in fact related by marriage as a *marked* subclass of the "in law" class, a subclass singled out by narrowing or specialization (that is, by the stipulation of an additional defining feature) from the general class. But if it were true that those who are related by marriage constitute a special, marked subclass of "in laws" in general, it would be inconsistent to assert that relationship by marriage is the relationship in law par excellence. According to Greenberg (1966: 72), whom Schneider cites on the matter of markedness (1968: 96 n. 4), it is the unmarked member of an opposition that represents either the entire "oppositional category" or par excellence the opposite member to the marked category.[8] Therefore it would be especially odd if, in this case, the sign of the marked category were also the sign of the "oppositional category" as a whole. So it is not surprising that, contrary to what Schneider claims, the alleged "in law" class is not designated *relative by marriage* or *in-law*.

Finally, Schneider (1968: 96) states, "It [marriage] is the very essence of the relationship in law of all of the different kinds of relationships in law within the domain of kinship." But he claims also that relationship by marriage is not the distinctive feature of the "in law" class. The two claims seem mutually contradictory. In Aristotelian terms, the "essence" of some kind of "thing" consists in the property or properties (features) of the thing, without which it would not be a thing of that kind; it is, in other words, the distinctive feature of that kind of "thing." If relationship by marriage were the "essence" of the "in law" class, it would not be just a special case of relationships in law (within the domain of "kinship") in general but, in fact, *the* case in terms of which or by comparison with which other kinds of social relationships also may be regarded, by generalization or "extension," as "relationships in law" (again, within the domain of "kinship"). Although I argue below that some categories of "relative" are in fact related to others by extension, that plainly is not the arrangement we have to deal with here; the fact of the matter, again, is that many of the alleged members of Schneider's "in law" class are not designated as *relatives by marriage,* or *in-laws,* even by extension.

AN ALTERNATIVE INTERPRETATION

Some aspects of how, in my opinion, the proper cultural account of the meanings and relations among the meanings of American kinship terms must differ from that proposed by Schneider have been presented in the preceding section. So far, my principal concern has been to show that the standards which govern interaction between persons who are related by blood or by marriage are not *distinctive* features of the categories "blood relative" and "relative by marriage" or of their more specific subcategories. It remains to be shown in greater detail how these categories are defined and how they are related to one another.

It is not feasible here to present a full-scale structural semantic analysis of the American English system of kin classification, much less of "American kinship terminology," that is, of all the meanings and relations among the meanings of American kinship terms. The most I can do is present, in brief, my understanding of how the major categories of "relatives" are defined and related to one another.

As Schneider (1968: 21) has observed, if asked "What is a relative?" American informants almost always reply, "A relative is a person who is related by blood or by marriage." This statement makes no mention of how those who are so related should conduct their social relationships with one another, nor does it provide for the fact that some individuals who are not related by blood or by marriage may be designated as *relatives,* for example, the foster and adoptive relatives. If asked about the foster and adoptive relatives, "Are they relatives, also?" the reply may be, "Yes, we call them relatives, too, but they are not really relatives." And if asked why they are "relatives," though not related by blood or by marriage, the answer is likely to contain some reference to the fact that they take the social places of "real relatives." The implications of all this appear to be that standards of interpersonal conduct are not distinctive features of the category "relatives"; foster and adoptive relatives are "relatives" by metaphoric extension.[9] Because they are "not really relatives" they are not mentioned in the definitional statement "a relative is a person who is related by blood or by marriage."

68

What, then, of the steprelatives and the in-laws, of whom also it may be said, "They are not real relatives." Are they too relatives by metaphoric extension?

Let us consider first the case of the "in-laws." The principal "in-laws" are one's spouse's parents and siblings and, conversely, the spouses of one's own children and siblings (cf. Schneider 1968: 77–78). They are "relatives by marriage" because they are "blood relatives" of one's spouse, or, conversely, spouses of one's own "blood relatives." Optionally, the expression *in-law* may be extended to "blood relatives" of the spouse's parents and, conversely, to "blood relatives" of the child's spouse. It is important to note, however, that not all "blood relatives" of one's spouse are designated as *in-laws,* nor are all spouses of one's own "blood relatives." Spouse's child, for example, is one's own child and a "blood relative," or is one's spouse's child by a previous marriage and therefore is one's stepchild. Similarly, parent's spouse is one's own parent or stepparent. Apparently, if asked to generalize about the meaning or use of the expression *in-law,* some Americans tend to overgeneralize and may appear to suggest that an "in-law" is "anyone related in any way by any marriage" (cf. Schneider 1968: 78). But inspection of actual use of the expression shows that this *is* an overgeneralization and that it is more correct (because more specific) to say that *some* "blood relatives" of one's spouse and *some* spouses of one's own "blood relatives" are "in-laws."

Plainly, the category of "relatives" that includes "in-laws" as well as "blood relatives" is derived by extension from the category "blood relative." The extension is accomplished by neutralizing or suspending the distinction made in the definition of the category "blood relative" between one's own parents and siblings and those of another person, specifically those of one's spouse. Because the neutralization is of a genealogical distinction, the extension is genealogically based; it has nothing to do with the quality of the social relationships, if any, between ego and his or her parents and siblings. Therefore, the extension is "simple" rather than metaphorical (cf. Scheffler and Lounsbury 1971: 7–10). But an "in-law" is a "relative" only by extension, and not a "relative" in the primary (logically prior) sense of the expression. Therefore, when it is said that "in-laws" are "not real relatives" (or "not really relatives"), the intention is to assert only that they are not "blood relatives," not that they are not "relatives" of any kind; they *are* "relatives": of another kind or in another (but not metaphoric) sense of the term.

The case of the "steprelatives" is both similar and different in some respects. The principal stepparents are parents' spouses who are not also one's own parents and, conversely, spouses' children who are not also one's own children. Optionally, the "blood relatives" of stepparents may be designated as *relatives*, too. The category of "relatives" then includes "steprelatives" as well as "blood relatives." The extension is accomplished by neutralizing or suspending the distinction between a parent's spouse who is one's own parent and a parent's spouse who is not one's own parent; and, conversely, between a spouse's child who is one's own child and a spouse's child who is not one's own child. Again, the extension is genealogically based and not metaphorical. As in the case of the "in-laws," when it is said that a stepparent or stepchild is "not a real relative" or "not really a relative," the intention is to assert only that he or she is not a "blood relative," not that he or she is not a "relative" of any kind. Thus, the case of the "steprelatives" is similar to that of the "in-laws" insofar as both are "relatives" by extension and the extension in both cases is genealogically based and nonmetaphorical. The two cases are different, however, in that they depend on different rules of extension.

There is a further difference. In the preceding discussion, it was assumed that it is irrelevant for designation by either expression—*stepfather* or *father-in-law*—whether or not ego relates socially to the denotatum. It must be noted, however, that not all mothers' husbands (who are not also genitors) are spoken of or referred to as *stepfather* or *father*. Consider, for example, the case of a man who marries a divorced woman whose children are in the custody of her ex-husband. Such a man is not likely to be spoken of as *stepfather* or *father* by these children, nor is he likely to refer to himself as their *stepfather* or *father*; and neither he nor they are likely to speak of one another as *relatives* or as *relatives by marriage*, though they might, if pressed, say that they are related by or through marriage. Similarly, if a woman remarries after her children are grown and have domiciles of their own, they are not likely to speak of her husband as a *stepfather*, *father*, or *relative*, unless their own father is deceased or they have no social relations with him, and unless they are particularly friendly with their mother's husband and he treats them in a warm, fatherly fashion. Probably, if asked of a mother's husband who has not participated in their rearing, "Is X your stepfather?," some people would reply that he is not a relative, much less that he is a stepfather. Others, however, might say something like, "Well, technically I suppose he is my stepfather, but I never speak of him that way. After all, he is not really like a father to me." It seems clear enough that people are reluctant to designate a mother's husband who has not participated in their rearing, or who has not otherwise acted "like a father," by the expressions *relative, stepfather,* and *father.*

In order to account for this it is not necessary to suppose that "stepfather" is a subclass of a lexically unmarked superclass whose distinctive feature is interaction according to a "code for conduct that demands diffuse, enduring solidarity" and that membership in the subclass is determined by the relationship of marriage to one's mother. Indeed, this supposition is ruled out by the fact that a man may seriously abuse his wife's dependent children and still be regarded by himself and by them as their stepfather (cf. Schneider 1968: 27; 1970: 375 on the "cruel stepmother"). Thus, while it may be that conduct according to the standards for father-child interaction is a condition that governs *use* of the expressions *stepfather* and *father,* such conduct is not a distinctive feature of the category "stepfather."

Here (as in the cases of the ex-uncle and the new uncle or aunt's subsequent husband, cf. Schneider 1968: 80–81, 92–93), it is necessary to distinguish between an account of the *use* of an expression and an account of its *meanings.* Its meanings, we may say, consist in part of the conditions which are necessary (as well as sufficient) for designation by it; these conditions constitute the definitive meaning of the expression, or its definitive meanings in the case of a polysemous or homonymous expression. Its meanings consist also of those conditions which are merely sufficient for designation by it; these conditions constitute its nondefinitive meaning or meanings, or its connotations. Knowledge of these several conditions is not sufficient, however, to enable us to predict use of the expression. Its use depends not only on its meaning or meanings but also on the situation in which the speakers find themselves, on their perceptions and conceptions of those situations, and on their intentions in dealing with the objects they perceive in those situations. Thus, for example, a speaker may choose to denote some object, to which the expression X might be applied, by some other expression, Y, which is figuratively (perhaps metaphorically) appropriate. Also, a

71

culture may feature rules (extra semantic or sociolinguistic rules) that prohibit the use of an expression where its connotations are expressive of some stigma (cf. the discussion of *natural father* in the preceding section, pp. 62–63 above) or where its connotations are inappropriate, even though, in that context, use of the expresison would be "technically" correct because those conditions which constitute its definitive meaning are present. This, it seems, is the kind of situation we have to deal with in the case of *stepfather*. Use of the expression to denote a man who has not participated in the rearing of his wife's children, or otherwise conducted himself toward them more or less as a father should, is connotatively inappropriate; therefore the term is not used to denote him, though it would be "technically" correct to use it.

If this is true, a man is one's stepfather if and only if he is one's mother's husband (but not one's genitor); this relationship is the distinctive feature of the category "stepfather." And, if so, the restrictions on the use of English *stepfather* are similar to the restrictions on the Yapese use of *citimongog* 'father' (cf. Schneider 1953). They are restrictions on the use of the term in specified social contexts in which its connotations (or some of them, anyway) are inappropriate, but they are not restrictions on or features of its definitive meaning.

We have seen that "steprelatives" and "in-laws" are both "relatives" by extension (but not metaphoric extension) and that the extension rules in the two cases are somewhat different. The two classes are similar, however, in that both are related to ego through marital as well as genealogical connections. For this reason, either kind of "relative" may be described as a "relative by marriage." Yet, as Schneider (1968: 95) has noted, some Americans are "uncomfortable" with the designation of steprelatives as *relatives by marriage,* though they are, it seems, unable to say why. The reason, I think, is that in the expression "a relative is a person related by blood or by marriage," the marriage referred to is ego's own, and the expression may be paraphrased as "my relatives are those individuals to whom I am related by my birth or by my marriage." In other words, the "relatives by marriage" referred to in this expression are one's "in-laws," and most especially one's spouse's parents and siblings (cf. Schneider 1968: 77). If so, it follows that, strictly speaking, "steprelatives" and others such as parents' spouses' siblings are not "relatives by marriage."

Even so, we speak of stepfathers—and of aunts' husbands and uncles' wives—as *relatives* and, if pressed for a reason, we can note that there is a marital relationship; one is related to one's stepfather through his marriage to one's mother. It is all too easy, however, to slip from "through marriage" to "by marriage" and thus to confuse the "relatives" to whom one is related through the marriages of one's own senior-generation blood relatives with the principal "relatives by marriage," namely, one's "in-laws." This, I suspect, is just what happened when one one Schneider's informants said, "Oh, yes. My aunt's husband is a relative all right. He is a relative by marriage. One of my in-laws, I suppose. I call him 'uncle' you know!" (Schneider 1968: 93).

If the primary "in-laws" are the parents and siblings of one's spouse (and, conversely, the spouses of one's children and siblings), spouses are not "in-laws" or "relatives by marriage." But according to Schneider (1968: 77), "Americans may properly say that their husband or wife is not a relative, but an in-law or someone related by marriage." Thus, he argues, the spouse categories are "in-law" categories; they are, indeed, the "in law" categories par excellence (Schneider 1968: 95–96; 1970b: 379–81). Although Schneider's hypothetical "in law" category is nonexistent, it may be that some Americans, when asked about it, do say that spouses are in-laws or, more likely, that they are *like* in-laws or relatives by marriage. It must be, however, that explicitly or implicitly these Americans are making an analogy rather than predicating membership of the spouse classes in the "in-law" or "relative by marriage" class. The analogy must rest on the fact that spouses are related by marriage in the special sense that they are married to one another. But, plainly, being related by marriage in this special sense is quite different from being related by marriage in the way required to be classified as an "in-law" or "relative by marriage." Indeed, in my experience, many people regard it as somewhat "odd" even to say that husband and wife are related by marriage. The perceived oddity lies, I think, in the fact that to say that one is related by marriage to his or her spouse is to suggest that his or her spouse is a "relative by marriage" or an "in-law," when in fact he or she is not a "relative" of any kind.[10] It follows from this that we must say that the spouse categories are not a part of the American system of kin classification, at least insofar as they are not subcategories of any category of "relatives." But they are part of that system insofar as they are categories by reference to which membership of other categories within that system is determined; one's spouse, that is, is the person by reference to whom membership of the category "relatives by marriage" or "in-laws" is determined.

The case of the steprelatives is somewhat different. As we have seen, there are reasons to suppose that the use of the expression *relative by marriage* in reference to a parent's spouse is nothing more than a rather loose, imprecise, and misleading use. We have seen that "steprelatives" are not "relatives by marriage" or "in-law"; neither are they "blood relatives." Yet they are related to ego through genealogical and marital connections and they are designated as *relatives* in one of the extended (but not metaphorical) senses of the expression. This must be a rather special category of "relatives," whose existence is not implied in the statement "a relative is a person who is related by blood or by marriage." A stepfather, for example, is a substitute father, the man who takes the place of ego's own father as ego's mother's husband and as the male head of ego's family of orientation. Although a stepfather is like one's own father in some respects, he can never be like one's own father in the way required to be a member of the category "blood relative." Moreover, a stepfather is not at all like a father-in-law. A father-in-law is not a substitute father; he is one's spouse's father. Therefore, a stepfather is very much a secondary kind of "father" and a secondary kind of "relative," not a relative "properly speaking." The situation of the steprelatives in general is the same; members of this category are like particular kinds of "blood relatives," not like particular kinds of "in-laws." The "step" category, like the "in-law" category, is derived by extension from the category "blood relatives," but the two derived categories are quite distinct and do not belong to any supercategory other than the most general category of "relatives" (see below, figure 1).

Some mention must be made of the spouses of uncles and aunts and their reciprocals, the children of one's spouse's siblings. Such persons are designated as *uncle, aunt, nephew,* or *niece* and as *relatives,* and they are sometimes described (though again, it seems, somewhat loosely and imprecisely) as *relatives by marriage.* Although they are related to ego through marriage, they are not "in-laws" or "steprelatives," so it must be that they constitute yet another class of "relatives" by extension, though this class has no special designation of its own.

We may now consider the adoptive and foster "relatives." Here, it is clear, we enter into the realm of metaphoric extension. This is evident if we consider the cases of adoptive and foster fathers. A man becomes an adoptive father by entering, usually along with his wife, into a legal contract to accept a child whom he did not engender and whom she did not bear, as the legal equivalent of his own or natural child. When a man thus adopts a child, the child becomes his legal heir. Although a man may adopt a child to whom he or his wife is genealogically related, the fact of a prior genealogical relationship does not give anyone a prior right to adopt, nor does it impose a duty to adopt. So, unlike the situation in many other cultures, specific kinds of relatives of the natural parents have neither the right nor the duty to succeed to the legal statuses of the parents or to claim those statuses should the parents wish to relinquish them. There are, in other words, no genealogical- or marital-relationship criteria of entitlement to the status of adoptive parent. Therefore, adoptive fathers are "fathers" and "relatives" only metaphorically; they are only like fathers, and they are like fathers in that they take the legal places of "fathers" (genitors). This legal status imposes on the adoptor all of the legally sanctioned rights and duties of the genitor, and in accepting the legal status he accepts the morally sanctioned rights and duties of the genitor as well. Thus, adoptive fathers are expected morally and legally "to act like fathers," because the act of adoption is a sign of one's voluntary consent to those expectations. The case of the foster father is similar. A foster father is a man who takes care of or looks after a child as its genitor should, but without entering into a legal contract to accept the child as his legal heir, though he may have entered into a legal contract to care for the child for a specified or unspecified period.

The fact that adoptive and foster fathers are men who have voluntarily undertaken "to play the father role" *in full* probably accounts for the fact that they are classified as "relatives," though again only metaphorically. For it seems probable that the expression *relative* does connote "diffuse, enduring solidarity," at least when used in reference to a "blood relative," and that this is expected of adoptive and foster fathers.

This brings us to the cases of those persons who are denoted by specific kinship terms such as *father, mother,* and so on, or by constructions based on kinship terms such as *den mother, housemother,* and the like, but who are not regarded as any kind of "relative." These are metaphoric uses of kinship terms because they are based on reference to nondistinctive or contingent features of membership of kin categories.[11] Consider the case of *den mother*. A den mother is a woman who is charged with the supervision of a group of boys in their activities as Cub Scouts, just as a mother is charged with the supervision of her children in their domestic activities. There is no reference here to genealogical relationship or to relationship by marriage, because no such relationships exist between den mothers and their charges (except accidentally in the case of a woman whose son happens to be a member of her Cub Scout pack). The reference is solely to some aspects of the social implications of membership of the kin category "mother." There is a similar (though by no means identical) reference in the case of an "adoptive mother." An "adoptive mother," however, is a kind of "relative," while a den mother is not; for, after all, "diffuse, enduring solidarity" is required of an adoptive mother but not of a den mother. A den mother, then, is a kind of "mother," but a special metaphoric kind which is not included in the metaphoric kind of "relative." Again, the general "mother" class to which all the more specific kinds of "mothers" belong is *not* "a single set which consists in differentiated kinds of mother roles or mother relationships" (Schneider 1970a: 88). It is instead a composite, disjunctively defined class whose central or logically most prior subclass is genealogically defined. Other subclasses ("stepmother" and "mother-in-law") are defined by genealogical and marital relationships, and yet others are defined only by social relationships. When a woman socially takes the place of a child's mother (genetrix) and contracts to fill the mother role in full, she is designated metaphorically as the child's *relative*. In contrast, when a woman's role is perceived as similar in some limited respect to the role ascribed to women as mothers, she is not designated metaphorically as the child's *relative*, though she may be designated metaphorically as one or another kind of *mother*, for example *den mother*.

The relationships among the major nonmetaphoric categories of "relatives" in American cultures are represented in figure 1. As the figure suggests (but does not adequately show), "the meaning of kinship" in American culture is many layered (cf. Malinowski 1930: 29) and encompasses several semantic domains. At base, it is a matter of "relationship by blood," where "blood" stands metonymically (cf. Schneider 1968: 23–24) for all the bodily substances shared by those who are related by birth; and persons who are related by birth are "relatives" by definition. The distinctive feature of this, the central, primary,

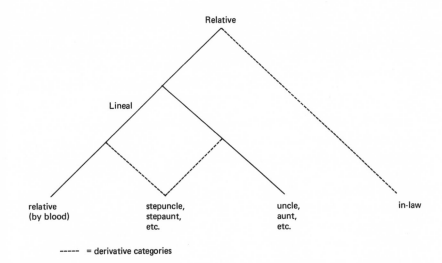

Relative

Lineal

relative
(by blood)

stepuncle,
stepaunt,
etc.

uncle,
aunt,
etc.

in-law

----- = derivative categories

FIGURE 1. MAJOR CATEGORIES OF "RELATIVES" IN AMERICAN
CULTURE

or principal category of "relatives," is relationship by birth; a person
is ego's relative in this sense if and only if he or she is ego's genitor or
genetrix, or offspring, or is related to ego through some chain of relationships of this kind. This category constitutes one of the semantic
domains of American culture—for a semantic domain is nothing more
than a supercategory, all of whose constituent subcategories have some
distinctive feature or features in common (if it is conjunctively
defined).

In addition, there is a category designated *in-laws* or *relatives by
marriage*. Because this category is defined by reference to the primary
category of "relatives" (it includes *some* of ego's spouse's "relatives,"
and so forth), it is logically derived from that category and is a category
of "relatives" by extension. Therefore the "in-law" category and the
primary category "blood relative" taken together constitute a larger
semantic domain also labeled *relatives*.

Within the category "blood relatives" a distinction is made between
those who are lineally related and those who are collaterally related to
ego. This is what distinguishes "father" and "mother" from "uncle"
and "aunt," for example. The domain of "relatives" is further widened
or extended by addition of the spouses of one's parents and, conversely,
the children of one's spouse. These are the "steprelatives." And the

77

spouses of one's parents' siblings and, conversely, the children of one's spouse's siblings are added as yet another (but not specially designated) category of "relatives" by extension. These are designated as *uncle, aunt, nephew,* and *niece.*

Beyond this, the "blood relatives" of one's own "in-laws" and "steprelatives" may be regarded as "relatives," but these extensions are optional. The previously noted extensions are not optional. It is appropriate to say that any of these other "relatives" are not "relatives" only if the speaker intends to assert that they are not "relatives" in the primary sense. It is not proper to say that they are not "relatives" in any sense of the term. This may be said, however, of the "blood relatives" of one's own "in-laws" and "steprelatives."

Similarly, the American system of kin classification makes no formal provision for the classification of persons such as the spouses of cousins and the spouses of nephews and nieces (siblings' children). "Technically," that is, these persons are not "relatives" of any kind, but the category may be further extended to include them. Because there are no definite rules governing the classification of such persons, and they must be classified by analogy with the classification of persons more closely and directly related to ego, it is possible for different speakers to classify them in at least two different ways, neither of which is "right" or "wrong." Thus, for example, a cousin's spouse might be designated as *cousin-in-law* by analogy with sibling's spouse (because cousin and sibling are in the same generation), or as *cousin* by analogy with the spouses of uncles and aunts (because cousins, like uncles and aunts, are collateral relatives). Because the American system of kin classification has no definite rules governing the classification of such persons (to whom one is or may be regarded as "related"), it is formally defective (cf. Greenberg 1966: 100, on "defectivation"), but it is not internally inconsistent or self-contradictory (cf. Schneider 1968: 106, n. 7).[12]

The broad semantic domain constructed by progressive widening of the category designated as *relatives* or *blood relatives* thus includes a number of lesser semantic domains, all of which are related to and derived from that single category or domain. This, however, is not the most inclusive semantic domain labeled *relatives* in American culture. An even broader domain is generated by metaphoric extension, that is, by letting the nondistinctive features of the category "blood relatives" (the connotations of *relative* in its primary sense) serve as sufficient conditions for designation as a *relative*. This results in the addition of two more categories, "adoptive relatives" and "foster relatives," whose distinctive features have to do with interpersonal social relationships and whose definitions exclude genealogical or marital relationships.[13] These categories, however, are most closely related to the category "blood relatives," because they are derived by metaphoric extension from the connotations of *relative* understood in its primary sense. They are not closely related to the "in-law" category, despite the fact that legally sanctioned relationships figure in the definition of at least one of them (the category "adoptive relative").[14]

The semantic domain that contains all of these categories of "relatives" is not a unitary domain, that is, not all of its constituent subdomains have a distinctive feature or set of distinctive features in common. Thus it is not possible to specify a conjunctive definition for this domain; it is possible, however, to specify a disjunctive definition for it. The disjunctive nature of the definition of this domain derives, of course, from the fact that it is elaborately constructed of many definitional and extension rules (cf. Scheffler and Lounsbury 1971: 105–6) which make the expression *relative* highly polysemous.

Finally, some American kinship terms are extended (metaphorically and in other figures of speech) beyond this domain. These extensions do not further enlarge the domain of "relatives" (or of "kinship"), as is shown by the fact that the expression *relative* is not extended along with the specific kinship terms in these cases. To all appearances, the expression *relative* is not so extended because, in its primary sense, it connotes "diffuse, enduring solidarity" (or what Fortes [1969] terms "prescriptive altruism"): this is expected only of those persons who are related by blood and of those persons who take their social places *in full*, which den mothers, priests, and the like never do. Thus, den mothers, priests, and the like are outside the domain of "kinship" in American culture. This is not to say that their designation by kinship terms is irrelevant to an understanding of "the meaning of kinship," the significance of kinship, in American culture. Plainly, the use of kinship roles as models for social relations between nonkin is part of that significance, even though it is outside the domain of "kinship" proper. The projection of kinship roles and terms into the domains of "nationality" and "religion" also is a part of the significance of kinship in American culture, but the three domains are quite distinct.

KINSHIP, NATIONALITY, AND RELIGION

Schneider (1969a) argues that, in fact, the "domain of kinship" in American culture may not be distinctly different from some other cultural domains, in particular "nationality" and "religion." Indeed, he goes so far as to suggest that these three domains are "defined and structured in identical terms" and "are all the same thing (culturally)" (1969a: 124; 1972: 43). He says that if this argument "has any merit, it follows that it will no longer be possible to study 'kinship' or religion or economics or politics, etc., as distinct cultural systems" (1972: 59), and "logically it will be necessary to treat the whole culture as a single cultural system" (1972: 60).In these contexts Schneider is not writing about American culture in particular but about cultural systems in general. Also Schneider's thesis is not the familiar (though not unchallenged) doctrine that cultural systems are "meaningful wholes" whose several parts all bear logical-meaningful relationships of one kind or another to each other; it is that all the major structural units or categories of the culture of any society are (or may be) "defined and structured in identical terms," that is, all have (or may have) the same distinctive features.

Before assessing the probable validity of this suggestion, I should state my understanding of Schneider's argument about the relations among the domains of "kinship," "nationality," and "religion" in American culture. Because of space limitations, I will deal only with "nationality." Schneider argues that the domain of "nationality" is constructed of the same two distinctive features as the domain of "kinship"—"relationship by birth" and "relationship in law." Thus, he argues, just as there are "relatives by blood alone," "relatives in law alone," and "relatives by blood and in law," so also there are "citizens by birth alone"(ex-citizens), "citizens by law alone" (naturalized citizens), and "citizens by blood and by law." And just as the "role" of "the person as a relative" is to love his or her relatives, so the "role" of the person as a citizen is to love his or her country.

Schneider (1969a: 123) emphasizes that this analysis is only an elaborate "guess" and that he presents it only so that it "can be taken into consideration in trying to reach a useful definition of kinship." Presumably, Schneider believes that it needs to be taken into account because of the use of kinship terms in certain expressions having to do with nationality (for example, *motherland*). As Schneider sees it, these usages of kinship terms make one wonder how the domains of "kinship" and "nationality" are distinguished, how they differ critically from one another. He concludes, as we have seen, that the differences are not in the distinctive features of these domains, for these features are one and the same, and as "pure" domains they are one and the same. The differences, Schneider argues, are in the ways "persons" within this single domain are subdivided into various categories and in the more particular qualities of the norms associated with membership of those categories. This single, large domain may be divided into "kinds of relatives" and "families," and so on, in which case we have to deal with "kinship"; or it may be divided into "states," "counties," "towns," and so on, in which case we have to deal with "nationality" or "citizenship" (cf. Schneider 1969a: 120–22).

The main defect in this argument is that it confuses the relationships "defined in terms of" and "defined in the same way as." The fact of the matter is that one's status as a citizen of the United States is dependent on one's parentage, that is, on whether or not he or she is a particular kind of "relative"—a natural-born child, legitimate or illegitimate, of an established citizen of the United States. Of course, anyone's identity as a relative of someone else may be dependent on his or her parentage, as in the cases of "child of" and "cousin of"; but it may not be so dependent, as in the cases of "parent of," "uncle of," and so on. It should be clear from this that "kinship" and "citizenship" are not defined in the same way but that "citizenship" is defined in terms of "kinship," or, more specifically, by the relationship "child of." Furthermore, the two categories are quite differently structured. Most importantly, "relative" is egocentrically defined and "citizen" is not; its focus is not on a person but on a place with certain political boundaries. Thus, "kinship" or "blood relationship" is symmetrical, transitive, and commutative, whereas "citizenship" is asymmetrical, intransitive, and noncommutative. So, if two persons are both relatives of some third person, they are relatives of one another and they must share a common "substance" ("blood"); but if two persons are both citizens of the same country, they are not citizens of one another, nor is there any necessary implication that they share a common "substance," though they may if they are relatives, too. Plainly, these two categories or domains are radically different; they are neither defined nor structured in the same way.

It may be added that, although it is true that "being a relative" and "being a citizen" both entail certain (though quite different) sets of rights and duties, in neither case are these rights and duties distinctive features of the categories. They are normative implications of membership, and therefore nondistinctive or contingent features, of those categories. Of course, both categories are subject to extension, and an individual may become a citizen by "naturalization," that is, by voluntarily performing certain specified duties of a citizen for a specified period to the satisfaction of specified officials who may then confer citizenship on him or her. So there is, indeed, a category of "citizen" whose distinctive feature is conduct according to a specified code for conduct, but it is a category of "citizen" by metaphoric extension and not a category of "citizen" in the primary sense of the term.

Kinship and nationality are distinctly different domains in American culture, and they do not belong to any one overarching domain because they share no distinctive features. This does not preclude the possibility of Americans perceiving and even constructing similarities among their respective features (both distinctive and nondistinctive) and, thus, of using expressions drawn from one domain to signify aspects of the other. It should be evident that this is what we have to deal with when we consider such expression as *mother country*. By and large, if not entirely, the extensions are from kinship to nationality, and not from nationality to kinship.

At this point we may be tempted to turn Schneider's claim—that we cannot understand the "meaning" of kinship in American culture without at the same time understanding the "meanings" of nationality and religion—on its head, or at least on its side. We may be tempted to argue that the two domains are related only insofar as one's kin ties determine formally (or informally, as in the case of religion) his or her status as a citizen (or his or her religious affiliation); and insofar as kinship terms are used to signify aspects of the significance of nationality (and religion). What those terms signify must be kinshiplike and we must understand what kinship is before we can understand that which is kinshiplike. Therefore, we cannot understand the "meanings" of nationality (and religion) without first understanding the "meaning" of kinship in American culture. But this would be a rhetorical over-generalization, and we should be more precise.

Here it is useful, indeed essential, to distinguish systematically (as Schneider does not) betwen the "meanings" of the words *relative* and *citizen* and the "meanings" of the objects or relationships that these words denote, or the "meanings" of the categories that these words designate. These latter "meanings" consist in the forms of significance —jural, moral, affective, and so on—attributed by members of the society to objects or relationships of the kinds designated by those words. The former "meanings" consist in the references of the words *relative* and *citizen* to the necessary (as well as sufficient) conditions for inclusion in the categories they designate, that is, to the distinctive features of those categories. Of course, the "meanings" of the words *relative* and *citizen* also include their reference to the forms of signifi-cance attributed to membership of the categories which they designate, that is, to the nondistinctive or contingent features of membership of those categories. Even so, it is important to keep the distinction between the "meanings" of words and "meanings" of cultural categories, and of membership of those categories, clearly in mind. It is important because the "meaning" of a cultural category is not (as Schneider has pointed out) the same thing as the "meaning" of its "name" or designation— *the "meaning" of a cultural category does not include its distinctive features!* So we must distinguish, following Charles Morris (1964), between "signification" and "significance," even though the former may encompass the latter.

With this distinction in mind, it is easy to see that understanding of the definitive meaning of the word *relative* is not dependent on under-standing of the definitive meaning of the word *citizen*, because the criteria for membership of the category "relative" are not dependent on the criteria for membership of the category "citizen." In contrast, however, to understand the criteria for inclusion in the category "citi-zen," it helps to know (although it may not be wholly essential to know) that the relationship "child of" is a kind of kinship relation and that a child is a kind of relative. Also, if we wish to understand the significance attributed to being a relative in American culture, or, in other words, the nondistinctive or contingent features of the category "relative" and the connotations of the word *relative*, there is no need to consider either the defining or the contingent features of the category "citizen" or the definitive or the nondefinitive meanings of the word *citizen*. This is because the significance of being a relative is not normatively contingent (though it may be pragmatically contingent) on being a citizen of the United States. But, if we wish to understand the significance of being a citizen of the United States, and therefore the nondistinctive or contingent features of membership of the category "citizen," it is useful, if not wholly essential, to know something about the significance attributed to being a relative or a particular kind of relative. This is because Americans often express this significance in kinship terms, by alluding to the forms of significance attributed to being a particular kind of relative. But they do not express this significance wholly in kinship terms; so understanding of the significance of being a citizen or fellow citizen of the United States is only partly dependent (to a still undetermined degree) on understanding of the social significance attributed to being a relative or a particular kind of relative.

Despite this strong dependence of understanding of the "meanings" (signification and significance) of *citizen* and "citizen" on understanding of the "meaning" (signification and significance) of *relative* and "relative," it is not true that it is not possible to study "kinship" and "politics" as distinct cultural systems, especially if we use *culture* in Schneider's very special, restricted sense. For we have seen that the categories "relative" and "citizen" are differently defined and structured, so that as "cultural systems," in Schneider's sense, they are not "the same thing." Even so, it cannot fairly be denied that any account of the significance of kinship in American culture would be incomplete without some reference to the ways in which Americans extend kinship roles and kinship terms to persons whom they deny are relatives in any sense of the term, and to other entities, animate and inanimate as well. In acknowledging this, however, we need not fall into the trap of supposing that these are extensions of the domain of "kinship" itself. That they are not, and that they are irrelevant to understanding "what a relative is" or "the American cultural definition of a relative" or even "the significance of being a relative," is demonstrated, again, by the fact that the parties denoted by particular kin terms are denied to be relatives in any sense of the term. It remains to be seen whether, in contrast, the evidence from other societies will support Schneider's more general suggestion—that the major structural units or categories of any culture are all "defined and structured in identical terms." The American evidence suggests that this is a rather dubious proposition.

CONCLUSION

It may be tempting to suppose that the differences between Schneider's and my interpretations of "the meaning of kinship in American culture" are related to profound differences in our respective theoretical orientations. There is, for example, a considerable difference in our respective uses of the word *meaning*. It seems to me that Schneider's rather casual and largely unanalyzed use of the word in its many ordinary, everyday senses produces confusion, especially insofar as it leads him to write of the distinctive features of a category as part of the "meaning" of that category. This leads, as I think I have shown, to a confusion between signification and significance, or between the meanings of words and the forms of significance attributed to the objects they denote and the categories they designate. (The confusion is apparent in the way Schneider treats the question "What is a relative?" as though it were one and the same as the question "What is the meaning of kinship in American culture?".) It leads, ultimately, to the conflation of distinctive and nondistinctive features and thus away from one of the major goals of "cultural" or "symbolic" analysis, which is, according to Schneider (and I agree), to determine how cultural categories are defined and articulated.

This difference aside, it may be that the theoretical differences are in large part by-products of a simple methodological difference—not a difference in principle but a difference in practice.

Schneider's argument—that independent analysis of the genealogical designata of American kinship terms is unwarranted—is predicated on his argument that social and genealogical relations are alternative distinctive features of the categories designated by those terms, and that the several different categories of "relative" are related paradigmatically rather than taxonomically or derivationally. This argument, in turn, is predicated on the assumption that the distinction that may be made analytically between unmodified and (restrictively) modified terms corresponds to a cultural distinction which, on analysis, turns out to be a distinction between two broad categories of "relative"—"in nature" and "in law." But this last (though logically most prior) assumption is falsified by the fact that some individuals denoted by the modified terms are not regarded as "relatives" in any sense of the term. Schneider notes the fact but fails to see its implication for his assumption. It would seem that he is misled by confusing the situation of the person who is a "relative"of one kind but not another—and so "may or may not be counted as a relative," depending on which of the senses of *relative* the speaker has in mind—with the situation of the person who is *not* a "relative" in any sense of the term, even though he or she may be denoted by a specific kinship term such as *father* or *mother*. Schneider confuses the case of the person who *may* or *may not* be "counted as a relative" with the case of the person who *can not* be "counted as a relative," even though he or she is denoted by some other kinship term.

Because he fails to distinguish these cases, as speakers of American English do, he is led quite reasonably (but nonetheless erroneously) to conclude that social and genealogical relations are alternative distinctive features of the categories designated by American kinship terms, including *relative*. This leads him to what he supposes is an exposé of the main defect of structural semantic analysis as practiced by Goodenough, Lounsbury, and others (including myself), and to the rejection of a number of concepts, distinctions, and methods that others have found essential to the study of "kinship" and other semantic and cultural domains.

I have tried to show that if we do take this distinction—between the uses of kinship terms to denote "relatives" and their uses to denote nonrelatives—sufficiently into account, we derive a model of the meanings and relations among the meanings of American kinship terms that is quite different from that proposed by Schneider. I suspect, however, that Schneider and others will find this model (or as much as I have presented of it) quite unsatisfying. Some will be quick to point out that the model fails to tell us much about "the meaning of kinship" in American culture beyond the minimal information required to distinguish between "relatives" and nonrelatives as Americans do. In other words, it might be argued that there is something more to being a relative in American culture than just being related by blood or marriage, and if a person is a relative only in this minimal sense he or she might just as well not be a relative—or so many Americans might say.

86

Also, it might be argued, much of that "something more" that a relative "is" must be part of the meanings of American kinship terms; so *any* account of the "meaning" of kinship in American culture, or of the meanings of American kinship terms, must say something, indeed a good deal, about that "something more."

Such an argument, however, would overlook or misconstrue the fact that a distinction is made in American culture between "being a relative" and "the significance of being a relative," that is, between the distinctive and nondistinctive features of a "relative," or between the definitive and nondefinitive meanings of relative. The "something more" that a relative "is," other than "a person who is related by blood or by marriage," consists of the significance that Americans attribute to the fact of being a "relative" of one kind or another, or to being some specific kind of "relative." Because this significance certainly is a part of the meanings of American kinship terms, it is true that an account of the definitive meanings of those terms (their reference to genealogical features and kin categories) is not the same thing as an account of all the meanings of American kinship terms; nor is it the same thing as an account of the meaning (in some global sense) of kinship in American culture. Plainly, analysis and description of both kinds of reference—to distinctive and to nondistinctive features—is essential to a full discussion of the meanings and relations among the meanings of American kinship terms. Even so, the logical-semantic relations between these two kinds of reference or meaning is such that reference to genealogical features and kin categories may and must be analyzed and described independently of reference to the nondistinctive features of those categories. That is to say, the categories themselves are logically prior to the forms of significance attributed to membership of them. It follows, therefore, that the structure of the system of connotations is logically dependent on (though not necessarily the same as) the structure of the system of kin categories (which, as we have seen, is not the same thing as the totality of categories designated by kinship terms). Therefore there can be no reasonable objection to Goodenough's (1965) analysis of the genealogical and marital category referents of American kinship terms *independently* of any other referents those terms may have (cf. Schneider 1965; 1972: 49).[15]

Thus far I have said nothing about other "kinship terminologies" or "systems of kin classification." As a final note, however, I should add that it has not been my intention to imply that all reputed kinship terminologies are like American kinship terminology, at least in that most important respect—the apparent reference of their terms to structurally independent, genealogically defined categories—that has led anthropologists to describe them as kinship terminologies. We may agree with Schneider and others that in far too many instances where it has been claimed that such a cultural category is present, the evidence (if any) presented in support of the claim leaves room for reasonable doubt about its validity. But the room for doubt is variable, especially because there is room also for doubt about the validity of many of the assumptions that have motivated criticism of the relevant bodies of data and various interpretations of them (cf. Scheffler and Lounsbury 1971). Thus, I think it is fair enough to say that the existence of genealogically defined and structurally independent cultural categories is not improbable and that it is not unlikely that they are quite common. In any event, Schneider's sweeping generalization that they do not exist anywhere is readily falsified merely by demonstrating that at least one such cultural category does exist—and at least one does exist in *American culture*.

My principal concern in this essay has been to show that the American kinship system really is a kinship system. This is not, I think, a trivial concern. It seems to me that ethnography is inevitably a comparative exercise, and we English-speaking anthropologists often find it necessary when studying, analyzing, and reporting on other cultures to allude to our and our reader's understanding of our own culture in order to make it clear what the features of those other cultures are and how they are similar to or different from the features of our own culture. Needless to say, if we do not understand our own culture, we are likely to have much difficulty in understanding others or in convincing people that we do. It is particularly important for comparative purposes that we understand those aspects of our own culture that have to do with the kinds of social actors we call *relatives* or (some of us) *kin*. It is particularly important because similarly defined kinds of social actors, together with systems of rights and duties associated with them, are components of many other cultures and societies in which they serve to order far wider ranges of social relationships than they do in our own.

NOTES

1. I am indebted to my colleagues Floyd Lounsbury, Harold Conklin, Susan Bean, and Richard Price, and to Karen Blu, Susan Montague, and Jean-Guy Goulet for many useful comments on earlier drafts of this essay. I am especially indebted to David Schneider for his comments on the first draft. They helped me to expand and, I hope, to clarify some aspects of the argument. As usual, Schneider has been most patient with this persistent and sometimes, I am sure, most trying critic. I want to emphasize that while in this chapter I am highly critical of the main features of Schneider's interpretation of American kinship, I am not unaware of the perceptiveness of many of his empirical and analytic observations. Also, Schneider is entitled to our admiration for his daring in attempting more, indeed much more, than the limited (but not arbitrarily limited) goal of understanding one kind of use of American kinship terms. His persistent and pointed criticism of the kind of work loosely known as "componential analysis" has stimulated me to examine my own concepts and assumptions and to make them clearer to myself and, I hope, to others.

2. Space limitations make it impossible for me to discuss many aspects of Schneider's interpretation as fully as I would like, and other aspects cannot be considered at all. Also, the range of ethnographic facts explicitly noted and discussed cannot be as wide as I would wish. This may leave me open to the charge of failing to take a sufficient number of facts into account. Be that as it may, I have considered a good deal more factual material than that mentioned in this essay, and I cannot see how taking a greater range of ethnographic facts explicitly into account would lead me to Schneider's conclusions.

3. The reader should note carefully that I distinguish between two categories, "in law" and "in-law." The former is a category posited by Schneider, and if it exists in American culture it has no leximic designation. There certainly is a category designated *in-law*, and Schneider maintains that it is a subcategory of his "in law" category.

4. Expressions whose meanings are being discussed are italicized where the reference is to the word itself. They are placed in double quotes where the reference is to the category, or one of the categories, designated by the word.

5. *Connote* is here used in the ordinary language sense, not in the sense sometimes attributed to it by philosophers who use it as the equivalent of *intension* (cf. Scheffler and Lounsbury 1971: 5–6; Scheffler 1972: 316–18).

6. Schneider's use of *polysemy*, it should be noted, differs from that of Goodenough, Lounsbury, and others who follow the conventional linguistic and philosophical usage, in which *polysemy* refers to the condition in which a word has two or more senses (significata) which are related in such a way that one may be said to be derived from another (cf. Waldron 1967; Scheffler and Lounsbury 1971: 6–9; Scheffler 1972: 313–16). In Schneider's usage the expression refers to the condition in which a word has "many meanings," irrespective of the nature of the relationships among those "meanings." Thus Schneider (1968: 4) finds it sensible to say, "A word never has a single meaning except in one, limiting set of circumstances" (that is, in scientific discourse where a special, restricted sense is stipulated for it); and he adds, "since words are seldom used in this way, and rarely if ever in 'natural' culture, this limitation can safely be ignored while the polysemic nature of words is kept firmly in mind." This, however, would permit us to say that a word is polysemous if it has more than one denotatum, even if all its denotata are covered by a single sense, that is, even if they

all share the same distinctive feature(s). While this seems to me a profitless use of *polysemy* (it might just as well be said that most words have more than one denotatum), it is not my intention here to legislate on the use of a technical term. I am not arguing that Schneider misuses *polysemy* but that his use of the expression differs from that of other scholars, and if we are not aware of the difference we may end up talking across one another.

7. It is doubtful also that it is a nondistinctive feature of this category. See below, "An Alternative Interpretation."

8. According to Greenberg (1966: 64), the marked category of an opposition has some feature which is absent from the unmarked category. Thus, for example, in the opposition *man* versus *woman*, *man* designates the unmarked category, whether *woman* is opposed to *man* in its broad sense "human being (irrespective of sex)" or to *man* in its narrow sense "nonfemale (=male) human being," because in each case the category "woman" has a feature ("female") which is absent from the other category. In this example, the narrow sense of *man* is unmarked and it is a derivative (residual) sense of the term. It is derivative because the concept "human being (irrespective of sex)" is logically prior to the concept "male human being." Thus the primary sense of *man* is "human being (irrespective of sex)." Logically, this is the par excellence sense of man, but it may be said that *man* "represents par excellence" the category "male human being" ("the opposite member to the marked category"), if by *par excellence* we mean "especially" or "in particular" rather than "above all."

9. Following Black (1962) and Lounsbury (1956: 192–93), the expression *metaphoric extension* here refers to those figures of speech which operate by suspending one or more of the defining features (critical attributes) of the primary sense of a word and substituting in its place some feature or features of connotative meaning associated with the primary sense or some simple widened sense of the word (cf. Scheffler and Lounsbury 1971: 10–11; Scheffler 1972: 318–19). In the process, features that are nondefinitive of the category designated by the primary or simple widened sense of the word become criteria for the use of the word; the category that the word then designates is defined by those features; they are the distinctive features of that class; and the word then signifies those features. Thus, for example, in the expression "man is a wolf" (cf. Black 1962), *wolf* designates a category defined by the features "behaves ferociously," "acts treacherously," and so forth, and in that expression *wolf* designates a behaviorally defined, "wolf-*like*" category; it does not designate the morphologically defined category "wolf" itself. It is important to be clear about this: when used metaphorically, a word does designate a category, and that category has certain distinctive features which the word then signifies. What makes the usage metaphorical is the relationship between those features and the features of the other category or categories which the word in question also designates. Metaphor consists in taking nondistinctive features of one category and treating them as distinctive features of another category of the same name as the first. In the case of foster and adoptive "relatives," the extension of *relatives* is metaphoric because it is based on the voluntary assumption, by individuals who are not genealogically related, of social relationships which are ascribed between persons who are so related, and because these social relationships are nondistinctive or contingent features of "relatives" and of particular kinds of "relatives" in American culture.

10. I am aware that some (not all) Americans, if asked about it, will say that spouses are "relatives." I see nothing wrong with saying that informants who say this are mistaken. After all, informants do make mistakes, some of which may be quite

informative if understood for what they are. Of course, it is difficult to know when an informant has made a mistake, and the attribution of error to informants must be used sparingly if we are to avoid imposing erroneous interpretations on cultural systems. My argument here is that American informants disagree on this point and we must account for the disagreement. Schneider attempts to account for it by arguing that there are alternative rules in American culture and that according to one set of rules spouses are "relatives." I have tried to show that, for a number of reasons, this argument is unacceptable. The alternative interpretation offered here is that informants sometimes confuse "being married to one another" with "being related by marriage." It is easy to understand how the confusion arises and how it is that informants may appear to contradict themselves from one occasion to another.

11. The designation of a priest as *Father* is not a case of this kind, since in Catholic dogma this designation is based on the priest's relationship with God, and not on his social relationships with lay members of the church. But this is a complex case, full exposition of which would require several pages, and so I leave it for another occasion.

12. Failure to understand the rules of a system has led other anthropologists to conclude, again erroneously, that other systems of kin classification also contain logical inconsistencies or imperfections (cf. Lowie 1917).

13. I am not conceding that, after all, interaction according to "the code for conduct which demands diffuse, enduring solidarity," is a distinctive feature of kinship in American culture. This would be a false or, at best, misleading way in which to restate the point being made here. While metaphorically derived categories must have distinctive features, it must be kept clearly in mind that these are not the distinctive features of the domain of "kinship" or, in other words, of the category of "relatives" par excellence. It may be useful to note also that while the distinctive feature of the metaphorically derived category of "relatives" does have to do with a "code for conduct," the criterion for inclusion in this category is not that the denotatum actually follows this "code" but that he or she has entered voluntarily into a moral or legal contract to do so.

14. It has been suggested to me that something like Schneider's "in law" category does exist in American culture, that it is better termed "relatives by law" or "legal relatives," and that it consists of all so-called relatives who are related to ego through some marital tie (a "legal" relationship) or through adoption or fosterage (also "legal" relationships). We have seen, however, that not all of these categories of "relatives" are subcategories of the same higher-order category or supercategory. The argument that they are depends on the false assumption that steprelatives, parents' siblings' spouses, and in-laws all belong to a single category designated *relatives by marriage*, and on a confusion between the "legal" quality of marriage, and the "legal" qualities of adoption and fosterage. While it may be true that marriage, adoption, and fosterage all entail legal processes and sanctions, this does not in itself imply that the several kinds of "relative" in question all belong to the same supercategory. The several categories are only vaguely analogous; and in the analysis of cultural systems we must be careful not to misinterpret such analogies, whether they are perceived by informants or analysts.

15. Although I think some valid criticism may be made of Goodenough's (1965) analysis of the genealogical and marital category referents of American kinship terms—because that analysis does not take their polysemy systematically into account—that is another matter I cannot deal with here.

4

'Wise Words' of the Western Apache: Metaphor and Semantic Theory

KEITH H. BASSO

University of Arizona

> The greatest thing by far is to be a master of metaphor. It is the one thing that cannot be learnt from others; and it is also a sign of genius, since a good metaphor implies an intuitive perception of the similarity in dissimilars.
>
> —Aristotle (*Rhetoric*, 3)

INTRODUCTION

The subject of metaphor, wrote Michel Bréal (1964: 127), "is inexhaustible." And so it would seem, for ever since the fourth century B.C., when Aristotle expressed his opinion that metaphor was the highest form of verbal art, this subtle instrument of language has been the object of serious thought and, in certain quarters, a source of richly informative debate.[1] Yet, as Clifford Geertz (1964: 58) points out, despite the accomplishments of this venerable tradition of inquiry—a tradition, it should be added, which now boasts an enormous body of literature and embraces disciplines as diverse as philosophy, rhetoric, and literary criticism—the study of metaphor remains marginal to the major concerns of most social scientists. This lack of interest is both ironic and regrettable because today, perhaps more than at any time in the past, anthropologists and linguists are in a position to construct theoretical

93

models that can contribute in useful ways to a clearer understanding of the semantics of metaphor and the role of metaphor in cultural systems (see, for example, Geertz 1964, 1972; Lévi-Strauss 1963, 1966; Hale 1971; Scheffler and Lounsbury 1971; Scheffler 1972; Fernandez 1972, 1974).

I assume that an adequate theory of metaphor must articulate with a theory of language—and by direct implication a theory of linguistic competence—that satisfactorily explains the ability of human beings to produce and interpret figurative speech. Such a theory has not yet been formulated within the paradigm of transformational linguistics nor does its development there seem probable. This is because the goals of modern semantics have been defined in such a way that a transformational grammar need only make explicit the tacit knowledge which enables the speaker of a language to assign literal or propositional meanings to sentence types (Katz and Fodor 1963; Chomsky 1965; George Lakoff 1971; Katz 1972). If such a grammar is taken to constitute a finished theory of language, as well as a complete model of the linguistic competence of its speakers, it is possible to conclude that the knowledge necessary to assign figurative meanings to sentences is "nonlinguistic" and that the ability to implement this knowledge lies outside the sphere of competence (e.g. Leech 1970: 89–93; Katz 1972: 441–52). This is what a number of transformationalists have claimed or implied, and in so doing they have exempted themselves—and their theory— from having to explain the fact that many sentences in a language can be, are, and in some instances *must* be interpreted in ways that are not predictable from an understanding of their literal meanings alone.[2]

Simultaneously, an image has been created of man as "ideal speaker-hearer" (Chomsky 1965: 3) which from an anthropological perspective is not ideal at all. Indeed, it is quite disturbing. For the ideal speaker-hearer as depicted by transformational grammarians is a person ("machine" is clearly a more accurate term) whose linguistic competence does not allow him to make meaningful sense of metaphorical speech. This hypothetical individual, we are informed, knows his language perfectly (Chomsky 1965: 3). Yet this same knowledge, complete, unflawed, and impeccable as it purportedly is, presents him with no alternative but to interpret a sentence such as "Cops are pigs" as a piece of poppycock arising from a confusion of policemen with a class of barnyard animals. It stands to reason that as long as this image of the ideal speaker-hearer persists unmodified, and as long as linguistic competence is restricted exclusively to the kinds of information contained in transformational grammars, attempts to construct an adequate theory of metaphor will be severely hampered.

One possible solution to this problem is to enlarge the concept of competence to include the full complement of skills and abilities that permit the members of a speech community to assign nonliteral meanings to spoken and written messages. But what are these skills and abilities? And how are they to be discovered? This much seems clear. The knowledge required to interpret metaphor in a culturally appropriate manner cannot be prescribed a priori. Rather, it must be inferred on the basis of detailed investigations of how actual instances of metaphor are constructed and construed. Initially, we must go about our business empirically, determining for particular societies what kinds of statements count as metaphors, what kinds of statements count as interpretations or "explanatory paraphrases" (Urban 1939: 39) of metaphors, and, perhaps most important of all, what kinds of standards are invoked to define some interpretations as more appropriate than others. In short, we must follow Hymes's (1964, 1971) suggestion and do "ethnographies of speech," in this case, ethnographies of metaphorical speech.

In this essay I shall outline a model for the analysis of metaphor and apply it to a small body of metaphorical statements made by residents of Cibecue, a Western Apache speech community located on the Fort Apache Indian Reservation in east central Arizona. Concomitantly, I will attempt to make more explicit what Aristotle and others have implied, namely that the production and interpretation of metaphorical speech involves a genuinely *creative* skill. Proceeding on the assumption that the successful interpretation of any metaphor entails the formation of at least one unitary concept, I will present evidence which suggests that these concepts are not lexically coded in the Western Apache langauge. On the basis of this discovery, I shall go on to argue that the interpretation of metaphor is grounded in an ability to form *novel semantic categories*. Such an ability is not accounted for by the standard transformational model of language, and I will conclude by discussing the implications of this deficiency for the revision of key linguistic concepts and the construction of an adequate theory of metaphor.

METAPHOR AS SIMILE

The most salient characteristic of metaphor consists in a blatant violation of linguistic rules that results in the expression of a proposition that is either logically false or, in Rudolf Carnap's (1955: 47) terminology, "conceptually absurd." Walker Percy (1958: 81) has put the matter nicely: a metaphor "asserts of one thing that it is something else" and is therefore inevitably "wrong." At the same time, of course, a metaphor is also "right" because, semantic disobedience not withstanding, the proposition it expresses can be construed as containing a truth. Interpreted one way, Thomas Brown's metaphor, "Oh blackbird, what a boy you are," is utter nonsense since it is simply not the case that blackbirds are boys, or vice versa. On the other hand, this statement can be taken to mean that despite numerous differences there is some sense in which boys and blackbirds are alike—in their penchant for loud noise, for example, or in their propensity for energetic play. Herein lies a dilemma: how is it that a metaphorical statement can be at once both true and false?

This question is most commonly answered by asserting that metaphor is simile in disguise, a view which rests upon the more basic claim that an analytic distinction can be drawn between semantic features which compose the *designative* or *literal* meanings of words and features which compose their *connotative* or *figurative* meanings. Designative features are relatively few in number and serve as a set to specify the necessary and sufficient conditions for membership in the class of objects referred to by the word in question (Scheffler and Lounsbury 1971: 4; Scheffler 1972: 311). Connotative features are much more numerous, are nondefining in the sense just described, and consist of any and all "associated commonplaces" (Black 1962: 32) or "contingent facts" (Katz 1972: 285) which the designative meaning(s) of the word call(s) to mind.

If designative meanings are relied upon to interpret a metaphor, the reasoning goes, the proposition it expresses will be understood as false or, at worst, contradictory. However, if the metaphor is construed as a covert simile, it will be understood as expressing a noncontradictory proposition whose truth value can be assessed—and, for those in a position to do so, established—on the basis of connotative meanings. The trick to interpreting a metaphor, then, is to reject it as a declarative proposition (e.g. Blackbirds are boys), interpret it as a comparative proposition (e.g. Blackbirds are *like* boys), and confirm the truth of the latter by adducing at least one valid similarity between the classes of objects being compared (e.g. Blackbirds are like boys *by virtue of* a shared fondness for whooping it up).

This theory has two important implications. One of these is that the same metaphor may be interpreted in different ways—as many, in fact, as there are features of connotative meaning shared by the metaphor's main constituents (Shibles 1971b; Richards 1948; Black 1962; Read 1952). We have interpreted Thomas Brown's metaphor on the grounds that blackbirds and boys share the attribute of being raucous, but other similarities could easily be adduced—liveliness, playfulness, an inclination to hide things, and so forth. It would be arbitrary, then, to insist that a metaphor has one "best" or "proper" sense; to the contrary, as many writers have noted, it is the special virtue of metaphor that it is capable of gathering unto itself several senses any one (or two, or three, or more) of which can serve as a basis for interpretation. This is a significant point because it accounts for the empirical fact that interpretations of a metaphor may exhibit wide variation even within the same speech community.

The theory before us also implies that the interpretation of a metaphor is ultimately grounded in an ability to form a concept (or two, or three, or more) which serves to establish an equivalence between the metaphor's main constituents, and of which, therefore, the constituents become exemplars par excellence (Brown 1958; Richards 1938; Urban 1939; Scheffler and Lounsbury 1971). In other words, if X and Y are the constituents equated in a metaphor, interpretation requires the formation of a concept that subsumes both X and Y and thus defines the terms of their identity. Our interpretation of Brown's metaphor presupposes and derives from a concept that may be glossed as 'animate objects that are raucous'. It is essential to assume both the possibility and validity of such a concept. Otherwise, there would be no way to account for our particular interpretation of the metaphor, or to explain the fact that it can be readily understood by others.

97

The concepts required to interpret a metaphor are not expressed by the metaphor itself. Rather, they may be said to underlie it and must be *discovered* through the adduction of shared features of connotative meaning. It is this act of discovery, coupled with the sometimes puzzling search that precedes it, that can make the interpretation of metaphor an original and personal experience. And it is this same act of discovery—this "finding" of a meaning that resolves the puzzle—that endows metaphor with the capacity to cause surprise, to structure the perceptions of individuals in unanticipated ways, and to make them "see" associations they have never seen before. Thus, as Herbert Read (1952: 23) has written, "A metaphor is the synthesis of several units of observation into *one commanding image*; it is an expression of a complex idea, not by analysis, or by abstract statement, but by a sudden perception of an objective relation" (italics added).

This brings us back to where we began. The meaningful interpretation of metaphor rests upon an ability to discern some element of plausibility or truth in a statement that asserts an implausibility or falsehood. It is clear, I think, that if we can characterize this ability— or, more precisely, if we can determine how the concepts that underlie the interpretation of metaphor are formed—we will have learned something interesting about metaphor itself. We will also have learned something interesting about cultural symbols and the way they work to impose order and meaning on that elusive entity sometimes known as the "real world."

'WISE WORDS' AS SIMILES

The class of Western Apache metaphors that will concern us in this essay takes the form of simple definitional utterances which represent expressions of a single surface syntactic type: subject + predicate + verb. In every case, the subject is a term designating some category of animate natural phenomena (e.g. *hadaditl'a*: 'lightning'; *kaage čo*: 'raven'; *koyiłčoože*: 'carrion beetle'), the predicate is a term designating some human category (e.g. *'iitsaa*: 'widow'; *'iškįįn*: 'boy'; *'indaa'*: 'whiteman'), and the verb is a copula (*'at'ee*: 'is'; 'are'). In every case, too, a semantic rule is violated: subject and predicate do not agree. To put it more precisely, the subject possesses designative features that are incompatible with designative features possessed by the predicate. As a result, a proposition is expressed which is contradictory and therefore always false. Eight of these metaphors are presented below:

(1) a. *hadaditl'a' 'iškįįn 'at'ee* ('Lightning is a boy')
   b. *kaage čo 'iitsaa 'at'ee* ('Ravens are widows')
   c. *koyiłčoože 'indaa' 'at'ee* ('Carrion beetle is a whiteman')
   d. *gooše čaɣąąše 'at'ee* ('Dogs are children')
   e. *mba'tsose 'indee 'at'ee* ('Coyotes are Western Apaches')
   f. *doole č'ikii 'at'ee* ('Butterflies are girls')
   g. *doole 'izeege 'at'ee* ('Butterflies are sweethearts')
   h. *toołkaiyee saan 'at'ee* ('Burros are old women')

Metaphors of this type are identified by Western Apache as prime examples of what they call 'wise words' (*goyąąɣo yaiti'*), a distinctive speech genre associated with adult men and women who have gained a reputation for balanced thinking, critical acumen, and extensive cultural knowledge. These persons, who form collectively a kind of intellectual elite, are typically well along in years and because of their advanced age are not expected to participate in the full round of daily activities that occupy most younger members of Western Apache society. Consequently, they have plenty of time for visiting and talking, especially with one another, and it is in the context of these conversational settings, called *baiyan diidała'at'ee* ('old people talking together'), that 'wise words' are used most frequently.

When an Apache—or an ethnographer—encounters a metaphor he does not understand, he may request an interpretation of it. The appropriate form of such a request is XY *haago 'at'eego dałętt'ee?* (X and Y, how are they the same?), where X stands for the subject of the metaphor and Y stands for the predicate. The appropriate response is an explanatory paraphrase that describes one or more ways in which the referents of subject and predicate are alike. I recorded sixty-four of these explanatory paraphrases—one for every metaphor listed in (1a–h) from each of eight Western Apache consultants—of which the following are representative:

(2) a. *Metaphor: hadaditl'a' 'iškįįn 'at'ee* ('Lightning is a boy')
   Interpretation: Yes, young boys are the same as lightning. They both dart around fast and you just can't tell what they are going to do. They both act unpredictably. They never stay still. Both are always darting around from place to place. They will shoot aimlessly, too. They will both shoot

99

anywhere, not aiming away from people's camps, not caring what they hit. That is why they both cause damage.

(2) b. *Metaphor: kaage čo 'iitsaa 'at'ee* ('Ravens are widows')
Interpretation: Ravens are widows, these people say. They say that because ravens and widows are poor and don't have anyone to get meat for them. That is why sometimes these women will stand near your camp and wait like that until you give them food. It is the same way with ravens. They stand around near roads so they can eat what is killed there; they just wait like that until some car hits something and kills it. That's what ravens are doing when you see them standing near roads. They are waiting to get fresh meat.

(2) c. *Metaphor: koyiłčoože 'indaa' 'at'ee* ('Carrion beetles are whitemen')
Interpretation: Well, there is this way that carrion beetle reminds us of whitemen—they waste much food. Carrion beetle, when he is young and before he starts to eat meat, just eats a little hole in a leaf and then moves on to eat a little hole in another. He leaves plenty of good food behind him. It is like this with some white people, too. Another way they are the same, these two, is that in the summer they only come out from where they live when it is cool. You only see carrion beetles early in the morning and again in the early evening. It is the same with some white people. In the summer they always want to stay some place where it is cool.

(2) d. *Metaphor: gooše ča_γǫǫ́še 'at'ee* ('Dogs are children')
Interpretation: I think this way about what that means. Both of them, children and dogs, are always hungry. They like to eat all the time, and when they don't get food they come to a place where someone is cooking. There is this way, too. Both of them get into everything and don't leave anything alone. So you have to shoo them away. If you don't, they might break something or soil it so you can't use it anymore.

These explanatory paraphrases, like all of the others I recorded, focus pointedly upon the specification of attributes in terms of which the referents of the constituents in a metaphor can be considered the same. Consequently, it seems safe to conclude that Western Apache metaphors of the type presented here are intended to be construed *as if* they were similes, and that failure to construe them in this manner will render interpretation extremely difficult, if not impossible. Of course, this does not explain how the concepts underlying particular interpretations are formed, or why some interpretations are judged more appropriate than others. I turn now to a consideration of these problems.

METAPHORICAL CONCEPTS: DESIGNATIVE FEATURES

The concepts that underlie interpretations of Western Apache metaphors consist of one feature of connotative meaning and one or more features of designative meaning. The connotative feature is criterial, is openly described in explanatory paraphrases, and may be viewed as the "outcome" of a search and selection procedure (see pp. 103–7). The designative features are noncriterial and are not described in explanatory paraphrases; they are contingent upon—and therefore must be inferred from—the position in lexical hierarchies of the semantic categories labeled by the metaphor's constituents.

Consider the following example. In paraphrase (2c) an equivalence is drawn between carrion beetles (*koyiłčoože*) and whitemen (*'indaa'*) on the grounds that both 'waste food' (*-'iit'an donaodi yodawołsida*). 'Waste food' is a feature of connotative meaning since it does not state a necessary condition for membership in either of the categories 'whiteman' or 'carrion beetle'. But 'waste food' is only one component of the metaphorical concept. The other components consist of two features of designative meaning that together define a superordinate category to which both 'whiteman' and 'carrion beetle' belong, namely, *ni'gostsangolįįhi* (living things that dwell on or below the surface of the earth'). Thus the complete metaphorical concept, defined by the features 'living thing' + 'earth dweller' + 'waste food', is *ni'gostsangolįįhi 'iitan donaodi yodawołsida* or 'living earth dwellers that waste food'.

The designative features of a metaphorical concept are always those features which the metaphor's constituents share by virtue of membership in the same semantic domain. As shown by the hierarchy presented in figure 2, the referents of 'carrion beetle' and 'whiteman' do not become members of the same domain until the node labeled by *ni'gostangolįįhi* ('living earth dwellers') is reached. At this point, they become exemplars of a single category, thus overcoming and resolving the semantic conflict—or, in Geertz's (1964: 59) phrase, the "semantic tension"—that distinguishes them at subordinate levels. It follows that a metaphorical concept will always be *more inclusive* than either of the

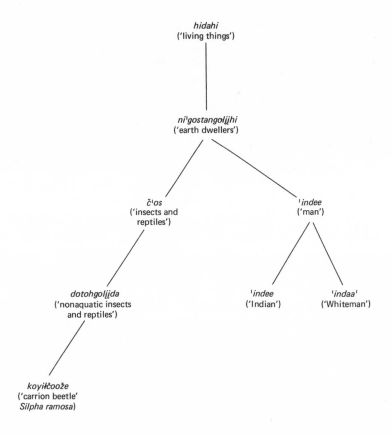

FIGURE 2. LEXICAL HIERARCHY SHOWING LOCATION OF WEST-
ERN APACHE CATEGORIES 'CARRION BEETLE' (*koyiłčoože*) AND 'WHITEMAN' (*'indaa'*)

categories labeled by the metaphor's constituents. The concept 'living
earth dwellers that waste food' is more inclusive than either 'carrion
beetle' or 'whiteman'; it must be because it subsumes them both.

The hierarchical level at which the categories labeled by a metaphor's
constituents are incorporated into the same domain is also the lowest
level at which features of connotative meaning can be adduced. This is
because shared connotative features must be compatible with designative features *shared by both constituents*, a condition that can only be
satisfied when the referents of the constituents become exemplars of a
single category. In terms of our example, this simply means that any
connotative feature adduced to establish a similarity between carrion

beetles and whitemen must be compatible with features that define 'carrion beetle' and 'whiteman' as 'living earth dwellers'. Any connotative feature that fails to meet this requirement (e.g. 'never die', 'cause snowstorms', 'make good cooking pots') will be prohibited.

This claim is supported by empirical evidence which will be presented later in the chapter. For the moment, however, let us agree with R. A. Waldron (1967: 174) who has observed that:

> Metaphor is by no means carried out in total contravention of the rules [of a language] but in part by courtesy of the system itself.... Linguistic categorization involves classification on the basis of similarity of attributes. Metaphorical categorization is only an extenson of normal linguistic activity; it is exceptionally *wide classification* [italics added].

The rules to which Waldron refers in this passage are what transformational grammarians commonly call "selection restrictions" (Katz and Fodor 1963; Bever and Rosenbaum 1971; Katz 1972). These rules define the conditions under which the semantic features of a language can cooccur, and therefore determine which combinations are allowable and which are not. We have hypothesized that Western Apache metaphorical concepts do not violate selection restrictions and therefore are defined by allowable combinations of semantic features.

METAPHORICAL CONCEPTS: CONNOTATIVE FEATURES

The connotative features of Western Apache metaphorical concepts are chosen in compliance with a set of sociolinguistic principles which specify the *kinds of attributes* that can be adduced to establish equivalences between the referents of a metaphor's constituents. From the point of view of the individual Apache hearer, these principles constitute a heuristic strategy or plan that guides and simplifies the search for shared similarities (Miller, Galanter, and Pribram 1960: 159). Simultaneously, they serve to define the criteria in terms of which the appropriateness of his interpretation will be assessed by other members of the speech community. The principles may be stated as follows:

A. To be appropriate, an interpretation of a Western Apache metaphor must specify one or more *behavioral attributes* which the referents of the metaphor's constituents share in common.

B. (Corollary) Interpretations that are based upon other types of attributes—such as size, shape, color, habitat, and the like—will be rejected as inappropriate.

C. To be appropriate, an interpretation of a Western Apache metaphor must specify one or more behavioral attributes that are indicative of *undesirable qualities* possessed by the referents of the metaphor's constituents.

D. (Corollary) Interpretations based upon attributes indicative of desirable qualities will be rejected as inappropriate.

The validity of principles A and C was given strong empirical support by regularities in the corpus of sixty-four explanatory paraphrases provided by my Western Apache consultants. Close examination of these statements revealed that principle A was never violated. In other words, all the paraphrases I recorded concentrated upon the identification of behavioral similarities and none adduced similarities of other kinds. Principle C was violated only twice, both times by the same consultant, and on each occasion his interpretation was challenged by older Apaches on the grounds that it "spoke too well" of the referents of the constituents of the metaphor in question.

Principles B and D were upheld by the Apaches' consistent rejection of metaphorical interpretations that violated the conditions defined by principles A and C. Discussions centering upon the reasons for such rejections were of special interest because, as shown by the three excerpts presented below, they yielded valuable information concerning the Apaches' own conceptions of how 'wise words' should be interpreted. The first excerpt, which describes an exchange between myself and two consultants, deals with the central importance of adducing behavioral similarities. So does the second, which presents a portion of a conversation between one of my consultants and his eleven-year-old daughter. The third excerpt, involving three consultants and myself, is from a discussion concerning the requirement that behavioral similarities be chosen which reflect unfavorably on the referents of a metaphor's constituents.

(3) a. *Consultant 1:* Butterflies are girls—try that one.
Ethnographer: Well, this is what I think of that one—they're both the same because they're pretty, brightly colored, like the dresses the girls wear.
Consultant 2: [Laughter] You could say that, but it sounds wrong to us . . . like when you said ravens are widows be-

cause they wear black. [More laughter] Maybe they are the same that way, but to us it doesn't mean anything.

Ethnographer: Why not?

Consultant 1: [Long pause] It doesn't mean anything because it doesn't tell us what they *do*, these things in the 'wise words'. You have to think about how they are the same in what they do—not what they look like. Think about how they act the same. That way you'll understand it. Butterflies are girls because sometimes they act mindlessly, just chasing around after each other having a good time when they should be working, helping out with chores and younger children. What they look like doesn't matter, it's how they *act* that makes them the same.

(3) b. *Consultant 1 (to daughter)*: Who said it to you: carrion beetle is a whiteman?

Daughter: X's wife. She said it yesterday at her camp.

Consultant 1: What did you say?

Daughter: Nothing. I didn't know what she meant.

Consultant 1: Wise words. That old woman likes to talk that way. She wanted to know if you knew how they were the same—whitemen and carrion beetles. Do you know how they are the same?

Daughter: No.

Consultant 1: Think.

Daughter: Because there are many of them.

Consultant 1: [Laughter] No. Think about what they do, those two—like leaving clear tracks so they are easy to follow, or like the way they waste food.

Daughter: But there *are* many of them.

Consultant 1: Yes. But when old people talk like that, using 'wise words', they want you to think about how carrion beetle acts . . . then they want you to think about whitemen that same way. So you have to watch both of them, and then you will see how they are the same. It's what they *do* that matters. Now, do you understand?

Daughter: [Pause] I think so.

(3) c. *Ethnographer*: Yesterday I was talking about 'wise words' with Y, the medicine man's wife, and she said something I didn't understand. Maybe you could help me out.

Consultant 1: What did she say?

Ethnographer: She said these old people use 'wise words' when they want to say something bad about someone.

Consultant 1: What made her say that?

Ethnographer: Well, she asked me why coyotes are Apaches and I said because they knew all about this country and were very smart.

Consultant 2: [Loud laughter] Maybe what you said about coyotes is true, but it doesn't sound right to us. Coyotes are like some Apaches who don't stay at home and roam around from place to place. Even at night they don't stay at home where they should be. They roam around from place to place and make lots of noise, yelling at night so you can't sleep. Some Apaches do like that, too, and it's no good; they should stay at home at night and keep quiet. That way they will stay out of trouble.

Consultant 3: It is true what that old woman told you. Those old people use 'wise words' when they don't like what someone has done. But they don't want to come out and use that person's name because that way he might hear about it and get angry. So they just say something like coyotes are Apaches and that is enough—everyone knows what they mean and who they are talking about.

Ethnographer: So when you are thinking about coyotes and Apaches you look for *bad* ways that make them the same? You look for what they do that is *no good?*

Consultant 2: Yes. I thought you knew that. It's the same for all 'wise words'. . . . One time when we were talking you said butterflies were girls because they were both pretty. That was wrong because it's good to look nice. I don't think butterflies are pretty, but you do, and that made us laugh. It's because they chase around after each other, like they had no work to do, that makes them the same. And that's no good.

Consultant 3: Let me tell you a story. One time my mother was sick and went to the hospital in Whiteriver. It was before my older sister got married. She was supposed to look after us, cook for us. She did all right, but then one day she took off with my two [female] cousins and they went to where some people were getting ready for a dance. They stayed there all morning. Then they went to another camp to drink beer with some boys. Then they went to another camp. At night they went back to the dance. Finally, they came home. My grandmother had come to take care of us, and I guess she knew that my sister had been running around. When my sister came in my grandmother didn't say anything at first. Then she said to my older brother, "Butterflies are girls and one of them just flew in." My sister knew what it meant, I guess, because she started feeling

bad. . . . That's how they use 'wise words', these old people—when they want to say something bad about someone.

It should now be apparent that the principles which govern the selection of connotative meanings are closely related to what Western
Apaches conceive to be the proper use of 'wise words' in ordinary conversation. As the material presented above suggests, metaphors of this
type are regarded by Apaches as vehicles for the expression of mild personal criticism. It is criticism of a highly oblique sort, however, and the
identity of the person (or persons) being denounced can only be inferred from other kinds of information. This is a complex and often
extremely subtle process whose analysis falls beyond the scope of the
present study. What is significant here is that the requirement to select
behavioral attributes—and, more specifically, behavioral attributes indicative of undesirable qualities—arises directly from the purposes 'wise
words' are designed to serve and the objectives they are intended to accomplish in the course of social interaction.

LEXICAL GAPS AND NOVEL
SEMANTIC CATEGORIES

Philosophers of language have long insisted that both the existence
and the use of metaphor can be understood as a response to incom-
pleteness in the vocabularies of natural languages (e.g. Urban 1939;
Ullman 1962; Alston 1964; Henle 1962). No vocabulary, these scholars
point out, is ever without interstices or "holes," and metaphor—because
it communicates meanings that the literal senses of available words do
not—functions to close or "plug" them. In this way, metaphor serves to
counter what Uriel Weinreich (1964: 57) has called the "designative
inadequacy" of lexical systems. Simultaneously, it alleviates this deficiency through the introduction of new meanings, thus extending the
semantic range of language and increasing its expressive potential.

Despite the widespread acceptance of this proposition, no systematic
attempts have been made to test it (Shibles 1971b). A search of the
pertinent literature reveals that the validity of the proposition—or how
one might go about demonstrating it—are matters which are simply not
discussed. This does not seem to worry the philosophers, but for those
of us who like to season our propositions with a dash or two of verification it inevitably raises doubts. In an effort to dispel such doubts, I shall

present evidence here which indicates that Western Apache metaphors do, indeed, operate in the manner described above. Specifically, I will suggest that the concepts underlying these metaphors correspond to *accidental lexical gaps* in the Western Apache lexicon.

In a stimulating essay, Bever and Rosenbaum (1971) have discussed the subject of lexical gaps in detail. A lexical gap is defined as any combination of semantic features that is not labeled by a lexeme. Some unlabeled combinations are prohibited by the selection restrictions of a language and in this sense may be considered *systematic* lexical gaps. Other unlabeled combinations are perfectly allowable (that is, they are not prohibited by selection restrictions) and therefore may be regarded as *accidental* lexical gaps. Our hypothesis, then, can be confirmed under two conditions. First, we must present evidence which demonstrates that Western Apache metaphorical concepts are composed of allowable combinations of semantic features. Second, we must show that these concepts are not labeled by lexemes.

To test the first condition, I went through my corpus of explanatory paraphrases and made an inventory of all the concepts used by my consultants to interpret the metaphors listed in (1a–h). Then, following the procedure outlined above (pp. 101–3), I defined these concepts in terms of their semantic components and constructed descriptions of the definitions in Western Apache (see appendix). Finally, I presented these descriptions to my eight Apache consultants, asking each of them if, according to his or her understanding, 'such things could be found in this world'. For example:

Ethnographer: Living earth dwellers that waste food—from what you know, can such things be found in this world?
Consultant: Yes.

An affirmative response such as this was taken to mean that the concept in question was linguistically and culturally valid—in other words, that it represented an allowable combination of semantic features and that it denoted a class of objects that existed, or could exist, within the Western Apache universe. A negative reply would have been taken to mean just the opposite. In fact, however, there were no negative replies. My consultants were unanimous in their agreement that all of the descriptive phrases listed in the appendix made clear and legitimate reference to 'things found in this world'. On the basis of this unblemished consensus, I conclude that Western Apache metaphorical concepts do not violate selection restrictions and are composed of allowable combinations of semantic features. This satisfies the first condition of our hypothesis.

To test the second condition, I began by asking my consultants if the phrases in the appendix could be said in shortened form. For example:

> *Ethnographer:* Living earth dwellers that waste food. This, what I have just said, can it be said in a short way and still mean the same?
>
> *Consultant:* No, I don't know of a short way to say it.

This query, which was designed to elicit synonyms or near synonyms that were also unitary lexemes, met with only two positive replies. One consultant explained that phrase 3.5 ('living earth dwellers that act fearlessly'; *ni'gostsangolįįhi dobiłgoyeeda*) could be replaced by the term *dobiłgoyedahi* ('fearless things'). Another consultant said that *dogoyąądahi* ('mindless things') could be substituted for phrases 6.3 and 7.1 ('living earth dwellers that act mindlessly'; *ni'gostsangolįįhi dogoyąąda*).

I also asked my consultants if the referents of the phrases in the appendix had 'names' ('*iži'*). For example:

> *Ethnographer:* Earth dwellers that waste food—do these things have a name?
>
> *Consultant:* No, they have no name, just what you have called them.

In Western Apache, a name, whether it denotes a person, animal, supernatural power, or whatever, typically consists of a unitary lexeme, and for this reason my query was understood as a request to provide linguistic forms that were more compact than the rather lengthy concept labels I had composed. The query was successful in uncovering five names, all of which were unitary lexemes. Two of these are the lexemes that replace phrases 3.5, 6.3, and 7.1 (see above). The other three are as follows:

(4) a. *tsitahohi* ('loners'; 'recluses') replaces phrase 2.6 ('living things that keep to themselves'; *hidahi tsitaaho*).
   b. *biłgoyeihi* ('lazy things') replaces phrase 6.4 ('living earth dwellers that refuse to work'; *ni'gostsangolįįhi do'ičeɣodadiida*).

   c. *haškeihi* ('mean things') replaces phrase 8.2 ('living earth
     dwellers that are short-tempered'; *ni'gostsangolįįhi dabižǫǫ
     dabik'e*).

It should be noted that the lexemes which replace phrases 6.3 and
7.1, 6.4, and 8.2 are not strict synonyms because, as further questioning
of my consultants revealed, these terms can be used to designate any
and all 'living things' and are not restricted exclusively to 'earth
dwellers'. If we choose to assign significance to this fact, we may conclude that 30 of the 33 metaphorical concepts in the Appendix are not
labeled by unitary lexemes; if we choose to ignore it (as my consultants
apparently did) the number of unlabeled concepts falls to 28 of 33. In
either case, it is clear that a high percentage of the concepts in our
sample are not lexically coded. This establishes the second condition
of our hypothesis and, together with the evidence presented earlier in
support of the first condition, serves to substantiate our claim that
Western Apache metaphorical concepts correspond to accidental lexical
gaps.

    This finding has several important implications. One of these is that
the interpretation of most Western Apache metaphors—and, I would
venture to guess, the interpretation of most metaphors that take the
form of disguised or hidden similes—requires of the individual an ability to form *novel semantic categories*. This must be so since the concepts that make interpretation possible are not lexically coded and
therefore are not accessible through the meanings of existing vocabulary
items. Almost certainly, it was this lack of accessibility that Aristotle
had in mind when he said that metaphor—and here, of course, I am
assuming he meant metaphorical concepts—could not be learned from
others.

    One can, of course, receive instruction in how to interpret metaphors
from other people. This is what explanatory paraphrases and some
English professors are all about. But because metaphorical concepts lack
names, such coaching is inevitably circuitous. Consequently, even with
instruction (and most assuredly without it) metaphorical concepts must
be attained on one's own through private acts of discovery and recognition that reveal the existence of relationships where previously none
were perceived. Such acts are *creative* in the fullest and most genuine
sense, for they presuppose and exemplify an ability to arrange familiar
semantic features into unfamiliar combinations, to form fresh cate-

gorizations of not so fresh phenomena—in short, to generate new categories of meanings.

Once again Aristotle perceived the fundamental point, this time when he observed:

> Most smart sayings are derived from metaphor and thus from misleading the hearer beforehand. For it becomes evident to him that he has learned something when the conclusion turns out contrary to his expectations, and his mind seems to say, "How true it is! but up to now I missed it" (*Rhetoric* 3; quoted in Shibles 1971a: 123).

It is the rare gift of the maker of metaphor—the "mark of genius" that Aristotle so admired—that he glimpses new categories of meaning before anyone else and, realizing that the linguistic resources at his disposal are inadequate to express them directly, turns to metaphor as a way to escape from his dilemma. His task is not an easy one, however, for by voicing a proposition that is literally false he runs the risk of being completely misunderstood. The maker of metaphor speaks in semantic contradictions and extends to his audience an invitation to resolve them. If the invitation is accepted, and if attempts at resolution are successful, the result is the acquisition of a concept that is in a very real sense unspeakable. Herein lies the essential ambiguity of metaphor and also its ultimate force—it "says" with ordinary words what ordinary words alone cannot say, thus facilitating the conversion of apparent absurdity into understandable truth.

Clifford Geertz (1964: 59) has spoken to this same point but in a slightly different way. Writes Geertz:

> The power of metaphor derives precisely from the interplay between the discordant meanings it symbolically coerces into a unitary conceptual framework and from the degree to which that coercion is successful in overcoming the psychic resistance such semantic tension inevitably generates in anyone in a position to perceive it. When it works, a metaphor transforms a false identification . . . into an apt analogy; when it misfires it is a mere extravagance.

TOWARD A THEORY OF METAPHOR

At the outset of this essay, I claimed that transformational linguistic theory could not explain the ability of human beings to produce and understand figurative speech. I also claimed that the transformational model excluded certain types of information which are essential to an adequate theory of metaphor. In conclusion, I would like to return to these issues and discuss them in relation to the foregoing analysis of Western Apache 'wise words'.

Let us suppose that we have in hand (or in head) a transformational grammar of the Western Apache language consisting of a syntactic component and a semantic component which conform in all respects to the specifications set down by Chomsky (1965) and Katz (1972). Let us also suppose that we are presented with the sentence *hadaditl'a' 'iškįįn 'at'ee* ('Lightning is a boy') and are asked to interpret it. How would our grammar respond? What would it tell us? It would respond by assigning the sentence a literal reading. Specifically, it would inform us that the sentence is contradictory because the subject possesses semantic features that are incompatible with features possessed by the predicate (e.g. 'sky dweller' vs. 'earth dweller'). This is *all* our grammar could accomplish. A figurative reading of the sentence would be out of the question. Why?

The inability of our grammar to provide figurative readings is directly related to a guiding principle of transformational linguistics which states that the goal of semantic theory should be to predict and explain the *properties and relations of sentence types*. "A semantic theory," according to Katz (1972: 7), "must explain why the meaning of a linguistic construction makes it a case of a certain property or relation, makes it exhibit the phenomenon of synonymy, ambiguity, contradictoriness, and so forth." Such a theory, Katz (1972: 62) goes on to say, ". . . must abstract away from features of utterance contexts and concern itself with inherent features of sentence types."

This conception of the aims of semantic theory is coupled with a principle by means of which transformationalists determine what constitutes "semantic" information and what does not. This principle is described by Katz (1972: 285–86) as follows:

> Semantic theory offers . . . a principle telling when a piece of information is part of the meaning of a lexical item, as opposed to being a factual comment on its referent. Given such a principle, each piece of information that qualifies as semantic by the principle enters the semantic representation of that item in the form of a semantic marker in one of the lexical readings in its dictionary entry. . . . This principle, then, must decide how to choose between

two lexical readings R_1 and R_2, which are the same except that R_2 contains (*ex hypothesi*) a component, putative semantic marker μ that represents *factual* information and R_1 does not contain μ. . . . Linguistics should resist the addition of any information to a lexical reading if its inclusion would fail to increase the predictive or explanatory power of the lexcal reading and thus of the dictionary. Since what must be predicted and explained by a dictionary, as part of the semantic component of a grammar, are the semantic properties and relations of anomaly, synonymy, analyticity, entailment, etc., by showing that R_2 does not predict or explain any of these properties or relations that are not already predicted and explained by R_1, it will be shown that μ, which is the only difference between R_1 and R_2, represents factual, not semantic, information. . . . If we cannot eliminate information from the lexical reading of a word W without losing predictions and explanations of properties and relations of expressions in which W occurs, then such information belongs in the dictionary entry for W and is hence rightly deemed semantic; and if we can simplify the entries of the dictionary by excluding a certain piece of information from all of them, then it is rightly deemed non-semantic.

In actual practice, the principle Katz discusses is used by transformational grammarians to exclude from dictionary entries all "factual comments" about the referents of lexical items. Such information is considered "non-semantic" because it is not needed to explain the properties and relations of sentence types. For example, with respect to *hadaditl'a' 'iškįįn 'at'ee* ('Lightning is a boy'), the fact that both boys and lightning 'dart around' (*-naadamase*) is not necessary to demonstrate that the sentence as a type exhibits the property of contradictoriness. In this way, transformationalists have defined as extraneous to semantic theory what we have been calling connotative meanings or, as Katz (1972: 451) puts it, ". . . the contingent properties that groups of people think belong to the referents of words." In so doing, they have committed themselves to a rigidly literalist view of language in which figurative speech has no place and cannot be explained. A theory of metaphor is *ipso facto* impossible. Is it any wonder that our grammar of Western Apache can tell us only that 'Lightning is a boy' embodies a semantic contradiction? Or, as Uriel Weinreich (1966: 399) has observed, that transformationalists have been constrained to deal with ". . . special cases of speech—humorless, prosaic, banal prose"?

It would be a serious mistake, however, to conclude that transformational theory is irrelevant to a theory of metaphor. On the contrary, it can play a significant role. For reasons that should now be clear, a theory of metaphor must be capable of assigning to the constituents of a metaphorical expression their literal or designative meanings. To the extent that a transformational grammar specifies these meanings, it forms a necessary part of a theory of metaphor. Also, since metaphor involves the violation of certain selection restrictions, a theory of metaphor must be capable of identifying the restrictions that are violated. Transformational grammar can accomplish this task with considerable precision (at least in principle) and for this reason, too, is needed in a theory of metaphor. It is apparent, however, that a theory of metaphor must do more than specify the literal meanings of words and the rules determining their cooccurrence; it must also account for the adduction of connotative meanings and specify the rules that govern their combination with designative meanings to form metaphorical concepts. It is this last set of requirements that a transformational grammar does not satisfy.

But let us suppose it did. For the sake of argument, let us imagine that our hypothetical Western Apache grammar contains a complete listing of designative and connotative features for every item in the lexicon, as well as a full set of selection restrictions that define the conditions under which these features can be combined. Could we now assign a figurative interpretation to 'Lightning is a boy'? We might, but we would have no assurance whatsoever that our interpretation would be culturally appropriate. For nowhere in our grammar is it stated that the connotative meanings adduced to interpret a Western Apache metaphor must be commensurate with behavioral attributes that reflect unfavorably upon the referents of the metaphor's constituents. This vital information is omitted entirely, and its absence points to another weakness in the transformational paradigm: a total neglect of the cultural norms and attitudes that influence the ways in which language is *used*.

This neglect is an unfortunate consequence of the transformationalist dictum that a theory of linguistic competence should concern itself exclusively with sentence types and ignore both sentence tokens and the contexts in which they occur. Such a proscription serves to disengage the study of language from social life, and neatly removes from

114

consideration and analysis all forms of knowledge that guide and shape the activity of speaking, the actual conduct of verbal communication. Gone at a blow are the skills that enable the members of a speech community to decide on what should be said and how to say it, to whom it should be said and under what circumstances, and how what is said should be interpreted. Gone, in other words, are the kinds of sociolinguistic principles that complement grammatical knowledge but go beyond it to define what is proper, fitting, and, as we have seen in the case of the Western Apache, fundamental to the evaluation of metaphorical speech. Gone is what Teeter (1970) has called the *command* of language, the ability to call upon it and apply it in ways that meet the standards and expectations of fellow speakers. Wrenched from their natural context like so many fish out of water and hung up for sale, the sentence types prized by transformationalists are arrayed and analyzed as if they had no place of origin, no relationship to the affairs of men, no purpose but to be dissected and, once laid open, awarded to the cleverest bidder. They exist in an ecological vacuum, isolated and unconnected, their formal properties and relations still intact, but their appropriateness—if ever they had any—a quality of no importance, a matter of no concern.

The drawbacks inherent in such an approach emerge most clearly when we consider metaphor in relation to the concept of linguistic competence. Chomsky (1965) restricts competence to the tacit knowledge represented in a grammar, that is, to the body of rules and information which enables a speaker-hearer to generate and interpret an infinite number of novel, well-formed sentences. It is in this sense, of course, that he has characterized language as a productive and creative system. Note, however, that if we accept Chomsky's definition we are obliged to conclude that because Western Apache metaphors are designatively ill formed they constitute evidence of flawed or imperfect competence and therefore reflect *deficiencies* or *defects* in the Apaches' "knowledge" of their language. In this view, metaphors are reduced to the level of linguistic *errors* or *mistakes* not unlike those a child might make. And far from being regarded as manifestations of a creative skill, they can be taken as indicative of just the opposite: an inability to speak according to grammatical rules. Here is a real dilemma. Either we declare all Apaches who use metaphor to be linguistic incompetents, or we admit that the concept of competence as defined by Chomsky (1965) is unsatisfactory and in need of modification. The latter is clearly the only alternative.

What is needed, as Hymes (1967, 1971, 1972, 1973) has suggested, is an expansion of the concept of linguistic competence to include the ability to speak *appropriately* as well as grammatically. The two should not be confused because appropriate speech is often ungrammatical and grammatical speech is frequently inappropriate. Part of an Apache's sociolinguistic competence is to know when it is appropriate to violate grammatical rules and which rules are appropriate to violate. It is this kind of knowledge that he acts upon when speaking metaphorically. 'Wise words' are prime examples of *appropriately ill-formed* utterances.

In the broadened view of competence proposed by Hymes, metaphor would no longer count as a linguistic blunder; neither would it imply impaired linguistic knowledge. To the contrary, it would be seen as a positive achievement, a linguistic invention won through the artful exploitation of connotative meaning and a willingness to challenge grammatical authority. Such exploitation and challenge is not for linguistic cripples; it is for persons whose competence allows them to experiment with linguistic principles in unorthodox ways. Since this ability presupposes intimate familiarity with the principles themselves, metaphor implies mastery of language rather than ineptness.

If the study of metaphor can contribute to a widened interpretation of linguistic competence, it can also contribute to a deeper appreciation of linguistic creativity. Chomsky (1965) has equated creativity with the ability of human beings to produce and understand an infinite set of novel utterances. Metaphor, on the other hand, entails the invention and acquisition of novel semantic categories. The two abilities, though related, are not the same. The former, as Hymes (1973: 119) has pointed out, is basically concerned with the "systemic potentiality" of language, while the latter is ". . . that kind of creativity which consists of the discovery of possibilities implicit in a [linguistic] system, but not yet discovered, not yet known" (Hymes 1973: 99). Creativity in Chomsky's sense consists in the unfolding of existing structures. Creativity in metaphor consists in the use of existing structures to forge new ones.

What distinguishes the two even more sharply, I think, is that the former is achieved through adherence to grammatical rules while the

116

latter is achieved by breaking them. Chomsky's type of creativity manifests itself in the form of utterances which, novel though they may be, do not depart from established canons of designative meaning. In contrast, metaphor flaunts these canons in order to capitalize on connotative meanings and expresses what designated meanings cannot. Herein lies a fundamental difference. The transformationalist's ideal speaker-hearer is consistently obedient to the strictly grammatical rules of language. The maker of metaphor is not.

As defined by Chomsky, creativity is commensurate with one form of "unboundedness" in language, that is, with the ability of individuals to make continuously original use of materials already present. Metaphor entails this ability, too, but *adds* to what is present by formulating and sponsoring new categories of meaning. In so doing, it functions to augment the lexical semantic resources of linguistic systems, and serves as an indispensable device for adapting these systems to the changing communicative needs of their speakers. Chomsky's ideal speaker-hearer is content with his language as he finds it and does not disturb the *status quo*. The maker of metaphor is dissatisfied with his language and seeks to enrich it through the introduction of untried means of expression.

It hardly needs to be said that cultural anthropologists owe a great intellectual debt to Noam Chomsky and his insight into parts of a theory of language. But metaphor cannot be ignored, and Chomsky's theory, though necessary to an explanation of it, is not sufficient. What the Western Apache tells us is true. Ravens *are* widows and lightning *is* a boy. *I* am a carrion beetle. And it is important to find out why. Our best hope for success lies in continuing ethnography, and this means trying to make sense of contingent facts, unlabeled semantic categories, rules for language use, and the like. For it is in metaphor—perhaps more dramatically than in any other form of symbolic expression—that language and culture come together and display their fundamental inseparability. A theory of one that excludes the other will inevitably do damage to both. And this, we can all agree, should not be allowed to continue.

In closing, it is well to keep in mind that well-turned metaphors are recognized and appreciated by persons other than ethnographers, philosophers of language, and literary critics. Shortly before I last departed from the field, one of my Western Apache consultants, who was standing by as I packed my belongings, suggested that I stop for a moment—there was something he wanted to tell me:

> It's too bad that you didn't try to learn about wise words before. When I was young, old people around here used to make them up all the time. Only a few of them did it and they were the best talkers of all. Some people would try but they couldn't do it so they stopped trying. Now you know what some 'wise words' mean— that's what you asked us to teach you. But you still haven't made any up. Maybe those old people would have taught you how they did it. It's hard to do and you have to know a lot about everything. Those old people were smart. One of them would make up a new one and right away other people would start to use it. They had never heard it before and if it was a good one it would make them happy and they would laugh. It's still that way when someone makes one up. Only the good talkers can make them up like that. They are the ones who *really* speak Apache. They are the ones who make up 'wise words' and don't have to use someone else's. I don't know how they do it. It's something special that they know.

APPENDIX:
Definitions and Descriptions of
Western Apache Metaphorical Concepts

1. Metaphor: *hadaditl'a' 'iškįįn 'at'ee* ('Lightning is a boy')
    1.1 'living thing' + 'dart around'; *hidahi naadamase* ('living things that dart around')
    1.2 'living thing' + 'shoot aimlessly'; *hidahi dailįįyo dadiłtoh* ('living things that shoot aimlessly')
    1.3 'living thing' + 'cause damage'; *hidahi dawąąne dayiłčǫǫ* ('living things that cause damage')
    1.4 'living thing' + 'act unpredictably'; *hidahi haga'aadadešįį dobegoziida* ('living things that act unpredictably')
2. Metaphor: *kaaγe 'iitsaa 'at'ee* ('Ravens are widows')
    2.1 'living thing' + 'unable to procure fresh meat'; *hidahi doyo'itsį' nadadineeda* ('living things that are unable to procure fresh meat')
    2.2 'living thing' + 'wait to be given food'; *hidahi 'iit'anbigąą č'idadodil'įį* ('living things that wait to be given food')

118

2.3 'living thing' + 'talk through nose'; *hidahi bičįįyeyadałti'* ('living things that talk through their nose')

2.4 'living thing' + 'talk in raspy voice'; *hidahi dihedlaat'goyadałti'* ('living things with raspy voices')

2.5 'living thing' + 'tire easily'; *hidahi dos'aa daiɣaada* ('living things that tire easily')

2.6 'living thing' + 'keep to themselves'; *hidahi tsitaaho* ('living things that keep to themselves')

3. Metaphor: *koyiłčoože 'indaa' 'at'ee* ('Carrion beetles are whitemen')

3.1 'living thing + 'earth dweller' + 'waste food'; *ni'gostsangolįįhi 'iitan donaodi'yodaawołsida* ('living earth dwellers that waste food')

3.2 'living thing' + 'earth dweller' + 'avoid heat'; *ni'gostsangolįįhi gostoodbit'inčǫǫ* ('living earth dwellers that avoid heat')

3.3 'living thing' + 'earth dweller' + 'leave discernible tracks'; *ni'gostsangolįįhi bike'dabigozįį* ('living earth dwellers that leave discernible tracks')

3.4 'living thing' + 'earth dweller' + 'make winding paths'; *ni'gostsangolįįhi dailįįyo'anataał* ('living earth dwellers that make winding paths')

3.5 'living thing' + 'earth dweller' + 'act fearlessly'; *ni'gostsangolįįhi dobiłgoyeeda* ('living earth dwellers that act fearlessly')

4. Metaphor: *gooše čaɣǫǫše 'at'ee* ('Dogs are children')

4.1 'living thing' + 'earth dweller' + 'are always hungry'; *ni'gostsangolįįhi ǰ'ida'dadnlįį* ('living earth dwellers that are always hungry')

4.2 'living thing' + 'earth dweller' + 'get into everything'; *ni'gostsangolįįhi dawǫǫ neyanakai* ('living earth dwellers that get into everything')

4.3 'living thing' + 'earth dweller' + 'do whatever they want' (i.e. act in an undisciplined manner); *ni'gostsangolįįhi dobadesdiida* ('living earth dwellers that do whatever they want')

5. Metaphor: *mba'tsose 'indee 'at'ee* ('Coyotes are Western Apache men')

5.1 'living thing' + 'earth dweller' + 'run around at night'; *ni'gostsangolįįhi tl'ege' anakaał* ('living earth dwellers that run around at night')

5.2 'living thing' + 'earth dweller' + 'make noise at night'; *ni'gos-*

tsangolįįhi tl'ege' hadagoł'aa ('living earth dwellers that make noise at night')

5.3 'living thing' + 'earth dweller' + 'stay away from home'; *ni'gostsangolįįhi gowąąyo donastąąda* ('living earth dwellers that stay away from home')

5.4 'living thing' + 'earth dweller' + 'act sneaky and sly'; *ni'gostsangolįįhi mba'tsose ga'adat'e* (living earth dwellers that act sneaky and sly')

5.5 'living thing' + 'earth dweller' + 'play tricks'; *ni'gostsangolįįhi łąągote'iłco* ('living earth dwellers that play tricks')

5.6 'living thing' + 'earth dweller' + 'get into trouble'; *ni'gostsangolįįhi nagontl'og yanat'liž* ('living earth dwellers that get into trouble')

6. Metaphor: *doole jekii 'at'ee* ('Butterflies are girls')

    6.1 'living thing' + 'earth dweller' + 'go around in pairs'; *ni'gostsangolįįhi nakii gonadakai* ('living earth dwellers that go around in pairs')

    6.2 'living thing' + 'earth dweller' + 'always want to play'; *ni'gostsangolįįhi nadawolzežǫǫ hadat'ii* ('living earth dwellers that always want to play')

    6.3 'living thing' + 'earth dweller' + 'act mindlessly'; *ni'gostsangolįįhi dogoyąąda* ('living earth dwellers that act mindlessly')

    6.4 'living thing' + 'earth dweller' + 'refuse to work'; *ni'gostsangolįįhi do'ič'egodadiida* ('living earth dwellers that refuse to work')

7. Metaphor: *doole 'izeege 'at'ee* ('Butterflies are sweethearts')

    7.1 'living thing' + 'earth dweller' + 'act mindlessly'; *ni'gostsangolįįhi dogoyąąda* ('living earth dwellers that act mindlessly')

    7.2 'living thing' + 'earth dweller' + 'chase after each other'; *ni'gostsangolįįhi łiłnadade* ('living earth dwellers that chase after each other')

    7.3 'living thing' + 'earth dweller' + 'can't concentrate'; *ni'gostsangolįįhi donatsi'dakesda* ('living earth dweller that can't concentrate')

8. Metaphor: *toołkaiye saan 'at'ee* ('Burros are old women')

    8.1 'living thing' + 'earth dweller' + 'rest with head hanging down'; *ni'gostsangolįįhi binii' nadaz'ąąna hanaadayoł* ('living earth dwellers that rest with their heads hanging down')

8.2 'living thing' + 'earth dweller' + 'are short-tempered'; *ni'gostsan-goliįhi dobidawołtǫǫda* ('living earth dwellers that are short-tempered')

8.3 'living thing' + 'earth dweller' + 'are independently minded'; *ni'gostsangoliįhi dabižǫǫdabik'e* ('living earth dwellers that are independently minded')

NOTES

1. I am grateful to all the members of the School of American Research symposium for their contributions to a general discussion of the first draft of this paper, but especially to Michael Silverstein, Roy G. D'Andrade, Susan Ervin-Tripp, Clifford Geertz, and Harold Scheffler—all of whom made particularly valuable suggestions which I have tried to incorporate into the final version. Others who read the early draft and whose comments influenced its revision include: Ellen Basso, Richard Bauman, Robbins Burling, Charles O. Frake, Philip Greenfeld, Dell Hymes, Scott Rushforth, David Sapir, Joel Sherzer, and Richard Thompson. I appreciate both their willingness to help and the stimulating quality of their ideas. Needless to say, whatever shortcomings remain are entirely my own responsibility.

I am most deeply indebted to the Apaches of Cibecue who introduced me to 'wise words' many years ago and, more recently, consented to give me detailed instruction in their interpretation and use. For this instruction, as well as for other gifts of a less tangible sort, I express my continuing thanks to Morley Cromwell, Nashley Tessay, Annie Peaches, Darlene and Calvert Tessay, Sarah and Francis DeHose, Eva Watt, Dudley Patterson, and Ernest Murphy. Ned Anderson, of Byles, Arizona, also provided indispensable help and counsel.

2. This position is most obviously characteristic of "interpretive semantic theory" as outlined by Chomsky (1965) and developed by Katz (1972). It should be noted, however, that many of the criticisms expressed in this essay apply with equal force to "generative semantic theory" (e.g. George Lakoff 1972; Reddy 1969) as well. Recently, generative semanticists have broadened their approach to the analysis of meaning to include features of discourse but, as Joel Sherzer (personal communication) has aptly observed ". . . they have not yet really faced up to the basic issue of the *use* of language in social and cultural life, and until they do the models they propose will be inadequate to deal with such crucial uses of language as metaphor."

5
Speech Acts and Social Learning

SUSAN ERVIN-TRIPP

University of California, Berkeley

INTRODUCTION

"Go ask your mommy to come to the phone."

"Is the lady of the house in?"

"Hey, Len, shoot the chart to me, willya?"

"Oh, by the way, Doctor, could you leave that chart when you're through?"

It is a standard assertion that natural languages have polysemy. Any dictionary reveals numerous examples of multiple meanings for single forms; this is the source of many jokes about inept selection of alternatives in translation. Languages can have maximal economy of forms by allowing for variation of meaning according to context. Misunderstandings are avoided because of our extraordinary ability to make our understanding vary according to the surround, both linguistic and non-linguistic. In fact, we find that the most glaring instances of misunderstanding are often just the result of a rare coincidence of context between two possibilities. Polysemy is an economy which seems to be advantageous to speakers, since when diversity of output is reduced search processes are simplified. In colloquial speech, forms with low semantic specificity are often preferred, such as "thing," "guy," "*ce truc*," "*ce machin*," or demonstratives.

Yet why is it that while we encounter polysemy in languages, we also find considerable synonymity? It is just as common to find many ways to say the same thing as it is to find many meanings for the same form. In fact, stylistically—at least in writing—adults prefer a low density of repetition and use syntactic compressions, required anaphoric pronouns, and synonyms in order to escape repetition. This chapter will explore in detail one system of alternative ways to say the same thing and will raise questions about the social functions of such diversity. The theme, then, is symbolic diversity.

In the lexicon, we normally find several names for the same things or people. In English, this diversity is especially rich in certain topical areas, such as body functions ("urinate," "go to the potty," "piss," "take a leak," "go to the little girls' room," "go to the bathroom," "be away from one's desk," "wee-wee," and so on). Diversity appears in address terms for the same person, who may, on various occasions, respond to "Mommy," "Aunt Louise," "Sis," "Lou," "Dr. Leland," "Grandma," and "Mrs. Jamison." It is clear at the outset that the focus of diversity in the lexicon or naming system is diagnostic of areas of cultural complexity or sensitivity.

Diversity also appears in the morphology of address, a familiar example being the system of person and number in pronouns and in inflections as a function of relations between speaker and addressee—e.g. *tu/vous, du/sie*. Thus what I translate as "This one is yours" may in some languages be homonymous with "This one is his" or "This one is theirs." Geertz (1960: 248–60) has reported on an even more elaborate set of alternations of cooccurring lexical and morphological variations, which he calls stylemes, that can be nuanced by honorifics—all being diverse ways of saying the same thing. In Geertz's examples, the alternations occurred within a common syntactic frame.

Linguists have noticed both the lexical and affixal systems of alternations because they assumed importance during the preparation of lexicons and grammars. The directives cited at the beginning of this chapter provide yet another kind of diversity. This type of alternation, which can occur with no syntactic or lexical similarity at all between the variants, is relatively common in human discourse. I now will examine the structure and implications of some of these systems of alternations.

We must agree at the start on what is meant by maintenance of meaning across variation. Of course I had traditional reference-centered semantics in mind when I made my initial points. The examples were those in which reference (such as urination, or a person addressed or spoken of) was held constant, but the form varied. Halliday (1975: 17) has spoken of three dimensions of language, which he views as being somewhat independent, that illustrate nicely categories of contrast which lead to diversity. One is the *ideational* axis, the traditional domain of semantics. Another is the axis of *text*. Diversity in form occurs when the same reference is made in different liguistic contexts. Anaphora is a good example. The difference between "The green one is on the table" and "The one on the table is green"—which some semantic analyses would make synonymous—can often lie in what we said just before. For example, if I say, "I have a green one and a blue one," I make the first alternative far more likely because I have defined what is presupposed, topical, or "old" information. The third axis discussed by Halliday is what he calls *interpersonal*. Thus the contrast between an utterance to greet and an utterance to evoke a service is an interpersonal difference, though both may have the same surface structure. A given utterance has values relative to all three axes at the same time. Thus if I say, "It's a fine day," I may be simultaneously greeting, introducing meanings about the external world, and starting a text. But this same utterance can have quite different values on these axes in other contexts.

Halliday's recent work with developmental changes in language in a very young child helps elucidate these distinctions. In his data, the axes were not yet distinct. In adult speech, for example, "more meat" might mean either a request or an observation; "green car" might also serve either function. But in the child's usage, a given utterance tended to have only one interpersonal function at first: "more meat" was always a request; "green car" was always a comment about a car, not a request for it. In addition, the contrast between request and comment was redundantly signaled by rising intonation for the first and falling for the second. In other words, the child was not yet using a given expression to have several functions. "Is Mommy there?" could only mean an information question.

Gumperz and Herasimchuk (1972: 106) have provided a more elaborate example from classroom interaction (I have added names):

Teacher: . . . how do you spell Ken?
Ann: Where's Ken? K–C–K–E, er—
Teacher: Ann, Ida is spelling it . . .

In terms of referential content, the teacher's last utterance is a statement about the act of spelling, with Ida as agent, addressed to Ann. In these respects, it would contrast with:

Is Ida spelling it?
Jack, Ida is spelling it.
Bob is spelling it.
Ann, Ida is going to spell it.

There has been considerable discussion in linguistics recently about problems of focus and of what is given or new in utterances. In these respects, it is clear in the example that the agent is at issue, not the action, and this difference is reflected in the stress on the agent. But is this really an adequate characterization of what is being said?

The utterance cannot be interpreted without reference to discourse rules. Normally, in this kind of classroom interaction, the teacher and the pupil alternate utterances. In normal discourse structure, when the pupil has performed, the teacher confirms or corrects the pupil (Sinclair and Coulthard 1974). This is the primary exchange in the formal classroom, but it is violated in our example. Instead, the teacher has made a comment about the proper participants in the exchange.

The teacher's utterance is syntactically a statement; any of the conventional semantic analyses would credit it with being an assertion of an ongoing event. But in fact Ida had said nothing. Interpersonally the utterance was a directive. It was functionally equivalent to the utterance Gumperz and Herasimchuk found a peer teacher using: "Don't tell 'im."

The use of statements which function as directives or prohibitions is common practice in classrooms, according to Sinclair and Coulthard (1974: 32–33). In cases which occur with sufficient frequency, such utterances conventionally function as directives, never as statements. The inferential link that makes novel instances interpretable is a hearer's knowledge of a social rule. In this case, the social rule is a general rule of turn taking in classroom conversation: the addressee of a question has prior claim to the floor, and only one person has the floor at once. This method of control simultaneously provides a directive in the particular case and alludes to the general rule.

It sometimes happens that teachers or parents make what appear to be directives without any evident wish to bring about compliance, or with an incongruous prosody. Jacquelyn Housh (1972), in observing classroom directives, found an instance in which the teacher said, "We must keep our feet on the floor!" while passing by some children who were lying on their backs with their feet in the air. This utterance may in fact emphasize the second function mentioned above; it reasserts a general rule by reminding everyone that the teacher is the proper custodian of rules, even their creator. However, enforcement in this instance was of minor importance.

This example is far from unique. We have enough instances to believe that it is common, as Halliday has asserted, for utterances to be plurifunctional. Let us return to the example:

Ann, Ida is spelling it.

On the *ideational* axis, this sentence contrasts with other possible agents, actions, addressees, objects. On the *interpersonal* axis, as a directive, it contrasts with a statement which would be descriptive of an ongoing event, that is, it contrasts with the other potential realizations of the same function. It is this system of alternations for the same function which I wish to discuss in greater detail below. I shall then examine the implications for socialization of such verbal systems.

DIRECTIVES[1]

Over a period of years I have been collecting evidence about the kinds of structural variation adults employ in accomplishing directives, including those that serve themselves and those that regulate others. These data suggest that such directives take five or more surface realizations:

1. Imperatives like "Bring me a sweater."
2. Embedded imperatives like "Could you bring me a sweater?"
3. Question directives like "Have you got a sweater here?"
4. Statements of need like "I'm cold."
5. Hints like "It's a cold night."

In some cases, a speaker may be aware of a condition but not specify a remedy. If the speaker speaks about a discomfort, but is as yet unfocused on the cure, the hearer may interpret the utterance as a directive, as we shall see. Under some social conditions, speakers may be aware of remedies but be unwilling to utter directives or even statements of need or condition. They suffer in silence rather than ask the prime minister to pass the salt.

Imperatives

Imperatives, if not the most common kind of directive, are certainly the most obvious. There is no way to make them ambiguous in function. But even imperatives can be modulated. Modulators include: greetings, honorific address terms, names, "please," pitch, tag modals, and tag "OK." One could argue that most of these, except the last two, are in fact potential modulators for any form of directive. They function as extra forms which can shift the effect of the central form of the directive and, in the case of sharp discrepancies, create a sarcastic effect. Indeed, where the situation is obvious, a name, "please," or a modal alone can function as a directive. These features are available, like honorifics such as "sir," as an optional extra marking to indicate deference, ingratiation, or sarcasm.

The distribution of modulators is socially defined. Where tasks normally involve imperatives—for example, where interchanges of money for services or goods, or coordinated services are required—names can modulate imperatives. Blue-collar workers: "More to the right, Joe." "Lift it higher, Bill." "Under the hinge, Joe." "OK, push, Bill." In shops, "please" is sometimes used to mark higher rank or age of addressee. Between waitresses and cooks, it may mark requests for services outside the realm of normal duties. In an office study, Gardner (1968) found that physical distance increased raised pitch, postposed modals, and address terms: "Bring the file" vs. "Bring the file, would you, Rose?"

Embedded Imperatives

Embedded imperatives are those in which the requested act is preceded by an introductory phrase, such as "Can you . . . ," "Would you mind . . . ," "Would you. . . ."

Sinclair and his colleagues have pointed out that this type of directive is common in English classrooms:

> An interrogative clause is to be interpreted as a *command to do* if it fulfills all the following conditions: (i) it contains one of the modals *can, could, will, would* (and sometimes *going to*); (ii) the subject of the clause is also an addressee; (iii) the predicate describes an action which is physically possible at the time of utterance (Sinclair and Coulthard 1974: 32).

The feasibility constraint is important. If one says "Can you swim?" in a living room, it is interpreted as an information question. Next to a swimming pool the same utterance would be interpreted as a command and followed by a splash.

In fact, many of these modal requests can *only* be interpreted as directives:

Hospital desk, nurse to aide:
Would you hand me Mr. Adam's chart, please?

Typist to professor:
Would you sign these this week, Professor Jones?

It is difficult to see how the directive interpretation of these items could arise, as has been claimed by Gordon and Lakoff (1971), by inference from a literal interpretation.

Another explanation for this class of instances is that they are routinely interpreted as requests within the feasibility limits suggested by Sinclair and Coulthard (1974). If this is so, any *can you* question that is feasible will be interpreted as a directive unless accompanied by a disclaimer of directive intent. The argument here is that given appropriate contextual conditions for a directive, the directive interpretation is automatic, unmarked, normal. Only if the situation is ambiguous, the effort great, and the spirit or the flesh unwilling will the prowess-questioning interpretation (the "literal meaning") be entertained.

Perhaps the best evidence that this apparent pragmatic neutralization is an illusion is noncompliance.

Can you bring me a Coke when you go to dinner?
No, I can't.

Can you sign the letter this afternoon?
No, I can't.

These answers are rude. Noncompliance with a modal imperative, like noncompliance with an imperative, requires an explanation. This is evidence that these utterances are normally interpreted as directives. We shall see that the same is not true of other forms of directives, which permit unexplained noncompliance. On the other hand, compliance with an embedded imperative permits a show of voluntariness.

Embedded questions were most frequent in addressing persons of different rank, peers in their own territory, or peers performing tasks outside their regular roles. Since imperative request forms tend to have fairly restricted conditions, they tend to cooccur with informal address terms, slang, and casual phonology.

The following quotations were collected in a research medical laboratory, where rank tends to be of great importance:

a. Hey, Len, shoot the chart to me, willya?
b. Shall I take it now, Doctor?
c. Oh, by the way, Doctor, could you leave that chart when you're through?

The technicians in this laboratory included some who switched to a solidary relation with the doctors, or some of the doctors, when outsiders were absent. On those occasions they used utterances like (a). When outsiders were present, rank was reinvoked to select address, phonology, lexical style, and directive type, as in (b). On those occasions, the switchers were indistinguishable from their more staid colleagues (c).

This effect of outsiders was apparent in other settings as well. For example, in an office setting peers normally used imperatives to each other unless at a distance or otherwise disadvantaged. In the presence of a high-ranking visitor, however, peers used complex, highly qualified directives of the sort they would address to a superior. The *outsider effect* in these samples is comparable to monitoring in style; it shifts speech toward social alternatives which would have been used had the outsider been the addressee, at least when the outsider is high enough in rank.

Question Directives

We are all familiar with common request questions which are standard forms for directives:

Hello. Is John there?
Pardon me. Do you have a double room for tonight?

It could be argued that we know these are directives because we interpret the questions literally and infer that a question about the presence of John could only be based on a desire to speak with him. On the other hand, in the production of these directives, we frequently find the forms are so normal that we use them even when we do not, in fact, need the information requested. One might, for example, watch John go into his apartment from a window across the way, and still say to his room-mate, "Is John there?" when he answers the telephone.

We have substantial evidence showing that under certain conditions questions are normally interpreted as requests and can become the normal, unmarked realization of directives.

A few examples will illustrate:

a. Professor telephones Room Permits office.
   Speaker's Intent: Getting information.
   "Do you have a seminar room for twenty, Monday nights?"
   "Just a minute. Yes I do, give me your name, department, and course number, please."
   Hearer's Interpretation: Directive to reserve room.
b. Office workers at lunch break.
   Intent: Getting information.
   "Is there any coffee left?"
   "Yeah, pass your cup."
   Interpretation: Directive.
c. Teacher to pupils in class.
   Intent: Starting lesson.
   "What are you laughing at?"
   "Nothing."
   Interpretation: Directive to be silent.
d. Caller to friend's wife on phone.
   Intent: Getting information.
   "Is John there?"
   "Yes, just a minute, I'll get him."
   Interpretation: Directive.

e. Host to guests, midnight.
   Intent: Offering a service.
   "How about another drink?"
   "Oh, no thanks, we'll be leaving soon."
   Interpretation: Directive to leave.

These are a sample of common experiences we have all had in which the usual way to realize a directive is through an information question. However, this directive represents a form that potentially neutralizes the contrast between directives and information seeking—it is a pragmatic neutralization. Speakers who are aware of this normal interpretation can avoid the directive interpretation by disclaiming it.

One can speculate on what such disclaimers might be:

a. "Would you mind telling me—I'd just like to know if there's a room available for twenty, Monday nights."
b. "Anna, should I make more coffee?"
c. "Let's look at an example; for instance, what is funny about that?"
d. "I don't want to talk to him, but is John there?"
e. (Disclaimer difficult) "While we're getting warmed up on that topic, how about a refill?"

Disclaimers remove neutralization by denying directive intent. In each of these cases, either directly or indirectly, one makes the directive intent less plausible than its alternative. Part of the reason for the difficulty in the last case is that direct imperatives are unlikely, so that the request question becomes strongly identified as a directive. The importance of the misunderstandings identified earlier lies in the evidence they provide that the normal unmarked form coincides with the syntax of information requests in such a way that speakers seeking information in these situations must remove ambiguity by disclaimers.

It would have been possible to provide direct imperatives for each of these instances, so we must account for the fact that the request question was used instead. The best account is a characterization of the social variables associated with request alternations. The variables that have appeared so far in observational studies have included territorial location of speaker and addressee (an addressee receives fewer imperatives in his own territory), familiarity, similarity of rank and age, and relation of the directive to expected activities such as the exchange of goods for money.

It can be expected that when we have richer data on individual speakers a selection order will become apparent, just as with address terms (Ervin-Tripp 1973: 305; Geoghegan 1973). The early selectors in the choice rule neutralize certain later variables. For example, directives to a familiar person in her own territory may be formally like those to a high-ranked person. In such a case we could say that territoriality neutralizes rank, just as status-marked situations such as trials neutralize familiarity in address terms. If familiarity precedes rank in the rule, then new colleagues who are peers are not given more imperatives than superiors.

These alternations can be seen in data for requests collected in an office by Carol Gardner (1968). We assume that place—the office—is given by a prior commitment. (Of course, actors may change location if a request is inappropriate to a place, or if necessary addressees are elsewhere. When we confine observations to one locale, we limit both the types of requests made and the personnel present in ways that could bias the more general description we seek.) In the office, if a high-ranking person was present, the speaker addressed her request to another person, using the politeness level that would have been suitable to the audience; if the service was dispensable, she kept silent. Elaine Rogers (1967a) found a similar effect of audience in a medical laboratory. The presence of outsiders or supervisory personnel resulted in a reduction of person-related requests; it also brought rank considerations into effect in both address and request forms. If the high-ranking person was the necessary addressee for the service, the most polite alternatives were selected that made the task evident, such as modal imperatives.

If a high-ranking person were not present, the next factor was whether there was pressure or tension in the office due to an extra work load. On these occasions, the speakers ignored social selectors toward their co-workers and used the more impolite forms. New coworkers received the more polite forms regardless of rank, age, or territorial considerations. Once the coworker became familiar, however, the other variables became important. If the person who was asked for a service was in her territory and the asker was not, requests became more polite and fewer imperatives were used. If territory was not a consideration, similarity in rank and age led to imperatives. These might be complicated by adding modal tags, "please," address terms, or rising pitch if the addressee was far away.

Several variables have appeared in request studies that are not evident in the studies of address, which otherwise have many parallels. Examples are territoriality, distance, the seriousness of the service requested, and whether compliance may be assumed because of the type of service, normal roles, or power relations. Some of the variables appear to involve continua, just as one might expect in the kind of cost-benefit situation that typically arises when requests for services and goods are involved. Because continua may require formal solutions different from those required by discrete "selectors," we need more detailed data. Agar's (1973) work on the choices of drug addicts seeking a "fix" raises parallel problems.

It is obvious that the specifics of a rule will vary with group and perhaps with setting. In an experiment, students making a simple request of strangers who were peers or superiors marked the rank primarily in greeting and address forms, only 15 percent complicating the request by asking such questions as "Do you happen to have a pencil?" In the office study, addressees lower in rank, like those higher in rank, received the more polite forms, but in some other studies—of doctors in a hospital and blue-collar workers on a construction site—imperatives were the norm to subordinates.

In all of these studies, some selectors appear to be prior and therefore to have the effect of "neutralizing" other social variables. In the Gardner (1968) office study, unfamiliarity neutralized rank and age differences. The neutralization of situation, social, or semantic features in ordered selection rules has important implications for analysis. A familiar example is the greeting form "How are you?" which has been called "insincere." This form involves pragmatic neutralization between greeting and information seeking. The respondent to this question need only check whether the asker is a close friend or not. If the answer is no, he need give only a routine answer such as "Fine" or another greeting, and does not have to check the actual state of his own health. For this reason, he is obligated in some social groups to make a semantic check and if the information is important—for example, if he just broke his wrist—he is expected to say so. The asker can anticipate the possible ambiguity by marking the question in various ways, thus disclaiming the normal interpretation of "How are you" as a simple greeting.

a. How *are* you, anyway?
b. I heard you were sick; how are you feeling now?

The fact that the routine interchange of greetings need not imply a semantic check of health does not rule out the capacity of some speakers to think of the other meaning of the sentence, just as some speakers can think of an alternate meaning for interrogative requests, or can pun.

I pointed out earlier that, just as in the case of an imperative, the discourse effect of a modal imperative is that noncompliance requires an explanation, but that compliance can be accompanied by an appearance of voluntariness because a question can be answered. In the case of the request question, the addressee is given a very good out. The noncompliant hearer can simply interpret the question as a request for information.

a. Do you have a seminar room for twenty, Monday nights?
   No, sorry, we don't.
b. Is there any coffee left?
   No, it's finished.
c. What are you laughing at?
   Well, you see, it was funny that . . .
d. Is John there?
   No, he's out.
e. How about another drink?
   Sure, I'd love one.

Replies such as these effectively legitimate noncompliance and make false information easy, as in the case of discriminatory landlords saying no rooms are available, and protective secretaries who report the boss is out. The imperative forms force a noncompliant addressee to find a refusal or excuse. Consequently, they force noncompliance to be made explicit.

There is a parallel, of course, in the case of information-seeking questions which contrast with polarized questions that preformulate a reply:

a. Where is the Women's Center?
   Sorry, I don't know where it is.
b. Do you know where the Women's Center is?
   No, I don't.

To answer affirmatively to (b) without supplying the locative information would be a joke, a pragmatic pun. The second question permits noncompliance by allowing an implied fifty-fifty occurrence of negatives. Noncompliance to (a) would require the respondent to admit ignorance.

In these examples, the utterances that speakers call more polite are those which allow the noncompliant addressee to reply without being explicit about his refusal. Discourse structuring is a major way of realizing politeness level. As Robin Lakoff (1972) has put it in a very general characterization, polite speech leaves the options open.

Need Statements

On the face of it, one might assume that the directive form which is minimally restricting is the statement, since in terms of discourse structuring it requires no reply at all. However, certain statements are relatively coercive.

Statements of need in which the requested object or act is made explicit are of course the most obviously coercive, especially if they are made by a person of higher rank.

   a. *Laboratory physician to technician:*
     "I need a routine culture and a specimen. Do you mind?"
   b. *Doctor to hospital nurse:*
     "I'll need a 19-gauge needle, IV tubing, and a preptic swab."

When communication is downward in rank, a direct-need statement is comparable in effect to an imperative. The directness is similar to "I'll have Pall Malls," which can occur when tasks are defined as including the transfer of goods and easy services only.

Some need statements are not intended as directives, although they may be interpreted as such nevertheless.

   Parent at breakfast.
   Intent: Thinking aloud.
   "Oh, darn it. I left my paper out there."
   "I'll get it."
   Interpretation: Directive.

Whether or not a speaker who is aware of a need frames a directive is dependent upon his calculation of the burden of cost he wishes to exact from others relative to his gain. For this reason, it is not always the case that persons who express states of need intend directives.

I have identified a second type of statement which is common in directives downward in rank or age. These involve a vagueness of agent:

a. *Office worker to a different age group of coworkers:*
   Who's going to take over these files?
   Has anyone gone to Accounting this week?
   Someone has to see Dean Anthony.
   Someone has to take dictation for Professor Spellman, Jane.
b. *Mother to daughter:*
   This room has to be vacuumed before that man comes.
c. *Doctor to technician:*
   We have a few things to do over.
d. *Nursery school teacher to children:*
   Let's all take our naps now.

In each of these cases the addressee is the obvious agent for the required act. The act is clearly specified. However, the speaker avoids directly identifying the agent of the act, so that the indefinites become a kind of euphemism to avoid overt imperatives. In some collective "someone" instances, the absence of an agent is a device for recruiting a volunteer.

Ayhan Aksu, a Turkish student, has provided a nice confirmation of the fact that this form must be downward in rank or age. She reports the following conversation (personal communication):

Student to landlady:
"Could we put the garbage can over here?"
"Why, Ayhan, I didn't know you had a roommate!"

Aksu states that she found this misunderstanding confusing, since she had interpreted the "we" directive as more polite than the second person form.

Hints

When the directives were to seniors in rank, an aversive state description might be used, at least by adults:

a. *Daughter to mother:*
   "Mother, you know I don't have a robe."
   "I know."
   "Well, we're having a slumber party tomorrow night."
b. *Wife to husband, who is rowing:*
   "Jock! I don't want to swim right now; here, I'll turn the boat."

The statement of aversive state permits a solicitous alter to aid with a display of voluntariness.

In the following cases, the state of affairs to be altered is made explicit:

  a. *Office worker to another of different age:*
     "It's stuffy in here."
  b. *Professor to office worker:*
     "Mrs. Terry, it's quite noisy in here."
  c. *Mother to son:*
     "Toby's cage is still dirty."
  d. *Wife to husband, who is rowing:*
     "You're throwing water all over me."
  e. *Wife to husband, who is rowing:*
     "You're going to bash a sailboat."
  f. *Husband to wife, who is rowing:*
     "You're heading . . . go over that way."

As Sinclair and Coulthard (1974: 32–33) have pointed out, in situations where there are rules or common agreements about prohibited acts, mere mention of a prohibited act or an unmet obligation functions to frame a command.

In the following examples, the speakers' intent was directive, but there is no direct mention of either a desired act, an aversive condition, or a prohibited act.

  a. *Adult sister to brother, standing near cupboard:*
     "Oh, dear, I wish I were taller."
     "Here, can I get something for you?"
     "Yes, please, some of those green dishes up there."
  b. *Lab director to secretary:*
     "We're waiting for Dr. Klepper from Texas. I'll be gone until two o'clock."
     Intent: Tell him.
  c. *Coworker to another of different age:*
     "I think Sarah opened the Xerox room, Joan."
     Intent: Go make copies.

Statements that fail to specify even the needed act are good candidates for misunderstanding. Here are some examples:

  a. *Office worker to another:*
     Intent: Thinking aloud.
     "It's almost twelve o'clock."

Hearer gets up and locks door.
Interpretation: Directive.
  b. *Woman to escort:*
  Intent: Small talk.
  "It's really cold tonight."
  "Here, take my jacket."
  Interpretation: Directive.
  c. *Guest to hostess, who serves green tea:*
  Intent: Small talk.
  "I've never had green tea."
  "Oh, I'll get you some black tea then."
  Interpretation: Directive.

In cases such as these, the person thinking aloud or making small talk does not really anticipate a reply at all. Consequently, the speaker is unlikely to be as aware of alternative rejoinders as a questioner who might anticipate misunderstanding of information questions as directives. Thus disclaimers are unlikely in the above instances. One can only refuse the service.

The social distribution of statement imperatives is distinctly different from that of imperatives in that they occur in two kinds of settings: (a) in work settings, where who is to do what is very clear, and the statements serve as reminders about time and condition to addressees differing in rank or age; and (b) in familial or quasi-familial relationships, when solicitude on the part of the hearer can be assumed and the service is too special to allow a direct imperative.

Statements do not require a response. The listener may or may not take up the implication, depending upon his state of attention, nurturance, goodwill, or power. Where compliance is unsure or a service is great, statements leave the greatest freedom of choice to a listener. On the other hand, if they are routine forms for standard requests in repetitive situations, there must be assumed compliance based on socialization to the role. The necessary conditions need merely to be stated for the well-trained alter to jump to. In the office studies, these forms never occurred between peers. It may prove to be the case that even in the family studies there are asymmetries of dominance reflected in the selection of indirect rather than explicit requests.

Adult directives range from explicit and slightly qualified imperatives to questions and statements formally identical to utterances that are not requests. Members learn to interpret such utterances routinely as directives when the service is feasible or is a part of their normal role and when interpersonal relations known to the participants can serve to account for the selection. The discourse constraints of statements, interrogatives, and embedded imperatives are successively more coercive. Statements allow the listener not to respond verbally at all; interrogatives allow the noncompliant listener to reinterpret the directive as an information question; embedded imperatives allow the compliant listener to reply as if he had complied by choice. The forms also differ in the amount of inference or knowledge they require. General statements and information interrogatives require the most, since the goods or services may not be mentioned.

When the normal forms are known, deviations can be construed as indicators of social meanings concerning the momentary affect of the speaker. In addition, the participants' knowledge of potential alternative interpretations for the utterance makes pragmatic punning possible, as in the following cases, which teach the addressee by implying a different intent:

a. *Student to friend on campus:*
"Are you going to share your candy bar with me?"
"I don't know."
b. *Child to mother:*
"Do you know where Daddy put the candy?"
"Yes."

Knowing the normal interpretation and production takes time and may require learning new norms. Jenny Gumperz (personal communication) points out the following contrast:

a. *American woman shopper:*
"Good morning. A dozen eggs, please."
b. *English woman shopper:*
"Good morning, it's a nice morning. May I have a dozen eggs, please?"

We can suppose that the American shopping in England, who uses the more imperative form, will be construed as brusque and rude.

Social correction of adults does occur, as the following instances indicate:

a. *Customer to shopgirl she didn't recognize:*
"I'd like some film, please, Ektachrome 35 mm."

"I'm not going to give you a thing, Susan, until you say hello."
  b. *Foreign client arriving in room sees repairman who has returned
     for a second visit and is at work:*
     "Croyez-vous qu'il faut remplacer la machine?" (Do you think
     we'll have to get a new machine?)
     "Bonjour, madame" (smiling as if joking).
  c. *Lunch-counter supervisor to customer in university lunchroom:*
     "You're carrying a lot. Do you want a box?"
     "Yes, do you have one?"
     "I wouldn't have offered if I didn't."

We know very little about the ways adults accommodate to culture
changes that require new sociolinguistic frames or the reclassification of
familiar situations. Not only children but adolescents and adults as
well are repeatedly resocialized through accommodation to new groups
which have an internal social structure that must be learned.

FUNCTIONS OF SYMBOLIC DIVERSITY

Alternations, at the level of lexicon and morphology and at the level
of speech act realization, serve major interpersonal functions. It must
be precisely because of these functions that alternations develop and
survive in language in spite of the countervailing pressure for simplicity
of form. These are some of the functions alternations serve:

  a. They repeatedly assert actual or claimed features of social re-
     lationships without making those assertions focal or topical.
  b. They can imply more extensive features connotatively through
     metaphorical extension in "equivalence systems."
  c. Boundary markers and situation-identifying utterances can in-
     teract with them to imply shifts in obligations.

Language is not, of course, the only means by which to assert social
relationships. Recent studies point to numerous nonverbal variables that
function in a similar capacity. For example, distance, posture (Mehrabian and Friar 1969), orientation of the body, eye direction (Argyle
and Ingham 1972), and touching (Henley 1973) can all be used to
assert dominance. Such features of speech as interruption rate (Zimmerman and West 1973), amount of speech, and intensity (Markel, Prebor,
and Brandt 1972) are sensitive to rank and sex. Zimmerman and West
(1973) found that males interrupted females and adults interrupted
children more than the reverse and were also less responsive to topic

initiation. It is not clear, of course, that complete consistency between verbal and nonverbal channels is necessary. In general, the findings suggest that when there are discrepancies, the information in the nonverbal channel may be more important than its verbal counterpart.

Within discourse one may find that a common language or style is maintained. It could be claimed that the monitoring this requires demands continual control by the speaker and is a continual assertion about social features, rather than a one-time assertion which is then maintained for the sake of consistency. A parallel problem appears in concord or agreement rules for number and gender. If there were a one-time selection rule, we would find perfect agreement that was automatic, the only "choice" occurring at the time of the initial selection. But there are interesting discrepancies, which become apparent when, for example, grammatical gender and sex conflict. In Switzerland, a young man required to undergo military training is *"la recrute."* In newspaper reports, where editing can maintain monitoring across the text, subsequent pronouns are feminine, but in colloquial speech the masculine pronoun tends to slip back in.

If cooccurrence rules alone governed what follows an initial selection, we would not find shifting as a reflection of interpersonal changes. Recent studies of bilingualism have shown that language shifting is a continual resource either for rhetorical purposes such as contrast, emphasis, or for symbolizing relationships to the addressee, especially solidarity and distance (Gumperz and Hernández-Chávez 1971), Hatch (1973), Gumperz (in press).

In the same way, we might question whether address terms are adopted by a single selection process at the first occasion of use. Many of the selectors of address terms (such as adult/child, relative age, occupational status, kinship) are external to the participants, but others (such as felt dispensation from formality of address, collegiality, believed relative rank, and familiarity) may be construed as having an expressive component which varies from moment to moment (Ervin-Tripp 1973: 331–42). Address terms do change within conversations. Friedrich (1972) has found particularly vivid examples of this in Russian literature, as have Brown and Gilman (1960) in French. In a study of classroom interaction recently, David Day (1968) found that during an argument the students shifted between titling, first name, and Mr. S—— to the instructor.

In English, each occurrence of an address term reasserts claims as to relative age, rank, collegiality, and so on. In certain respects the directive system may be more refined, in others, such as occupational titling, less so. For example, a two-year-old studied in detail differentiated addressees by rank or age when giving directives. Thus although in address all nursery school children were first-named, in directives the child distinguished other two-year-olds from three- and four-year-olds. She gave no commands to the four-year-olds and employed only questions, including permission requests, such as:

a. Can have an apple, Nida, please?
b. Can have the pen, Nida, please?

To the three-year-olds she gave commands, but 4 out of 5 instances included postposed "please" or "OK." Out of a total of 100 directives only 12 had these features, so the statistical imbalance is clear.

At home, this child used repetitions and politeness modifiers in three-fourths of her directives to her father, but rarely to her mother. To test whether there really was a difference between directives to her parents, each parent failed to pour her milk. To her mother, the child said, "Mommy, I want milk." To her father, she beat about the bush:

What's that?	Milk
My milk, Daddy?	Yes, it's your milk.
Daddy, yours? Yours, Daddy?	OK, yours, OK, it's mine.
It's milk, Daddy.	Yes, it is.
You want milk, Daddy?	I have some, thank you.
Milk in there, Daddy?	Yes.
Daddy, I want some, please? Please, Daddy, huh?	

The evidence is clear that although the address system only gave her "Mommy" and "Daddy" and children's names, her directive system allowed her to nuance the relative ranks of addressees.

Discourse is not uniformly rich in interpersonal information for every dimension. While it is probably true that all discourse contains some social information, there is significant variation in amount. For example, some lexicons have alternatives, some do not. Geertz (1960: 249), in describing the extraordinarily elaborate Javanese system in connection with Prijaji etiquette, gave "table" as a lexical item lacking alternatives in that system. Bilingualism and diglossia are probably the strongest cases, where nearly all lexical items have two morphophonemic realizations.

But even where the lexicon or morphology does not supply contrasts, register or style contrasts may be available. For example, in explaining a toy to younger children, four-year-olds use shorter sentences, more deictic or defining types of structures, and more imperatives than they do to age peers (Shatz and Gelman 1973). To children younger than two, prosodic and phonological features of baby talk may also be present. Thus limitations in baby talk–marked lexicon do not mean that discourse lacking those terms cannot be marked for age of addressee.

Directives are especially rich in alternations, possibly because the speaker is asking some action of the listener and must pay in social effort. (Perhaps this is why one feels irritated with an overly obsequious speaker, as though overpayment implies false coinage.) In general, the higher the cost of the goods or service, the greater the option offered the listener, so that as cost goes up one moves from imperative to request question and then to statement. In terms of formal elaboration, address and style upward in rank are more elaborate. To some extent, these effects are counterbalanced by the normality of the request to the role. If the activity usual to a task involves directing, the simpler, more imperative style may occur more often than one would expect on an analysis purely of rank.

It is important to realize that selections are available at many levels. At various points in the life cycle, options occur that commit one to communicative choices. For example, a choice to emigrate or a choice to attend school may entail language learning and therefore involve a shift in code usage. The choice to be present in certain settings or with certain participants has consequences for choice of communicative device. And even in a selected setting, one can opt for silence or omit certain content.

These choices seem to be relevant to a complete model of alternations, precisely because each of them represents certain important extremes. A person who finds himself in a setting with high-ranking participants may be unable, for example, to ask to borrow money for lunch. In a case such as this, the verbal alternatives we have proposed as being related to the cost of the exchange become irrelevant. One has to go without lunch, wait for an offer, or go elsewhere in hopes of finding other addressees more familiar or closer in rank.

Nancy Tanner (1972: 131) and Richard Howell (1967: 93) have both shown that for speakers with a multilingual repertoire ambiguous social relationships may result in language shifts to the variety which does not force specification of relative rank. Howell observes that in Korean, where even a very small difference in age requires calling a woman "older sister," friends may select English in order to avoid such distancing. Tanner describes a preference for Indonesian over native Javanese among speakers of different social class, since in Indonesian that difference would be less apparent. "Use of *krama* (high Javanese) would seem incongruous to a friend and neighbor so similar in age, education, and religious philosophy" (Tanner 1972: 131).

These avoidance reactions indicate that the social information carried by the selection of particular alternatives is not automatic and neutral, but may be as much a part of a speaker's sense of appropriate choice as how he dresses. Awareness of such choices seems to be maximized when selectors to the choice give ambiguous results, for instance when current familiarity would conflict with past rank difference.

METAPHORS AND EQUIVALENCE STRUCTURES

One can wonder at the social utility of developing elaborate linguistic indicators of social differences when those differences are in fact often apparent. For example, in many societies there are markers for the sex of addressee. Why should sex be indicated verbally when it is obvious already? Why should the fact that an addressee is an infant or a child be indicated? Even these obvious features generate selections which complicate choice.

Social alternations are rarely single sets for single social variables. The forms which signal male-female contrasts in Japanese also signal higher-lower. Thus whenever a woman speaks to a man she not only tells him he is male; she tells him he is of higher rank as well. "Equivalance structures" is a term I used to refer to these systems. The social significance of equivalence structures is that some meanings from one set of contrasts carry over to the other as a kind of metaphor. When avoidance is possible, we might expect that women would refrain from using these forms, for example by speaking English if the family is bilingual. Bilingual Japanese women in this country borrow the word "husband" into Japanese; they say it is because the Japanese word means "master."

The principal claim here is that meanings learned with respect to one set of symbols affect other, homonymous symbols. In fact, this principle extends further to include not merely lexical symbols and morpheme contrast systems like inflections, but also features such as phonological features in baby talk or in code shifting.

We have evidence that when only some expressions in a system of contrasts have real-world semantic correlates, there is generalization of these meanings to expressions without semantic correlates or to those whose meaning is ambiguous. Connotations of sex difference do generalize to gender, but under restricted conditions. The generalization is unlikely to occur if realistic attributes of objects are present which contradict the implication of the generalization, if the system includes considerable unpredictability of the grammatical gender of people or of conspicuously sex-typed animate referents, or if the formal contrast is a dead metaphor and no semantic choices need to be made on any occasion (Ervin 1962: 249–53). Gender in many languages is not a dead metaphor; it is still necessary to decide the sex of a human referent in choosing gender.[2]

Blom and Gumperz (1971: 294–96) have used the term "metaphorical shifting" to refer to cases in which features of predictable, situationally rule-governed shifting between languages or dialects are extended. They found that certain meaning components derived from clear-cut cases of contrast were generalized. Thus if it is a general pattern to use a village dialect to villagers and a standard language to outsiders, the solidarity-distance meaning dimension may come to be symbolized by features of the linguistic contrasts between village dialect and standard language. These contrasts become available resources for expressing nuances of relationships between villagers.

The claim here is not simply that metaphors derive from predictable contrasts, but rather that between the predictable contrasts themselves "leakages" in meaning occur. The fact that meanings have been extended may not be obvious except in marginal cases or errors, but the underlying process of meaning extension is the same as that used in metaphor.

Biased neutralizations represent a different kind of metaphorical extension. For example, it is often said that the English pronoun system neutralizes gender for singular general reference. The neutralization is biased, however. The books say "he" should be employed for such occasions, and will then refer to both male and female antecedents. However, in common usage it is clear that there is a resistance to the assumption that "he" is neutral. It clearly is not, but is highly semanticized and refers to male sex, since in genuine indefinite reference, the plural, which really is neutral as to gender, is preferred (note: "If anybody wants this spare copy they can have it").[3] If there is a class of persons antecedent to the pronoun the gender depends on the stereotype of the class. For example, we can say "every judge should be careful to keep her knowledge of law up to date," "every nursery school teacher has his favorite greeting," and "every airplane pilot should buckle her seat belt too"; and we can say "any nurse who doesn't show up tomorrow will find he has been flunked out," "every American president has her own style of managing the Congress," and "in our department, each secretary has his own typewriter."

It is clear, I think, that these pronouns are not neutral. The supposedly neutral masculine pronouns are just as jarring applied to typically feminine occupations as are feminine pronouns applied to masculine occupations; if the pronouns were neutral this would not be the case. The same, of course, is true for theoretically neutral nouns, as in "early man invented the wheel, made extraordinarily beautiful cave paintings, and developed elaborate religious beliefs." We find it hard to envisage women in these activities, and indeed in popularized pictures of early man such as those published by Time-Life, only men are shown talking around campfires, making hand axes, butchering animals, manufacturing statues, and performing ceremonial burials. In the most extraordinary extension of the metaphor, all reconstructed early men are shown as male, and indeed at least one noted anthropologist[4] has remarked that some errors concerning size of homonids in reconstructions have occurred because it is routinely assumed that an isolated bone must come from a male. All of this seems another variety of the kind of metaphor that Roman Jakobson spoke of when he said that "a Russian child, while reading a translation of German tales, was astounded to find that Death, obviously a woman . . . was pictured as an old man. . . . *My Sister Life*, the title of a book of poems by Boris Pasternak, is quite natural in Russian, where 'life' is feminine, but was enough to reduce to despair the Czech poet Josef Hora in his attempt to translate these poems, since in Czech this noun is maculine" (Jakobson 1959: 237). But Life and Death are abstractions without sex; early men and women were not.

How strong is this metaphorical extension of meaning features in cases where terms are extended? A good example is the address term "Father" applied to priests. There are many respects in which the metaphor is weak. In reference, the term is treated like a kin title, so we can say "Father Shukletovitch," which would not occur in speaking to or of one's own father (though it does occur with parents-in-law). Likewise, Sister Eugenia is modeled on the general address rule for senior kin: title + (first name). However, this particular form would never be used by members of a family. The stylistic alternates used to a father are absent: one does not call a priest "Pop" or "Daddy". And one does not climb on his lap to plead for money or candy. Indeed, the term "father" as an address term in families is now relatively rare in this country. If not completely dead, the metaphor is at least very weak.

These examples, in which kin titles are used, remind one of the relationship and role terms such as "Baby" and "Sister" and "Little girl" used by children playing house. Many, but not all, children use kin terms rather than assigned proper names. The function of this practice seems to be that it keeps the dramatis personae clearly before the actors at all times. If a four-year-old boy is clearly called "Daddy" on numerous occasions, it is harder for him to slip out of character (though certainly not impossible). In addition to titles, many role properties go along with playing a particular part. For example, babies have to say certain things like "goo goo"; Mommies can say "honey," but nobody else can without being rebuked. One can argue that the presence in playing house of kin titles in direct address which do not exist in actual address to kin peers implies that they are in some sense latent in the kin system. They are derived from the same general rule that says a mommy can be called "Mommy," an aunt can be called "Aunty," and so on. That this rule is highly productive even for same-generation cases can be shown, for example, when one spontaneously calls slightly older cousins or small children "Cousin Bill" in order to make their specific kin relation clear. One could also argue by the same principle that even if "Father" has died out in direct address, it is potentially there if people know that the referential term is Father as well as Daddy. One can argue that address terms like "Father" to

priests or "Sister" to nuns or coreligionists have at least as much semantic force as these terms do when used in role playing.

BOUNDARY MARKING

Boundary markers, which define changes in the situation, interact
with markers of interpersonal roles. For example, in a classroom, the
teacher may say "Now . . ." as a starter for a shift to a new topic or
approach. Children do not use this form to the teacher; its use seems
to be confined to the person in control of the agenda. This term at
once reasserts authority and itself alters the structure by cuing listeners
for a change.

Greetings and farewells have a similar function. Clearly, however,
like markers of sex and age, they are redundant, marking what is already obvious. Everyone knows when participants arrive and leave, so
why mark the change in participants with a formality? It can happen,
however, that a third party will arrive in the midst of a dyadic conversation and remain excluded. If the other parties do not acknowledge
his presence, at least by eye contact, he is tacitly left out as a non-
participant and will normally not be expected to take part. The greeting
is an acknowledgment that the new arrival is a coparticipant equal with
others. Indeed, it may be followed by information regarding the topic
which appears to encourage or discourage his participation—information
which otherwise would not have been given—for example, "We were
just talking about nursery schools."

Emily Post, a valuable ethnographer of prescriptive norms, reports
that where it would be inappropriate to introduce someone to a person
lower in rank, the new participant can be brought into the conversation
through this topical invitation slot:

> "Mr. Smith is suggesting that I dig up these cannas and put in
> delphiniums" (Post 1922: 14).

In addition to defining who shall be a participant, these elements in
interaction can function to identify what type of speech event is being
enacted. Thus when a teacher passes from informal conversation to
the onset of the class, he requires a formal signal. Such signals need
not be highly explicit; they may involve a stance and a tone of voice
and little more. At this moment, however, an array of rules of inter-

action proper to classrooms comes to the fore. A shift occurs in the system of possible directive forms available to pupils in addressing each other.

The examples cited by Gumperz and Herasimchuk (1972) remind us that the child who has been socialized into appropriate classroom behavior does not precisely emulate the teacher. The child's emulation proceeds only so far as to include the intent (to instruct) and perhaps the content (instruction in spelling). But the effective child instructor accomplishes these ends by different means. Lacking the support of authority, the child cannot handle interruption by alluding to a rule stating that the teacher allocates the floor; this rule does not apply to child interaction. Thus we find a contrast: the adult says "Ann, Ida is spelling it," but the child instructor says "Don't tell 'im." (Gumperz and Herasimchuk 1972: 106). In this case the child must validate his claim by alluding to a different rule; only one person can be instructor at a time. And he cannot rely on the persuasive force of allusion to a rule alone, as can the teacher; he must prohibit bluntly.

INSTRUCTION AND CONTROL

I have argued that the diversity of realization of speech acts has several functions in adult speech: communicating major social relationships directly or through metaphor and marking the boundaries of situations within which rules apply. The acquisition of this system by children provides a new form of complexity in child skill and both reveals and defines social features that the child must come to know.

Our evidence so far suggests that some children begin to nuance directives very early in terms of the manifest honorifics which differentiate rank or age of addressee. They do not at first markedly conceal overtness in requests; they specify known desires. It could be argued on the basis of this evidence that there are two different types of "politeness" utilized in the directive system. One type is overt, and consists of names, tags, and imbeddings which decorate the bare command. The other type is the systematically framed question or statement which *does not refer* to the desired act. In some cases, these forms of request are so highly routinized as to be a kind of directive idiom. In other cases, only the listener with inferential knowledge, a knowledge of interpretive rules, can connect the statement with an act.

Children are able, as early as three years of age, to interpret the latter kind of request if the inferential steps are available to their thought. They seem, like adults, to assume that speech is motivated and to search for intent, at least under optimal conditions of attention. Unless they are able, in addition to understanding intent, to gain information from the utterance form as to social features of speaker or addressee, we cannot assume that the possibilities of language in conveying social nuances are used. These variations in realization would then seem random. How children learn to realize variations in response to social features, or to recognize the social implications of different forms, we are just now beginning to explore.

It has been argued in the past that the presence of contrasts in the linguistic system can accelerate the child's recognition of semantic differences; this is the theory that language can aid thought. There is a rather considerable body of literature in psychology showing that lexical learning, like other kinds of "mediators," can indeed facilitate learning and recognition of categories. On the other hand, it has been argued by Slobin (1973: 184) that the basic categories of child language are cognitive universals, and that it is precisely because the child learns these categories without the aid of, and prior to, language that he is able to discover the coding of them. The best candidates for this assertion are of course the earliest and most universal categories.

The obvious extension to sociolinguistic alternations is that the child and the adult learn the social system in part because they seek significance for the linguistic variations they encounter. This chicken and egg controversy is not as paradoxical as it seems. That is, in daily interaction there are both clear cases and ambiguous ones. The extension of the conjugational metaphor of power to sex contrasts in Japanese conveys a repeated tacit message of the weakness of women. For children there are clear cases where they already recognize the social feature present: sex and age, for example. These can be the "instructing" cases, which first define the meaning of the alternation. In the more ambiguous cases, where similar contrasts are used, we can assume the child will search for social features that account for a formal contrast he has already found to be significant. For instance, once the child discovers differences that correlate with age of addressee in many features of language, he will see these same features extended to rank contrasts when no age differences exist. He may never be explicitly told there is a rank difference, but the metaphor of power will instruct him that X is treated like an elderly adult and Y is treated like a child.

From this analysis one might suggest that the fact that alternation systems themselves are "polysemic" has a social utility since it facilitates this sort of extension or metaphorical learning. Another conceivable system would require a different speech act realization for every possible combination of sex, age, rank, territoriality, distance of addressee, and so on. Roger Brown (1965) had the brilliant insight that there are likely to be universal dimensions underlying these metaphors: the power semantic and the solidarity semantic may everywhere have a kind of inverse relation. The devices used to signal social distance or unfamiliarity tend also to be those used to indicate higher rank. While the "naturalness" of these transfers may make learning easier, and spontaneous generalization more likely to be right, it does not remove the necessity for learning. In the studies we have done, we have ourselves been surprised at the dimensions that affect the realization of directives; category boundaries (e.g. what is a child, what is "older") must be ascertained. So there are plausible grounds for believing that the presence of the system of alternations in realizing speech acts not only reminds adult participants continuously of the social features of the participants, but also provides an instructional milieu for learners regarding the major social dimensions and categories of groups they join.

The speech act I have discussed in greatest detail, the directive, happens to be among the most frequent acts of young children. It is also particularly rich in structural variability. However, we assume that many other acts, such as greetings, farewells, remedies, and various kinds of accounts, may show similar diversity. The evidence that systematic organized diversity of realization exists, and that it exists in very young children, is indisputable.

What remains hypothetical until more careful experimentation is carried out are our guesses about the functions of diversity. An array of evidence has been compiled here which supports the argument that diversity has major social consequences. While it apparently violates the economy principle in communication about reference or ideation, it embodies instructional contrasts intimately tied to social dimensions, thus providing continuous information to participants in interaction about their proper roles vis-à-vis each other.

NOTES

1. Major portions of the empirical material in this paper have been included in "Is Sybil There?" a paper to appear in *Language in Society*. The data cited here are drawn from many unpublished sources, including studies of requests made by my students over several years, particularly those of Ayhan Aksu, David Day, Carol Gardner, Craig Lawson, and Elaine Rogers. My debt to John Gumperz is apparent throughout. The opportunity to write this paper was supported by the School of American Research, the Center for Advance Study in the Behavioral Sciences, and the Guggenheim Foundation.

2. There is some reason to believe that gender, under conditions which retain the semantic vigor of the category, is not simply a formal feature. That is, it is probably the case that young children learning gender languages attach some semantic features to the referents themselves or to whatever constitutes the stored concept. The evidence is that (a) bilingual French speakers sometimes use gender pronouns in English for words which have gender in French, suggesting that they either retrieve the noun before the pronoun or in going from meaning to pronoun already have gender information; (b) bilingual speakers of gender languages, tested in English about the masculinity-femininity of objects and abstractions, differ from native English judges in a direction congruent with the gender; (c) there are said to be age differences favoring younger children in the acquisition of noun gender in second-language learners during the period when older learners usually learn purely grammatical features faster than younger learners; (d) children who forget or "repress" a well-learned child language later recover gender almost faultlessly; (e) when words are borrowed, the gender of the native word which best translates the borrowed word may be adopted. Sometimes whole semantic classes are affected, as in the French-Canadian preference for feminine gender for names of machines and masculine gender for cloth. Haugen has pointed out the paradox of this observation: loanwords are "used precisely because the native word escaped the speaker or because he had never heard a native word for the idea in question. There is no reason to suppose that his subconscious should have whispered the gender of the native 'equivalent' to him when it failed to deliver the equivalent itself" (Haugen 1953:2:449). But of course Haugen fails to consider either the possibility of semantic changes derived from gender or that word retrieval is often partial, as we all know from trying to recover proper names from memory. What all of this evidence suggests is that gender is a property of a semantic concept rather than of a word (or that gender features attach to the semantic features of a word rather than to its morphophonemic pattern).

3. Ann Bodine (1974) examined the interpretation of "um" as "them" or "him" following various antecedents and found that the proportion of "them" interpretations ranged between 86 and 99 percent for various indefinites, in contrast to 5 percent for "that streaker."

4. Sherwood Washburn (personal communication).

6

A Propositional Analysis of U.S. American Beliefs about Illness

ROY G. D'ANDRADE
University of California, San Diego

INTRODUCTION AND BACKGROUND

People think about things. Much of our thinking is vague and associative in form, yet the stream of consciousness which we experience has its foundation in abstract conceptual models of the world. In this chapter I will attempt to describe one such model, which Americans use to understand illness and disease.

The model presented here is different from a previously published model which was based on the techniques of multidimensional scaling (D'Andrade et al. 1972). In that study, multidimensional scaling enabled us to find order in the data we had collected about what people believe to be true about different diseases. But while these scaling techniques ordered the data in a simple and effective fashion, it became apparent that this order did not correspond to the way people store and process information about diseases. The multidimensional techniques gave us one representation about what people believe, but not a representation of how people go about believing.

In general, multidimensional scaling produces results that correspond to a quantified version of the *feature* model. That is, each object is assumed to be placed in relation to other objects on the basis of the conjunction of a limited number of attribute values. One of the main arguments of this chapter is that feature models, whether based on multidimensional scaling or on componential analysis, cannot adequately represent belief systems.

The data for the multidimensional scaling model were collected as part of a larger project by the Stanford Anthropology Research Laboratory, directed by A. K. Romney, a study of American, Mexican, and Tzeltal beliefs concerning illness. As part of this project, a study was begun to determine the salient categories of illness in U.S. American and Mexican cultures. After several unsuccessful attempts to elicit taxonomies and componential paradigms of disease based on distinctive features, it became evident that a simpler method of determining semantic structures needed to be developed. Research by Frake (1962) and by Metzger and Williams (1966) indicated that reliable information could be obtained about semantic relations through the use of a sentence-frame technique. Generally, sentence frames can be conceived of as "open propositions" which designate properties that informants believe to be true, false, or inapplicable to a domain, in this case the domain of diseases.

From a series of informal interviews with informants, a variety of statements about illness were collected. These statements were then put in sentence-frame form by replacing the particular name of the illness with a blank (for example, 'It is safer to have _____ as a child and get it over with'). Next, on the basis of informant and interviewer judgments, a sample of the more general, unambiguous, and semantically independent sentence frames was selected. A list of disease terms was also collected during these interviews, and a similar selection procedure used to determine the best understood terms. Sentence frames and disease terms were obtained first for the American-English sample. The Mexican-Spanish items were obtained both from translations from American-English items, in order to ensure some degree of comparability, and also from free interview statements made by the Mexican respondents. The final lists contained 50 sentence frames and 50 disease terms in both the American-English and Mexican-Spanish forms.

From this collection of sentence frames and disease terms a test was constructed in which each informant was asked for every sentence frame whether or not the insertion of each disease term into the frame would make the sentence true or false. Thus, an informant taking the American-English test would be asked for sentence frame number 1—'You can catch _____ from other people'—whether that was true for 1. 'appendicitis', 2. 'arthritis', 3. 'asthma', and so forth. To the Mexican-Spanish-speaking informants, the test was given orally, while a printed form was filled out by the American-English informants. A pretest indicated that the American-English informants preferred to answer on a scale, rather than give "yes-no" answers. A five-point scale was developed for the final American-English test form. The Mexican-Spanish-speaking informants, on the other hand, did not seem willing to accept this type of continuous scale, preferring just three alternatives: "yes," "sometimes," and "no." The American sample consisted of ten Stanford undergraduates judged to be of standard American middle-class background. The Mexican sample consisted of eighteen Mexican-Spanish speakers from Villa de las Rosas, a rural village in the highlands of the state of Chiapas.

From the test records the data from each informant were placed in a matrix form, with each row of the matrix containing the scores for a particular disease term, and each column containing the scores for a particular sentence frame. The first step of the analysis was to remove the poorer items. Using group mean scores, the variance of each sentence frame across disease terms was computed. Low variances appeared to be due to two factors: either to lack of agreement among respondents or to a failure of the sentence frame to differentiate between the various diseases. The 30 sentence frames with the greatest variances were then selected for further analysis. Next, the same procedure was repeated for disease terms, and the 30 terms with the greatest variance across sentence frames were selected. The final 30 disease terms for the U.S. American samples were:

(1) appendicitis	(2) bronchitis	(3) cancer
(4) chicken pox	(5) a cold	(6) dental cavities
(7) epilepsy	(8) gonorrhea	(9) heart attack
(10) influenza	(11) laryngitis	(12) leukemia
(13) malaria	(14) measles	(15) mononucleosis
(16) mumps	(17) pneumonia	(18) poison ivy
(19) polio	(20) psychosis	(21) rheumatism

(22) smallpox	(23) strep throat	(24) stroke
(25) syphilis	(26) tonsillitis	(27) tuberculosis
(28) typhoid fever	(29) ulcers	(30) whooping cough

The final 30 sentence frames were:

(1) You can catch _____ from other people
(2) _____ is caused by germs
(3) Most people catch _____ in bad weather
(4) _____ comes from being emotionally upset
(5) _____ runs in the family
(6) When you are overtired, your resistance to _____ is lowered
(7) _____ can't be cured
(8) _____ has to run its course
(9) _____ should be treated with miracle drugs
(10) _____ gets better by itself
(11) _____ is serious
(12) _____ is a fatal disease
(13) You never really get over _____
(14) _____ is a crippling disease
(15) You can have _____ and not know it
(16) _____ spreads through your whole system
(17) _____ is contagious
(18) If a woman comes down with _____ during her pregnancy it harms her child
(19) Feeling generally run-down is a sign of _____
(20) _____ affects the heart
(21) Your skin breaks out with _____
(22) Runny nose is a sign of _____
(23) Sore throat comes with _____
(24) _____ brings on fever
(25) Once you've had _____ you can't get it again
(26) _____ is a children's disease
(27) Most people get _____ at some time or other
(28) Some people have a tendency to get _____
(29) It's safer to have _____ as a child and get it over with
(30) _____ is a sign of old age

The next step was to assess the degree of similarity between disease terms, and also the degree of similarity between sentence frames. In order to do this, two matrices of product-moment correlation coefficients were computed, the first containing the correlations for each pair of disease terms calculated from the mean scores across sentence frames, the second containing the correlations for each pair of sentence frames calculated from the mean scores across disease terms. Correlation matrices were computed separately for the American and the Mexican groups.

Kruskal's multidimensional scaling technique, called M-D-SCAL (Kruskal 1964), a hierarchical clustering technique similar to that developed by Johnson (1967), and factor analytic techniques were used in the analysis of the data. All three techniques gave convergent results, indicating that the structures obtained in the analyses were not technique specific.[2] Based on the cluster analyses, the columns and rows of the original dichotomized matrix of diseases and sentence frames were then reordered in cluster groupings in an attempt to display the patterns of association to be found between diseases and sentence frames.

The results from the American sample displayed a structure in which two major dimensions or clusters were formed around the concepts of *contagion* and *seriousness*. Related to contagion were subclusters involving *children's contagious diseases* and *weather-induced colds*. A third cluster combined both *serious* and *contagious* diseases, such as syphilis, polio, and tuberculosis. The *noncontagious* illnesses appeared to be divided into two subclusters: the first contained the *serious* and often *crippling* or *fatal internal diseases*, such as cancer and heart attack; the second contained the *inheritable, old age–related*, or *emotionally affected illnesses*, such as rheumatism, arthritis, psychosis, ulcer, and so forth.

The results of these analyses throw some light on why our first attempts to develop classifications of illness yielded unreliable and idiosyncratic answers. It had been our assumption that the distinctive features of illness (that is, the features used to define particular illnesses) were also most likely to be salient features. But the characteristics that our informants discussed in the informal interview sessions and which formed the core of the different belief clusters appeared to be consequences and preconditions of the illnesses rather than the features which

159

were used to *define* them. This was true of both the American and Mexican sample data (D'Andrade et al. 1972).

COMPLICATIONS

Although the general ordering of data fits relatively well our intuitions about how middle-class Americans think about disease, the multidimensional scaling lacks the capacity to do a number of things which our informants do quite easily. First, informants who hold a particular set of beliefs are able to respond appropriately to a very large number of previously unencountered statements relevant to the domain in question. For example, the original American-English test contained 2,500 statements about diseases (50 sentence frames by 50 diseases), many if not most of which the informants had probably never encountered in any form (for example, 'Most people catch psychosis in bad weather', "Poison ivy affects the heart', 'Gonorrhea runs in the family'). Yet none of the informants seemed unable to assess such novel statements nor did any of them complain that the test was too difficult (the major complaint was that the test was too long). Of course, the informants admitted that they did not know the answers to some of the questions, adding that they felt a physician would (they asked questions like "Is it mumps or chicken pox that comes with a sore throat?"). But the number of questions the informants answered without trouble and with high agreement is unbelievable if one imagined that before a question could be answered it had to be already known in the form in which it was asked.

Since it seems unlikely that people have stored in their heads judgments about the truth or falsity of enormous numbers of statements concerning every domain about which they have knowledge, there must therefore be some *productive* or *generative* capacity to belief systems. The model of beliefs about diseases given by the multidimensional scaling techniques does not contain any kind of simple generative capacity and therefore cannot predict answers to newly formed questions.

A second limitation of the multidimensional scaling model is that it does not present information about the kinds of relations which occur between objects. Multidimensional scaling techniques place objects in a space on the basis of overall similarity. The objects may be alike because one is a subset of the other, or because one is a member of the class named by the other, or because one is caused by the other, or because one is a part of the other, or because both are members of some third class, or because one is the antonym of the other, or because one physically cooccurs with the other, and so forth. All of these relations lead to the assessment of objects as similar (Flavell and Stedman 1961). Once the information about the different kinds of relations has been reduced to one overall similarity measure, there is no way to retrieve information about how objects are specifically related to each other.

For example, 'germs' and 'contagion' as properties of diseases were found close together in our multidimensional scaling analysis. We may understand why this is so, but nothing in the analysis makes this information explicit. When dealing with results from another culture, in which the investigator cannot fall back on his own intuition and implicit cultural knowledge, this gap in the multidimensional scaling model becomes incapacitating. The map of objects that emerges from the analysis is as uninformative yet as intriguing as a picture of the stars from a planet in some distant and unknown galaxy.

It should be made clear that the objections presented above are not objections about multidimensional scaling models as such. Rather, the objections concern the use of multidimensional scaling models as models of belief systems. While multidimensional scaling models can be used to help determine patterns of similarity with respect to objects or properties in a belief system, these models do not represent the processes by which individuals generate answers to novel questions; neither do they represent the specific kinds of relations by which properties and objects are conceived to be interconnected.

REANALYSIS

In order to construct a model of a belief system with both generative capacity and specificity concerning the logical relations involved in beliefs, the data from the previous study of U.S. English speakers were reanalyzed in terms of simple subset-superset relations. This was done not because the basic relation in belief systems is assumed to be the subset-superset relation, but because other kinds of relations often manifest themselves as subset-superset relations. Thus, for example, if germs are a necessary cause of fever, then there will be no examples of diseases which have fever as a symptom and which are not germ caused. Or in terms of the relations between sets of diseases, the set of diseases which have fever as a symptom will be a subset of the set of germ-caused diseases.

The first step in the analysis of the set relations was to determine which sentence-frame properties occurred as subsets of other sentence-frame properties. In order to examine all 335 possible pairs of sentence-frame properties a computer program was written which constructed two-by-two tables for each pair of sentence frames that showed a significantly strong degree of association (phi greater than ±.32, p less than .05). These pairs of sentence frames were then scanned a second time for evidence of subset-superset relations.

Subset-superset relations can be determined from a two-by-two table by the presence of one or more zero (or near zero) cells. (We assume that for the domain of diseases the absence of a property designated by a sentence frame is itself a property—that is, that 'noncontagiousness', for example, is a psychologically salient property.) In the six examples of zero-cell tables given below, each case corresponds to a type of subset-superset relation:

		Property B		
		+	−	
1. Property A	+	10	0	If any disease has property A, then
	−	10	10	it has property B, i.e. "A ⊂ B"

		Property B		
		+	−	
2. Property A	+	10	10	If any disease has property B, then
	−	0	10	it has property A, i.e. "B ⊂ A"

		Property B		
		+	−	
3. Property A	+	0	10	If any disease has property B, then
	−	10	10	it has the property of being not A
				($\overline{A}$), and if any disease has property
				A, then it has the property of being

not B $(\bar{B})$; i.e. $B \subset \bar{A}$ & $A \subset \bar{B}$ (Rather than using the subset-superset terms, it is clearer to say no disease has both properties A & B, or that property A contrasts with property B, i.e. "A/B")

Property B

	+	−
4. Property A +	10	10
−	10	0

If any disease does not have property A $(\bar{A})$, then it has property B, and if any disease does not have property B $(\bar{B})$, then it does have property A; therefore: $\bar{A} \subset B$ & $\bar{B} \subset A$; or everything is either A or B, or both, i.e. "A ʊ B"

Property B

	+	−
5. Property A +	15	0
−	0	15

If any disease has property A, then it has property B, and if any disease has property B then it has property A, therefore $A \subset B$ and $B \subset A$, or $A \equiv B$

Property B

	+	−
6. Property A +	0	15
−	15	0

If any disease has property B, then it does not have property A $(\bar{A})$, and if any disease has property A, then it does not have property B $(\bar{B})$, therefore $A \subset B$ and $B \subset A$, or $A \approx B$

As an actual example, figure 3 presents the results of the computer print-out for the 2 sentence frames '_____ is a sign of old age' and 'you can catch _____ from other people'. It can be seen that for the 30 diseases there is no case of a disease which is said to be both a 'sign of old age' and 'catching'. This is an example of the third case of possible zero-cell tables, which has been termed the relation of *contrast* (nothing has both properties *A* and *B*), and which is formally identical to the subset-superset relation in which diseases that have the property of being a 'sign of old age' are a subset of the diseases that do not have the property of being 'catching'.

		_____ is a sign of old age	
		yes	no
you can catch _____ from other people	yes		whooping cough typhoid fever tuberculosis syphilis strep throat smallpox polio poison ivy pneumonia mumps mononucleosis measles laryngitis influenza gonorrhea a cold chicken pox
	no	bronchitis cancer heart attack psychosis rheumatism stroke ulcers	appendicitis dental cavities epilepsy leukemia malaria tonsillitis

FIGURE 3. ILLUSTRATION OF CONTRAST RELATION BETWEEN DISEASE PROPERTIES

Figure 4 presents another two-by-two table. In this table the diseases that 'bring on fever' are a subset of the diseases that are 'caused by germs' with but one exception. After looking at the computer print-outs and discussing the results with a number of informants, it was decided

	_____ brings on fever	
	yes	no
_____ is caused by germs yes	whooping cough typhoid fever tonsillitis strep throat smallpox pneumonia mumps mononucleosis measles malaria laryngitis influenza a cold chicken pox bronchitis	tuberculosis syphilis polio gonorrhea
no	appendicitis	cancer dental cavities epilepsy heart attack leukemia poison ivy psychosis rheumatism stroke ulcers

FIGURE 4. ILLUSTRATION OF EXCEPTION TO CONTRAST RELATION BETWEEN DISEASE PROPERTIES

that exceptions should be treated as part of the propositional system, in that people recognize and utilize subset-superset relations which have some exceptions. For example, most mammals do not lay eggs, although the marsupial duckbill platypus and the spiny anteater do, and most birds fly, although the emu, ostrich, and penguin do not. Given that the major undertaking of this chapter is to develop a model which corresponds to the way people understand and think about diseases, it seems reasonable to include subset-superset relations which are not perfect, but in which the number of exceptions are limited enough to make learning the relation an efficient strategy of information processing. For the data presented here the number of exceptions has been limited to three cases. The number three was not selected a priori, but because the data made the best sense when the number of exceptions permitted did not exceed that amount.

While two-by-two tables can be used to indicate the presence of subset-superset relations, it should be stressed that subset-superset relations can come about as the result of a wide range of specific relational conditions. For example, in cause and effect relations where the cause is necessary but not sufficient, the effect condition will be a subset of the causal condition. Lightning, for example, is a necessary cause of thunder. The two-by-two table which we would expect would have the following form:

		thunder	
		yes	no
lightning	yes	many cases	many cases
	no	o	many cases

If the cause is generally sufficient by itself to bring about an effect, but not necessary in the sense that other causes may also bring about the same effect, then the causal condition will be a subset of the effect condition. Being hit on the toe with a sledgehammer is generally a sufficient cause for having a sore toe, but not a necessary cause in that a number of other events can also bring about sore toes. The table for this type of causal relation would be expected to look as follows:

166

		toe sore	
		yes	no
toe hit with sledgehammer	yes	many cases	o
	no	many cases	many cases

If the cause is neither sufficient nor necessary but only one of a number of possible causes which bring about the effect with only a moderate degree of probability, then the two-by-two table will not have a zero cell. However, other things being equal, it will show a positive association between the cause condition and the effect condition.

Causal relations are not the only kinds of relations that produce zero cell tables. If the criteria for determining A are the same as the criteria for determining B, except that A has even more criteria which it must meet, then A will formally be a subset of B. The relation between the condition of being a parent and the condition of being a father is of this sort, and gives rise to a table of the following form:

		is a parent	
		yes	no
is a father	yes	many cases	o
	no	many cases	many cases

Another relation which also can yield zero-cell tables is the part-whole relation. In the domain of persons, for example, persons with fingers form a subset of persons with hands. Generally the relation will also go the other way; if a person has hands, he also has fingers. But this relation is open to exceptions of various kinds.

Other specific relations, such as the actor–common action relation (dog-bark), the object-attribute relation (lemon-sour), or the contiguity relation (Ghana-Togo), could also be discussed with respect to the likelihood of their forming subset-superset relations. In general, the likelihood of a particular kind of relation forming subset-superset relations varies by domain, although most domains appear to have at least one substantive relation which creates subset-superset relations.

RESULTS OF THE SUBSET-
SUPERSET ANALYSIS

Figure 5 presents the results of the computer analysis of the zero-cell (or near-zero-cell) set relations for the disease and sentence-frame data. Of the six kinds of possible zero-cell set relations discussed above, only four occurred in those data: the subset relation, the superset relation, the contrast relation, and the equivalence relation. Since the contrast relation and the equivalence relation are symmetrical (that is, if A is in contrast to B, then B is also in contrast to A), the same symbol appears in cell$_{ij}$ and in cell$_{ji}$ of figure 5. The subset relation, on the other hand, has as its converse the superset relation (that is, if A is a subset of B, then B is a superset of A). This means that if in figure 5 cell$_{ij}$ contains one of these two symbols, then cell$_{ji}$ will contain the other symbol. (For an exemplary analysis of this type of matrix, see Atkins and Curtis 1969.)

To simplify tables of this type, the first step is to find equivalence relations. In this case, the only pair of properties that display an equivalence relation are the sentence frames involving 'catching' and 'contagious'. These two properties can then be grouped into a single property, since whatever is true for one will also be true for the other.

The second step in simplifying tables of this type is to use the transitivity of relations to eliminate redundant information. Consider figure 6, which presents a small section of figure 5.

If the subset-superset relation is symbolized by an arrow (with the point directed toward the superset), and the contrast relation is symbolized by a dotted line, then the complete graph for figure 6 can be shown as in figure 7.

It is possible to simplify figure 7 by eliminating graph lines which can be inferred from the transitive character of subset-superset relations and contrast relations. The transitivity of the subset-superset relation is perhaps most familiar and easiest to illustrate. In figure 7, for example, it can be seen that the class of 'contagious' diseases (17), is a subset of the class of 'germ' diseases (2). Furthermore, the class of 'children's' diseases (26) is a subset of the class of 'contagious' diseases (17). Since the subset relation is transitive (that is, if A is a subset of B, and B is a subset of C, then A is a subset of C), the arrow between 'children's'

Column properties (1–30):
1 Catch · 2 Germs · 3 Bad Weather · 4 Emotion · 5 Family · 6 Resistance · 7 No Cure · 8 Course · 9 Miracle Drugs · 10 Better Itself · 11 Serious · 12 Fatal · 13 Never Over · 14 Cripple · 15 Not Know · 16 Spreads · 17 Contagious · 18 Pregnancy · 19 Run Down · 20 Heart · 21 Skin · 22 Runny Nose · 23 Sore Throat · 24 Fever · 25 Once · 26 Children's · 27 Get Sometime · 28 Tendency · 29 Safer Child · 30 Old Age

_is a _ of

Row	1	2	3	4	5	6	7	8	9	10	11	12	13	14	15	16	17	18	19	20	21	22	23	24	25	26	27	28	29	30
Catch 1	•	C	⊃	I	I					⊃							≡					⊃	⊃	⊃		⊃	⊃	I	⊃	I
Germs 2	⊃	•	⊃	I	I				⊃	⊃							⊃					⊃	⊃	⊃	⊃	⊃	⊃	I	⊃	I
Bad Weather 3	C	C	•	I	I	C	I					I	I				C		I		I	⊃	C	C	I		C	I	I	I
Emotion 4	I	I	I	•	C	C	I	I	I			C					I					I	I	I	I	I	I	C	I	
Family 5	I	I	I	⊃	•	C	I	I	I			C					I					I	I	I	I	I	I			⊃
Resistance 6			⊃			•				⊃												⊃	⊃	⊃			⊃			
No Cure 7		I	⊃	⊃			•			I		C										I	I	I			I			⊃
Course 8				I				•								⊃		⊃												
Miracle Drugs 9	C		I	I					•																					⊃
Better Itself 10	C	C		I	I	C	I			•			I	I			C					⊃					⊃			I
Serious 11											•	⊃		⊃					⊃								I			
Fatal 12											C	•							⊃								I	I		
Never Over 13		I	⊃	⊃		⊃				I			•									I	I	I			I			⊃
Cripple 14			I			I					C			•								I	I	I			I			
Not Know 15															•															
Spreads 16								C								•		C	⊃											
Contagious 17	≡	C	⊃	I	I					⊃							•					⊃	⊃	⊃		⊃	⊃	I	⊃	I
Pregnancy 18																⊃	⊃	•	⊃	⊃							I			
Run Down 19								C								C		C	•											
Heart 20											C	C					C			•							I			
Skin 21				I													C				•									
Runny Nose 22		C	C	I	I	C	I			C			I	I								•	C	C	I				I	I
Sore Throat 23	C	C	⊃	I	I	C	I						I	I			C					⊃	•	C						I
Fever 24	C	C	⊃	I	I	C	I			⊃			I	I			C					⊃	⊃	•			⊃	I		⊃
Once 25	C	C	I	I	I												C					I			•			I	⊃	I
Children's 26	C	C		I	I												C									•		I	⊃	I
Get Sometime 27	C	C		I	I	C	I			C	I	I	I	I			C		I				C				•			I
Tendency 28	I	I		⊃	⊃							I											I	I		I		•	C	⊃
Safer Child 29	C	C		I	I												C					I		C		C	C	⊃	•	I
Old Age 30	I	I	I			C		C					C				I					I	I	I	I	I	I	C	I	•

C   Row property is subset of column property
⊃   Row property is superset of column property
≡   Row and column properties are equivalent
I   Row properties are in contrast with (disjunctive of) column properties

FIGURE 5. SET RELATIONS AMONG SENTENCE FRAME PROPERTIES

diseases (26) and 'germ' diseases (2) is redundant, and can be inferred from knowing the other two subset relations. Therefore, the arrow between 'germs' (2) and 'children's' (26) can be erased without loss of information. Notice that this type of ordering simplification cannot be done with 'emotion' (4), 'old age' (30), and 'runs in family' (5), be-

	(2)	(17)	(26)	(5)	(4)	(30)
(2) Caused by Germs	•	⊃	⊃	I	I	I
(17) Is Contagious	C	•	⊃	I	I	I
(26) Children's Disease	C	C	•	I	I	I
(5) Runs in Family	I	I	I	•	⊃	⊃
(4) Caused by Emotion	I	I	I	C	•	
(30) Sign of Old Age	I	I	I	C		•

FIGURE 6. PORTION OF SET RELATIONS PRESENTED IN FIGURE 5

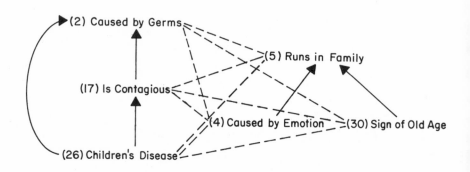

FIGURE 7. GRAPH OF SET RELATIONS REPRESENTED IN FIGURE 6

cause although both (4) and (30) are subsets of (5), (4) is not connected to (30) by the subset-superset relation.

It should also be noted that the transitivity of the subset-superset
relation runs both up and down the chains of arrows. Positive instances
are carried up the chain of arrows, while negative instances are carried
down the chain of arrows. Thus, given the chain going up from (26) to
(17) to (2), if we know of a given disease that it is a member of (26)
(a positive instance), then we know it is also a member of (17) (by
direct linkage), and also a member of (2) (by positive transitivity of

170

the subset relation). To go down the chain we must begin with a negative instance (that is, a given disease is not a member of (2)). From this we know it is *not* a member of (17) (by direct linkage), and also *not* a member of (26) (by negative transitivity of the superset relation).

The transitivity of the contrast relation is somewhat more difficult to describe, but fundamentally works in the same way as the subset-superset relation. For the rule of transitivity to apply, however, one of the pair of classes which is connected by the contrast relation must be a superset of some third class, as in figure 8.

FIGURE 8. CONDITIONS FOR APPLICATION OF RULE OF TRANSITIVITY

By definition of the contrast relation, if anything is a member of A, it is not a member of B. By definition of the subset-superset relation, if anything is not a member of B it is not a member of C. It follows then that if anything is a member of A it is not a member of C. Again the ordering chain runs both ways, so that if any disease is a member of C, then by definition of the subset-superset relation it will be a member of B, and since that disease is a member of B it will not be a member of A by definition of the contrast relation. As a result of the transitivity of the contrast relation, the dotted line between A and C can be erased without loss of information.

The result of using transitivity simplifications with respect to the graph given in figure 7 results in figure 9.

The transitivity ordering and simplification measures could be used without difficulty if no exceptions were permitted in determining subset-superset, contrast, equivalence, and other relations. Since exceptions are permitted, however, perfect transitivity cannot be maintained automatically. For example, if C is a subset of B with three exceptions, it might be the case that there would be six exceptions in treating C as a subset of A. In order to control the problem of exceptions accumulat-

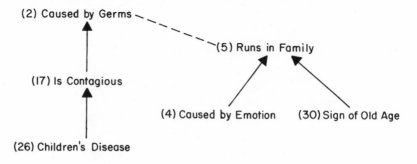

(2) Caused by Germs

(5) Runs in Family

(17) Is Contagious

(4) Caused by Emotion   (30) Sign of Old Age

(26) Children's Disease

FIGURE 9. TRANSITIVITY SIMPLIFICATIONS APPLIED TO GRAPH
PRESENTED IN FIGURE 7

ing, only those relations for which there are three or fewer exceptions
have been retained in the analysis.

A diagram of the ordered and simplified relations is presented in figure 10. Included in the figure are the actual diseases that belong within
each class (diseases always belong to classes above them to which they
are connected by an arrow, except for the starred disease terms, which
do not move up the arrows to the next higher class). The diagram in
figure 10, while not without drawbacks, does have the capacity to generate on large numbers of propositions about diseases. This generative
capacity is due to the transitive nature of subset-superset and contrast
relations. There are 31 basic relations indicated in figure 10. Using the
transitivity rule, 81 new relations between sentence-frame properties can
be inferred.

It should be emphasized, however, that the subset analysis does not
satisfactorily accomplish the goal of determining the specific kinds of
relations which link relevant properties. In fact, discussion with informants concerning relations found between certain sentence-frame
properties indicates that in a number of places the diagram presented in
figure 10 misrepresents "actual" relations, often because crucial properties have not been included in the analysis. Discussion with informants
also brought to light a number of ambiguities in the phrasing of the
original sentence frames. Many of these ambiguities come about as a
result of the dichotomization of the five-point "likelihood scale" which
informants used in answering the original sentence frames. For example, diseases such as colds, tonsillitis, bronchitis, laryngitis, mononucleo-
sis, and strep throat were all treated as true of the sentence frame
'_____ brings on fever'. But, in fact, the informants only indicated
that there was some relatively high *likelihood* that these diseases would
"bring on fever." A more accurate interpretation of the sentence frame
would therefore be "_____ is *likely* to bring on fever." As a result of

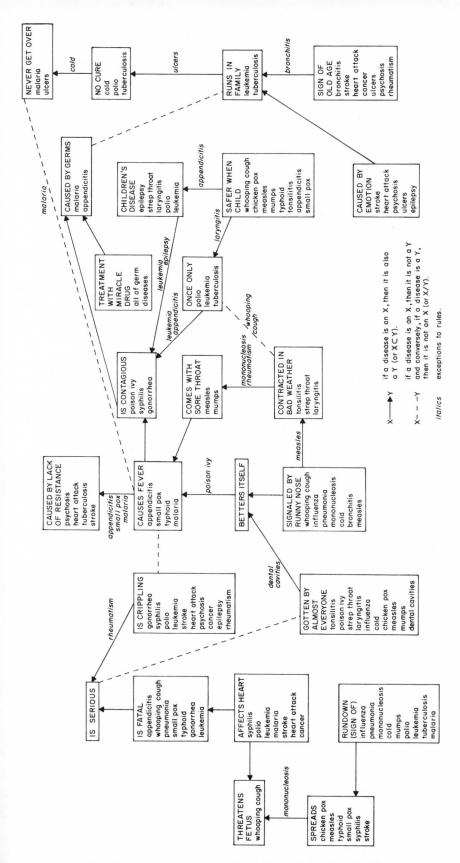

FIGURE 10. SET RELATIONS AMONG AMERICAN DISEASE PROPERTIES

the dichotomization process, implicit degrees of likelihood occur throughout the sentence frames. To avoid such implicit modifications, future work with sentence frames could perhaps employ a scale in pre-listing frames in order to select the most appropriate modifiers ('always', 'usually', 'sometimes', and the like) for explicit use, and then request respondents to answer only "true" or "false."

PROBLEMS IN DISCOVERING CONCEPTUAL RELATIONS

The difficulties involved in trying to interpret observed subset-superset relations can best be illustrated by discussion of a part of the larger network of relations. Figure 11 presents a part of the subset network that clusters around the concept of germs.

The problem which arises in trying to interpret the arrows in figure 11 is that the arrows do not correspond to informants' ideas about causal or other relations. For example, no informant will say that 'fever' causes a disease to be 'catching', or that being 'catching' causes a disease to bring on 'fever'. The subset-superset arrow between these sentence frames appears to be an artifact of the relations that both these properties have to a third property, 'germs'. According to a sample of informants who have been interviewed about these relations, germs (broadly categorized) are a potential cause of infection, and infection is a potential cause of fever. Germs are also believed inevitably to cause a disease to be potentially catching, or contagious. These causal relations are diagramed in figure 12.

The relation observed between 'fever' diseases and diseases which are affected by fatigue-induced lack of 'resistance' is also derivable from the causal relations given in figure 12 and illustrates again how subset-superset relations are often an indirect derivation from specifically conceptualized relations. Similarly, the subset relations between potentially 'catching' diseases, diseases which one can catch only 'once', and the 'children's' diseases can be derived from a causal network that involves notions about how contagious infections can cause the production of various kinds of 'antibodies' which 'cure' the disease and result in more or less permanent 'immunity'. In like manner the subset relations between 'fever' diseases, 'sore throat' diseases, 'bad weather' dis-

174

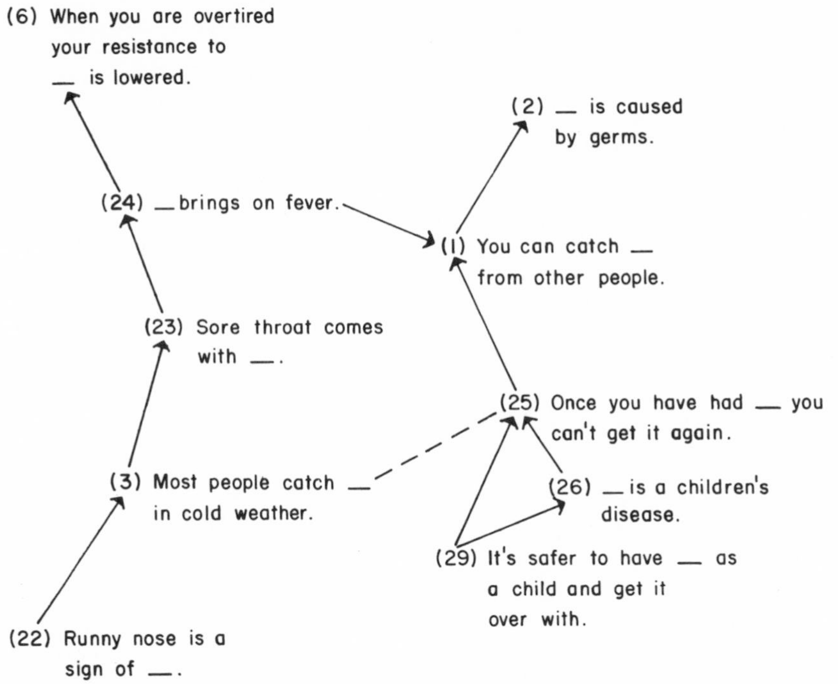

(6) When you are overtired your resistance to __ is lowered.
(2) __ is caused by germs.
(24) __ brings on fever.
(1) You can catch __ from other people.
(23) Sore throat comes with __.
(25) Once you have had __ you can't get it again.
(3) Most people catch __ in cold weather.
(26) __ is a children's disease.
(29) It's safer to have __ as a child and get it over with.
(22) Runny nose is a sign of __.

FIGURE 11. NETWORK OF SUBSET RELATIONS CLUSTERED AROUND CONCEPT OF 'GERM'

FIGURE 12. CAUSAL RELATIONS

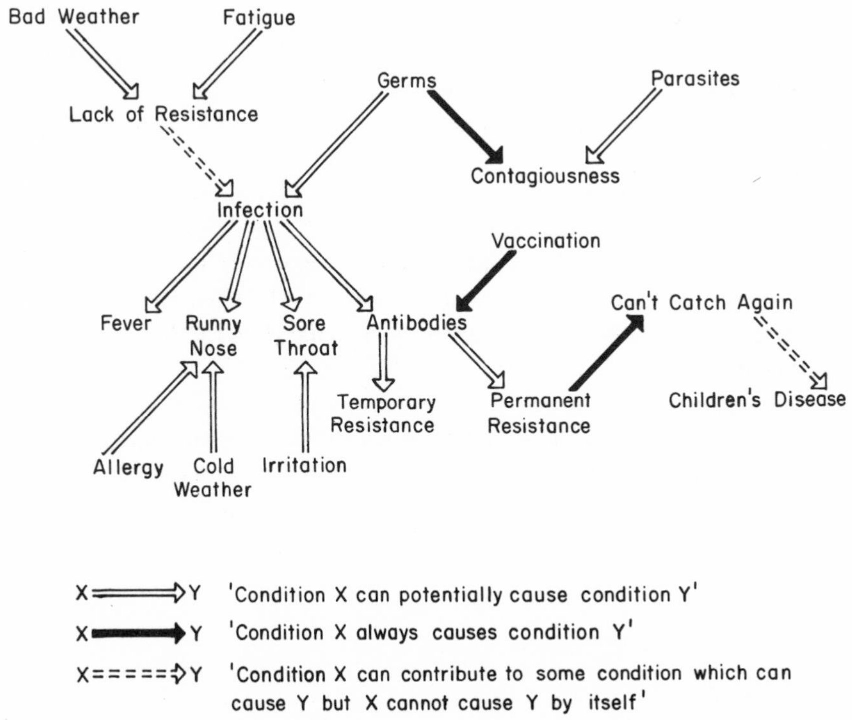

Bad Weather
Fatigue
Lack of Resistance
Germs
Parasites
Contagiousness
Infection
Vaccination
Fever
Runny Nose
Sore Throat
Antibodies
Can't Catch Again
Temporary Resistance
Permanent Resistance
Children's Disease
Allergy
Cold Weather
Irritation
X ⟹ Y 'Condition X can potentially cause condition Y'
X ➡ Y 'Condition X always causes condition Y'
X=====⇨Y 'Condition X can contribute to some condition which can cause Y but X cannot cause Y by itself'

eases, and 'runny nose' diseases appear to result from conceptualized relations of cause in which bad weather is seen as a *contributory* cause to 'respiratory infections'. 'Respiratory infections' are in turn conceived of as beginning in the throat area, and then, depending on the degree to which the germ infection 'spreads', moving first to the sinus areas and causing runny noses, and then, if virulent enough, moving to the chest and causing pneumonias and bronchitis. Here more than just the notion of cause is involved, since there appears to be some conception of an ordering by which infections 'spread' from area to area.

UNSOLVED PROBLEMS

An initial attempt has been made to construct a cultural model of how Americans think about diseases. The major modifications that have been added to the previous multidimensional scaling work are: (1) the use of the transitivity of subset-superset relations, which yields a model with generative capacity; and (2) determination of some of the specific conceptual relations which link properties. While the mapping of subsets and use of the transitivity rule in simplifying relation networks is relatively easy to routinize, the techniques for working out which conceptual relations are basic to a given domain are not so well formulated. It appears that the complex ideas of causality and potentiality are of major importance in understanding how U.S. Americans think about diseases. Other relations such as 'spread' and 'contributes to' may also be important conceptual relations in the domain of diseases. Interviewing problems become crucial here, since some informants are willing to agree to almost any complex proposition. Using only sentence frames about various types of causes, for example, and asking informants to fill in which properties were connected by which type of causes, resulted in inconsistent information. Only when the statements about causal relations were related to specific diseases did informants become less variable.

Another problem which arises in the mapping of subset-superset relations is that some of the set relations which are uncovered appear to be underivable from the information informants can produce. For example, the sentence frames (24) '_____ brings a fever' and (14)

'_____ is a crippling disease' were found to be in contrast in our sample of diseases. So far no informant has been able to explain why a contrast relation should occur between these two classes of diseases. It appears that while most of the observed subset relations should be accountable for by use of some inference procedure from informant-articulated statements about relations, some subset relations may nevertheless remain unaccounted for within a model of informant inference processes.

IMPLICATIONS

Much of the work in cognitive and symbolic anthropology has been concentrated on the analysis of features or attributes. Features are typically divided into two classes: *distinctive* and *connotative*. Distinctive features are those attributes which make up the necessary and sufficient conditions for membership in a class. Connotative features are attributes which are found in association with the members of a class, but which are not criteria for the definition of the class.

To date, much of the emphasis in the study of cultural symbol systems has been on the analysis of distinctive features. In many ways this emphasis on the study of "defining" attributes is counterproductive. Viewing the distinctive feature–connotative feature contrast with respect to the canons of logic, it is clear that distinctive features constitute definitions, and that definitions are tautologies and nothing but tautologies. To limit logic to the study of tautologies is a sound strategy, but to center the study of how people understand the world around them on the study of definitional truth is a much less reasonable procedure.

One of the objections to placing major emphasis on the analysis of distinctive features can be illustrated with the data concerning beliefs about illness. From both the multidimensional scaling analysis and the analysis of causal relationships, it appears that the attributes of disease with which informants are most concerned and which they use in making inferences about diseases are not the defining or distinctive features, but the connotative attributes of 'seriousness', 'contagion', 'curability', and the like. For example, what people know about cancer is not what defines a cell as cancerous, but rather that having cancer is often fatal and painful. If tomorrow a biologist discovers a serum that cures all cancers the defining features of cancer will not change. Such a discovery, however, would certainly change the way cancer is thought of, and that is what is culturally and socially, as well as psychologically, important. (For a similar argument, see Spiro n.d.)

A second objection to the emphasis on distinctive features is that in assuming an essential set of conditions for the definition of terms, the investigator is led to search for the sole domain in which terms can be defined. For example, in determining the features of American-English kin terms, a relatively enduring controversy has developed concerning whether or not these terms can be defined solely within the genealogical domain. There appear to be two problems with this search for the essential domain. First, there is some doubt that terms have a "core" meaning and hence one unique domain. This doubt has been expressed by such eminent students of symbolic systems as Wittgenstein (1963) and Needham (1972). Second, and more important, the search for a single essential domain tends to lead the investigator away from the study of how different cultural domains are interrelated. In the case of American-English kin terms, for example, certain uses of these terms have reference to genealogical facts. Other uses, however, reflect normative concerns, and still others have reference to ordinary and routine activities of family members. People seem to assume that with respect to kinship relations the genealogical domain, the legal domain, and the normative domain, along with the domain of routine family activities, normally all fit together in a simple, regular fashion. However, it is also recognized that in particular cases these domains may be out of correspondence. To use an anecdote for illustration, a friend once said "I want you to meet my real father" when he took me to meet his older brother. The use of "real" in this case was as much a comment on what in this world is 'real' as it was a hedge concerning special use. When the various domains of kinship fail to fit together in a conventional fashion, people reorder symbolic forms to emphasize and evaluate the discrepancies. It would seem to be more profitable to assume that all terms have somewhat different definitions in different domains and to investigate the interrelationships among domains than to assume a doctrine of essences and search for some one basic domain from which all departures can be treated as metaphorical extensions or accidental associations.

Even more basic than the problems associated with the connotative feature–distinctive feature contrast are the inherent limitations of any feature approach. As indicated by the American disease data discussed above, the feature model is severely limited in its capacity to serve as a structure for making inferences. With features it is possible to classify and discriminate objects (of whatever kind), but thinking consists of more than classification. Thinking involves inferences, and an effective structure for making inferences requires at least the use of relations. Relations when applied to appropriate objects become decisions. Inference occurs when a decision is made about the truth of a proposition based upon what is believed about the truth or falsity of other propositions.

Useful research has already been carried out in the investigation of various types of relations, including *part-whole relations* (Basso 1967; Spradley 1971), *use* and *ingredient* relations (Frake 1964; Metzger and Williams 1966), *cause* relations (Metzger and Williams 1963), and *if-then* contingency relations (Atkins and Curtis 1969; Triandis 1972). Werner's work (1970, 1972) on Navajo conceptual systems has been explicitly based on the hypothesis that there is a set of fundamental relationships which structure lexical fields, and these relationships are also part of the lexicon. In a pioneering study, Casagrande and Hale (1967) analyzed Papago folk definitions into a relatively small number of basic relations which they then found to be highly similar to the kinds of relations found in American-English word-association tests, a finding which holds out the promise of a universal typology of relations.

These studies constitute a beginning in the development of an adequate set of techniques and theoretical concepts for the investigation of belief systems. But even as commonplace and accessible a subject as American beliefs about illness has only been partially studied, and no clear consensus exists concerning how to elicit and represent relational structures. At present, the most frequently used (and perhaps most effective) technique for the study of cultural belief systems is for the individual ethnographer to immerse himself in the culture as deeply as possible and, by some series of private, unstated, and sometimes unconscious operations, to integrate large amounts of information into an organized and coherent set of propositions. To make these operations explicit, public, and replicable, or to develop a means of testing the

179

accuracy of the results of these operations, is likely to be a difficult and lengthy task. Nevertheless, it is a necessary task if the study of culture is to continue as a science.

NOTES

1. In addition to the members of the School of American Research Seminar, I gratefully acknowledge the following persons for criticisms and constructive comments: William Geoghegan, Paul Kay, Rodney Needham, Naomi Quinn, A. Kimball Romney, Theodore Schwartz, Melford Spiro, Mark Swartz.

2. These results are presented in D'Andrade et al. (1972).

7
Dialectics in
Zapotec Thinking

FADWA EL GUINDI
University of California, Los Angeles
HENRY A. SELBY
Temple University

INTRODUCTION

In this chapter we examine dialectical thinking in three areas of Zapotec (Mesoamerican) Indian moral philosophy: identity, morality, and society. The data are taken from two villages in the valley of Oaxaca, Mexico, where we have been working since 1965. A joint paper is possible not just because we have communicated frequently in the field, but because we share a common orientation. We are both empiricists who have been frequently and forcibly drawn to symbolic analysis and the postulation of unconscious structures in order to account for our empirical distributions and the accountings of our informants.

We should outline our general orientation to this kind of analysis. First, we agree with Ricoeur (1963) that at least a small part of heaven should be reserved for those who are concerned with the concrete meaning, or content, of symbols. However valiantly we might strive to encounter those realities "plus profondes" in the delineation of pure form without content, our field orientation has thus far prevented us from reaching that goal.

Second, we think that dialectical logic is fundamental to Zapotec thinking. Dialectical logic refers to a habitual mode of thinking in which polarities are defined on dimensions and usually mediated by categories that perform a defining/differentiating, or linking/transforming role.[1] A mediating category is said to be *defining* when it plays a semantic role in the definition and maintenance of a structural opposition. In Zapotec, 'life' and 'death' can be said to be mediated by the category 'child' in the sense that a child is both alive and dead: alive in the sense of having movement and warmth, dead in the sense of having a precariously infixed soul. The category 'child' thus incorporates both poles of the opposition 'alive/dead' or 'life/death'. In a related sense, a mediator can define by differentiating categories, as in the Zapotec example of death and marriage. El Guindi (1973) shows how marriage serves to differentiate death into a binary opposition of *angelito* ('death of not-married') and *difunto* ('death of married'). Here we find that the two kinds of death can only be defined in relationship to marriage as mediator (El Guindi 1973).

A mediating category is said to be *transforming* if it provides the conceptual locus for the change of one polar category into another. 'Graveyard' in Zapotec is a transforming category that takes the creatures of the outside, or of the wild, or of the field, and changes their nature so that they become creatures of the inside, of the domestic arena: 'Christians' or 'human beings'. In this sense it is also a linking point between opposing categories or worlds. For example, the Zapotec witch must pass through the graveyard between house, where witch is human, and field, where witch is superhuman (El Guindi 1973). Similarly, deceased relatives must go through the graveyard when they come once a year to visit their families on All Saints' Day (El Guindi 1974). 'Graveyard', then, serves as a linking point between the two worlds of human and superhuman.

Turning now to the nature of belief systems, we believe they can be analyzed with a view to exposing two kinds of constraints. The first arises out of a necessary level of dialectical tension which we view as having productive power; the second is a constraint implicit in the limited information-processing capabilities of human beings. We call this the problem of "dialectics versus decidability" and view these constraints as representing boundary conditions on the existence of belief systems. We hypothesize that a sufficient amount of dialectical tension must be present for the system to adapt, both to novel inputs and to infrastructural and superstructural changes over time. This sufficiency can be regarded as a lower bound. But since belief systems are systems of thought, people must think them, and think *with* them. As a consequence, there must be "fixed points" in the system; otherwise nothing could ever be decided. Decidability, we hypothesize, is an upper bound on the productivity, complexity, or richness of the system.

Dialectics and decidability are obviously related. In a pure (unmediated) dialectical system, decidability poses no problems: the law of the excluded middle holds, and a subject can readily decide whether an event is P or $\sim P$. But such a system lacks flexibility both structurally and over time. The more complexly mediated a dialectical system becomes, the less well defined the concepts of the belief system become, since P and $\sim P$ mutually define each other via mediating categories. Subjects may therefore readily "move" from one pole of an opposition to another, which ultimately has the effect of breaking down the categorical distinctions in the belief system, thereby subverting its structure.

In this chapter we have adopted El Guindi's (1972) vocabulary and perspective, which distinguishes between two polar characteristics of concepts: *closedness* and *openness*. These attributes do *not* apply to particular concepts, or semantic categories; for example, 'child' is not always an open category. Rather, a concept is closed or open in some particular context, set of events, or topical domain. Closedness and openness are properties of conceptual categories, but they are context-sensitive properties. We emphasize this point because in previous presentation of this material audiences have quite reasonably associated the properties with concrete categories and thereby have given the scheme we are developing a false fixity; also, it has been assumed that we hold that belief systems themselves are closed, which is patently false and utterly antithetical to our position. Human beings may be constrained in their creativity and thought, but they are certainly not incapable of it.

El Guindi has defined concepts as exhibiting closedness when they are "rigidly defined sets of logical (symbolic) statements about the relationships between coded aspects of the real and symbolic world. They are deterministic statements that do not allow contingency. They are algorithmic in nature; that is, they yield determined solutions for appropriate inputs" (El Guindi 1972: 81). When a concept is closed, it displays a high degree of decidability. Informants do not hesitate to classify an event if it can be assigned (in a given context) to a closed concept. In Zapotec, for example, an event is either "field" or it is "not field" in most contexts. "Closed concepts," El Guindi (1972: 55) goes on to suggest, "are associated with a complex ideology, relative inflexibility, and a high degree of sociological differentiation. Conversely . . . open concepts are associated with a less complex ideology, relative flexibility, and weak or neutral affective relations. *Closed concepts are mediated by open concepts*" (emphasis added).

However much closed concepts provide fixity and ideological richness to the system, their rigidity and high level of definition have the disadvantage of discouraging two kinds of events: (1) handling novel inputs, and (2) permitting subjects to "move around" in their own belief system. Open concepts are important for both reasons. Because open concepts (in a given context) are comparatively ill defined, they pose great problems of decidability; at the same time, however, they can encode novel phenomena. The openness of concepts permits change and adaptability. El Guindi (1972: 79) provides an example of this from the Zapotec funeral ritual.

A very old woman, who had never been married, died. The problem was whether she was a 'child' or an 'adult'. The solution lay in altering the child form of the significant mediating open category in this ritual: the music. The woman was buried as a child with adult music. It could have been no other way, since changes in the closed concepts would have changed the ritual from a burial into something else, or worse, into *nothing*. People feel very strongly about closed concepts; such concepts change very slowly in response to the ineluctable infrastructural processes that threaten to undermine the whole system. Another way of contrasting openness and closedness and the mediating function of openness is to imagine the Zapotec to believe that what is new is medial to what always was and always must be.

Lying behind the distinction between the properties of openness and closedness is the problem of decidability. If all were decidable and fixed, then novel inputs could not be entertained. This, in turn, would render belief systems extremely fragile and undefended against infrastructural changes. However, it would certainly permit rapid, efficient assessments of states of affairs, and would therefore minimize liminality and ambiguity. In the structural semantic sense the system would be a global paradigm: it would have clear distinctive features, easy access, rapid processing time, with the added feature of core memory requirements approximately the size of Nova Scotia. A hypothetical system in which all the concepts had the property of openness, on the other hand, would pose endless problems of decidability. A subject would never know the structural assignment of any event in the system, and the system would serve little or no interpretive function. Belief systems, in short, are suspended in a dialectical field between the opposed characteristics of closedness and openness.

ZAPOTEC IDENTITY

Three topics are to be discussed in this chapter in order to illustrate the ways dialectical thinking is realized in Zapotec moral philosophy and behavior. We start with the idea (and problem) of *identity*, which we translate into an appropriate Zapotec query: "Where does one belong?" This involves us immediately in a discussion of how villagers identify themselves at different levels of inclusiveness. We note that they identify themselves spatially in terms of their village, or 'house', and ontogenetically in terms of their social status, as 'sinners' or 'innocents'. Identity turns out to be a convenient starting place for our analysis since it involves us from the outset with the two other topics that are to be our concern: *sociology* and *morality*. We will show that there is a natural unfolding of a dialectical series that leads one via open concepts to the discovery of new oppositions that in turn serve as the conceptual underpinnings of Zapotec community life.

'My Village'/'Other Village'

The primary source of identity to the Zapotec villager is his village, as opposed to all other villages. Villages are nucleated, and boundaries are locally well defined and well defended. "People" live within the village boundary, while beyond it lie persons who are not quite people. They are malicious and malevolent—frequently witches. People in other villages cannot speak properly; their Zapotec is blurred and indistinct. They do not have proper customs.

Each village has its own, usually eponymous, patron saint and annual fiesta. It may have its own distinctive costume; it has its own distinctive oral tradition which invariably declares that its own foundation was very early and that the neighboring villages are colonies which hived off in the recent past. Each village is "an original."

The 'my village'/'other village' opposition is unmediated. It is the only oppositional relationship that we deal with in this chapter which has no mediating category. In this sense, it serves unambiguously to provide the setting for Zapotec thought and action: either an event is 'my village' or it is not; if not, then it cannot carry the sociological or moral weight that would admit it into the discussion that follows.

'House'/'Field'

At a lower level of inclusiveness we find a mediated opposition between 'house' and 'field.' The concept of 'house' is concretized through the rituals of lustration that accompany village processions (as at the Christmas and Easter celebrations), as well as the lustrations of the *fandango*, or wedding celebration. The last provides a context for fuller understanding. In the wedding celebration the person who directs the festival is the *casero* ('dweller of the house'), a person of authority and dignity, defined as 'one who commands'. The major categories of kinsmen are also commanded by 'members of their house', such that a *casero* heads up the party of the bride (the affines), while yet another heads up the party of the godfather of the bride (the fictives). The ritual communty divides the world of people into two kins: 'people of the house' and 'people not of the house'. This is a basic distinction in Zapotec thinking, which is replicated on many levels and is a fundamental aspect of morality and society.

Standing in conceptual opposition to 'house' is 'field'. They are distinguishable on a nominal scale of attributes (El Guindi 1973):

House	Field
inside	outside
has boundary	has no boundary
trust	distrust
good	evil
sacred	not sacred

186

safe	dangerous
edible food	inedible food
blessed water	unblessed water
licit sex	illicit sex
body + soul	*tono* ('animal soul')
Jesus + saints	Devil + *matlacigua* ('evil woman')
ritual	nonritual

'House' and 'field' in the contexts so far studied have attributes of closedness; that is to say no informant would have any difficulty in assigning an event to 'house' or 'field'. They are well defined and elaborate in structure.

'My House'/'Other House'

The contrast between 'my house' and 'other house' is defined for a number of contexts. In the context of ritual it distinguishes between the 'people of the house' versus 'other well-defined and closed groups of people who take part in the ritual'. In the wedding, for example, the distinction is made between *caseros* on the one hand and affines and fictives on the other. In the everyday context it can refer to the distinction between 'my own house' and 'my neighbor's house'.

In the everyday world the boundary between 'my house' and 'the street' marks an elaborate change of demeanor, speech, posture, and manner as one passes from 'that which is not a house' (that is, the street) into the house. 'My house' includes not just people but domesticated animals as well. Wild animals do not belong in the house (or in the patio that surrounds it). 'My house' is defined as the furthest extension of my personal demesne; and the way I handle, or define, the permeability of the boundary around 'my house' serves to define me in or out of the community (see below, on the 'abnormal person').

'My House'/'My Patio'

A final contrast exists between 'my house' and 'my patio', where the contrast is between the structures of wattle and daub and adobe and the open space around them that is still within one's personal demesne. The patio is the place where the domestic animals live, though they may enter the house under ritual conditions. Children live in the patio, and their presence there is taken utterly for granted. Any child may enter any patio, though he may not enter the house, and the child's presence is not marked in any way. The patio, not the house, is the locus of official business. The house is the locus of ritual. No ritual can take place in the patio; no business can take place in the house. Ritual drinking takes place in the house; casual drinking may only take place in the patio (or the cantina). In figure 13 the several meanings of the concept 'house' are presented in schematic form.

FIGURE 13. ZAPOTEC MEANINGS OF THE CONCEPT 'HOUSE'

MEDIATING CATEGORIES: THE GRAVEYARD

One of the most productive (and problematic) mediating categories (in the 'house'/'field' context) is the 'graveyard'. It also provides a convenient point from which to pursue our analysis, because in under-standing the conceptual place of the graveyard in Zapotec philosophy and cosmology, one can readily see how the moral and social domains are linked. The relationship of 'graveyard' to the categories 'house' and 'field' can be diagramed as follows:

HOUSE _____ GRAVEYARD _____ FIELD

El Guindi's (1972) work is again germane. The identification of the 'graveyard' as a mediating category followed upon its recognition as a locus of transformation. Relevant data can be summarized from the "myth of the witch" (El Guindi 1972: 105–7):

> There was once a witch who lives with her husband in the village. Every day during the "heavy hours" the witch goes out into the village, kidnaps children and takes them away with her to the field. After returning them, the children die. The mothers do not notice that the children are gone, because the witch puts a grindstone pestle in her arms.
>
> A neighbor warned the witch's husband that his wife was a witch and told him to be careful, because when the witch cannot find a child in another house to play with (and kill), she kills her own child.
>
> It happened that one day the witch circled the village during the heavy hours and could not find any child that was not being carefully attended by a wakeful mother. When she came home at evening, her husband was already in bed holding the child in his arms. She tried to lift the child out of her sleeping husband's arms, but the husband woke up and she desisted. Later, when he was asleep she tried again, but found that the child was tied to the father by arms, waist, and ankles. When she tried to loose the child, the husband woke up and heard a buzzard on the roof, which convinced him that his wife was a witch.
>
> By this time the wife had left the house, and the husband hurried out to see where she had gone. He left the child at a neighbor's with the warning that the mother was a witch and followed her.
>
> She went to the cemetery. Just in front of the hermitage she saw many heads. The witches leave their heads in front of the hermitage, and then go forth into the field to do their evil. So, the witch left her head in front of the hermitage and went away. The husband immediately switched heads. He switched his wife's head with a male head.
>
> When the witch returned to the cemetery to put her head on, she couldn't find it, so she put on a male head and covered it with a shawl. She went home, but when she talked, she spoke with a man's voice. She never could remove her shawl, and eventually died of shame.

From this evidence, as well as that from other sources, we can see that the "field" is the locus of the dangerous spirits. *Chaneques* (local familiar spirits who steal children's souls) are only defined locationally for 'field', where they abound. The witch belongs to the field as a wild animal, a scavenger in two forms. Its *tono* ('animal soul') is either that of a flying *leoncillo* ('mountain cat') or that of a buzzard. It must be transformed in the following way: the preincarnation of the witch-soul, the wife, can go to the graveyard, change her identity, and in transformed guise penetrate the 'field', where her dirty work can be done. She can then return to the graveyard, reassume her human guise, and repenetrate the 'house'.

'Graveyard' is therefore, in this theory, a mediating category and bears closer examination, since it is the stalking-horse for the creation of a wholly new set of oppositions in another domain. In El Guindi's (1972) analysis of the graveyard, she discovered that it was divided into two parts: the 'old graveyard' and the 'new graveyard'. People who died 'unnatural deaths' (deaths that could not be reasonably attributed to their *suerte*, or destiny) by accident, homicide, suicide, or witchcraft were buried in the old graveyard, whereas the *angelitos* and *difuntos* were buried in the new. The distinction between *angelitos* and *difuntos* is important, because it is not what it might appear to be to Spanish speakers, who normally translate it as "children" versus "adults." This translation may be fine, but it is essential to recognize that the distinction between children and adults does not depend on age; it depends on moral status. An adult is a sinner, and a person cannot be a sinner unless he or she has married. Thus, the graveyard creates an opposition of a new kind on two related but conceptually separate levels: the distinction 'married'/'unmarried' and 'sinner'/'innocent'.

INTERLUDE: WHY ARE MARRIED PEOPLE SINNERS?[2]

The reason that married people are sinners in Zapotec has nothing to do with sex. As Selby (1974) points out repeatedly in his study of Zapotec deviance, the act of sexual intercourse (as distinct from the symbol) is as natural as breathing, and about as problematic. All people engage in sexual intercourse as soon as they are capable, and as long as they are capable, and by our standards this is a very long time indeed. If anything the correspondence should be the other way around: 'single people' should be sinners, since they are living unnaturally, not forming households, remaining dependent on kinfolk for their food and upkeep, and not having children.

We contend that married people are sinners precisely because they *do* have children, and the logic of this apparent paradox will take us a fair way into Zapotec sociology and morality, forcibly introducing us to another mediating category of signal importance: 'affinal and fictive relatives'. But first a brief discussion of kinship.

In the sociological domain, the open category par excellence is the category of 'relatives of respect' which includes in-laws, godparents, and godchildren. Utilizing the test of decidability as a symptom of openness in this context, we may note that the kinship terms assigned to the categories of 'relatives of respect' by a componential analysis (see Selby 1974: Appendix 2) are plagued with problems of definition and decidability. This problem shows most clearly in two terms: *mbal* ('fictive relative',) and *sagul* ('relative-in-law'), both of which apply to relatives of higher than first degree of removal. Whether a person is *mbal* or *sagul* is very difficult for us, as well as for the local people, to decide. Some informants took the range of the term *sagul* out to fifth-degree affines; others would exclude third-degree affines of a close affine; still others excluded spouse's brother's wife. Similarly with *mbal*: some informants took as fictive kinsmen the fourth generation agnatic descendants of the original godfather-godchild relationship, while others cut it off after the first generation of descendants. Informants stated, in effect, that strategic thinking dominated the definition of *sagul* and *mbal*; one could 'permit the tie to cool', or one could 'keep it warm', depending on the relative advantage that accrued from opening up one's kinship network as compared to restricting it.

Pursuing the productivity of the concept 'affines and fictives' in the sociological dimension, we note that these categories of kinsmen serve as reservoirs which can be drawn upon for the manipulation of one's kinship network. Each villager is engaged in working out a saddle-point solution to two competing demands: the demand for psychological, social, and economic security on the one hand, and the demand for autonomy, freedom, and privacy on the other. Kinsmen whose relationships are known and recognized have vested interests in one; they can ask for favors, and according to the rhetoric of kinship, their requests have privileged priority on one's resources. To respond to all favors asked of one is impossible, in particular if one expands one's kinship network widely, since it would require an inhuman degree of altruism and abandonment of one's own responsibilities and privacy. Decisions about affines and fictives are in one sense casual. These relationships are the most important outside the nuclear family, so much so that two major rituals are devoted to the definition, exploration, and reaffirmation of these relationships: the *fandango* in the case of affines and saint's day in the case of fictives. The villagers regard these two relationships as the most laden with 'respect'—the local concept for discussing and describing the rules that create the social order.

It is now clear why married people are sinners; they abrogate the equilibrium that one and one's innermost family (later to be called 'people of the inside') have hit upon. In order to realize the structures of kinship and, in particular, in order to create a complete network of the 'inside', it is necessary either to reaffirm previously cold kinship relations, or to create relations not heretofore in existence through the medium of creating fictive ties. Children are tools, in the sense that they are used by adults to create fictive (godparental) relationships. Children have no say in this; they are an excuse for the elaboration and definition of ties of the "inside."

Upon marriage the family equilibrium changes dramatically because a married child thrusts a whole new universe of potential kinsmen at one—his newly acquired affines. Now, as was mentioned, the fascinating thing about affinal and fictive ties is that the degree of extension is highly malleable. In the fictive case one can activate a cogodparental tie with someone who parallels one in being four generations agnatically removed from the original fictive relationship, but one can equally well cut it off at the first generation. The same is true for affines, if we transform generational removal to degree. A child is a pliable and useful tool, but a married child (an adult) is dangerous, since on his or her own initiative he or she can create whole new networks through the extension of affinal ties and eventually the creation of new fictive relationships. These new definitions are thrust upon one and serve to abrogate one's categorical ('inside'/'outside') definition of the constitution of society, as well as to abrogate one's saddle-point solution to the 'security'/'privacy' problem. Adults are sinners, because adults are fully autonomous human beings with complete moral personalities capable of sociological iniquities.

When affines and fictives are mapped into the moral plane, an opposition is created between a 'morality of the inside' and a 'morality of the outside' that is central to the moral and ethical system of the Zapotecs. The concept 'affines and fictives' mediates two opposed categories in the kinship domain, 'people who live close to one' versus 'people who live far away'. By choosing to activate a relationship with an 'affine/fictive' one defines (or redefines) the chosen person as 'someone who is close to me'. For brevity's sake, we will call these 'insiders'; 'people who live far away' will be called 'outsiders'. The dualistic distinction made here runs throughout Zapotec thinking about society and morality but shows up most clearly in the study of two related problems, the definition of deviant sexual behavior and the process of witch finding.

Jurally, deviant sexual conduct is defined by the rules of incest and the rule confining proper sexual relationships to one's (monogamous) spouse. In practice, both these rules are consistently broken.

Incest can be defined (conventionally) as sexual intercourse with a close relative. If we were to define "close relative" genealogically, it would extend to cousins, second-degree affines, and third-degree fictives, but because there is much variability of definition, we do much better by stating that incest is sexual intercourse with an 'insider' not one's spouse. There are instances of every kind of incest imaginable, up to and including a man having continual connubial relations with his own daughter.

Adultery is institutionalized. There is neither man nor woman who is not having, has not recently had, or is not actively and continually contemplating an extramarital liaison. There are sanctions on such behaviors: institutionalized wife beating; fining, jailing, and severe paternal and godfatherly reprobation for the husband.

If one examines the instances when wife beating and/or reprobation take place, however, it becomes quite clear that another set of rules supersedes the jural ones. For one, incest is chuckled at; no one pays it much mind. Affines are particularly desirable for liaisons, the most desirable being the sister-in-law/brother-in-law relationship. To our knowledge no one is punished for incest, though jurally they should be. The same is true for adultery: extramarital liaisons are only punished when the relationship is with 'outsiders', the very people defined as potential sexual partners by the incest taboo. The reasons are twofold. The first has to do with the equilibrium solution mentioned earlier. By taking up a relationship with an outsider and making it public knowledge, one is acknowledging that a person, formerly of the outside, is now of the inside. One is importing obligations for one's self and one's close kinsmen without their acquiescence or knowledge. The equilibrium solution is abrogated, the insiders are outraged, and sanctions follow. But more importantly, in our view, the categorical distinctions between 'people who live close to one' and 'people who live far away' are confounded. On the moral plane, immorality consists in the blurring of the distinction with an improper mediation. The categorical order is put into jeopardy, and the relationship must be terminated. Generally, it is.

The process of witch finding, and the ideas generated by the open concept 'relatives of respect' are closely associated. The association of the two sets of ideas is but a reflection of the Zapotec notion that morality and society are coterminous.

Very briefly, witches are drawn from the category of 'people who are nothing to me' or 'outsiders'. The event that precipitates a witch finding is a sudden illness which requires explanation, the definition of "sudden" and "requiring explanation" being left up to the witch finders themselves. Often the witch-finding process starts in the period immediately after the sudden death, but sometimes it takes quite a while (and quite a string of untoward events) for one and one's inside group to decide that the death was sudden *and* that it requires explanation. The resulting distribution of witch candidates in the community is as expected: everyone has his own list, which partly (and only partly) overlaps with the list of other people. Even people within the same 'inside' group will not display complete consensus on the identity of witches.

Lists overlap because there is a constant flow of information over kinship and neighborhood lines about the conduct of outsiders, who by definition are the mendacious, malignant, and immoral. To the degree that the negotiated identification is successful from one's own point of view, a witch is labeled for the whole community. And the test for success is very simple: if the candidate's neighbor or close kinsperson believes that he or she is a witch, the prediction is safe that the rest of the community will agree. As a result the witch's 'inside' will consist of the designatee, spouse, and coresident children.

SUMMARY AND CONCLUSIONS

In belief systems, as in the discussion of cultural systems in general, one can start anywhere and get everywhere. We chose to begin with the discussion of 'house' for two reasons. First, it introduced our thinking about dialectical tension and the role of mediation. Second, it served to introduce the cast of characters who would take their places on the stages we had planned for them. The major characters were the graveyard, the child, the relatives of respect, and the witch.

As the argument developed it became obvious that there was an unfolding of oppositions in a clear and consistent fashion that laid bare the conceptual underpinnings of the Zapotec world. The topology of the graveyard yielded up distinctions on the sociological and moral planes that directed our attention to Zapotec moral philosophy and sociology. The graveyard challenged us with the problematic nature of the child, which gave rise to the opposition between 'sinners' on the one hand and 'innocents' on the other. This in turn required us to look into Zapotec sociology and inquire about the role of the child in the creation of social networks, and into the especially problematic nature of the 'relatives of respect'. Children lost their innocence upon marriage because they were no longer passive vehicles for the creation of kinship networks at their parents' disposal, but rather active creators of new social ties—"dangerous" in the sense that they could disturb the equilibrium solution that had been hit upon by the 'people of the inside'.

The discussion then turned to a full-blown interpretation of the implications of 'relatives of respect'. Though nothing like a full discussion of Zapotec community kinship could be given, it became clear that such relatives occupied a mediating position between 'people who were something to me' (that is, my recognized kinsmen) and 'people who are nothing to me'. And this distinction in turn could be mapped into the moral plane in three ways (1) in the definition of a 'proper' adulterous sex partner, (2) in the process of finding a witch and negotiating the identity of witches with the rest of the community and (3) in the allocation of authority among ritual categories.

We believe that this chapter has a medial place in the study of symbolic systems at the present time. Obviously we believe that there is much understanding to be gained by viewing belief systems as unfolding dialectical series. Obviously, too, we see this play of concrete ideas, and the dialogue between the properties of ideas (closedness and openness) as having comparable importance in our understanding. But, as we stated at the outset, we are also empiricists. At a basic level we want to explain events and distributions: the distribution of witches in the community, the frequency of wife beating and judicial processes in the case of divorce, the permissible substitutions of personnel in ritual activity, and so forth. What we have tried to show is not only that there is a place in heaven for those who care about symbolic content; there is also a need for dialectics in positivist, empiricist programs of research, for each informs and requires the other.

NOTES

1. This vocabulary with a fuller theoretical development and examples is to be found in El Guindi 1973: 15–34.

2. The discussion of the married = sinner conundrum was originally carried on by Selby with Charles G. Myers of Temple University. Our warmest thanks are due Mr. Myers, who took the trouble to read through all of the related materials, including some field notes, in order to enter the discussion and add to it.

196

8
Notes toward a
Theory of Culture

DAVID M. SCHNEIDER

University of Chicago

I

The object of a theory of culture is to contribute to an understanding of social action, because culture, which I define as a system of symbols and meanings, has a role in determining that action.[1] Whether culture plays a leading or major role among the determinants of any act is beside the point since there is no way to establish what a "leading" or "major" determinant is. It is clear that culture can never be the *sole* determinant, however, since other classes of determinants always play a role. These are the biological system, the psychological system, the social system, and the environment in which the act takes place. It is the anthropologist's special task to deal with the cultural aspects of social action, although he necessarily deals extensively with norms as well.

The assumption that culture cannot be reduced to any other system makes it possible to study culture on its own, apart from all other aspects of behavior, and the premise that culture should be studied for its own sake is tenable only if it is seen in this light. If one accepts the view that culture is an irreducible analytic construct, one must also accept in principle some general social theory, for example, Parsons's theory of social action. Of course, the study of culture can articulate with theories other than the one developed by Parsons. But I would insist that to study culture without reference to some broader social theory is a pointless endeavor. By the same token, any theory of "cultural determinism," which rests on the naïve position that "culture determines this or that act," is necessarily in error and cannot survive close scrutiny.

The concrete behavior of human beings is the basic problem as well as the basic datum of study; it is the analysis of what people do that is our aim. From the observations of actual behavior, many kinds of abstractions may be made for purposes of analysis. Two of these abstractions, which I shall discuss in much greater detail below, are norms and culture. An abstraction is simply an analytically defined operation that is applicable to, and can be drawn from, observations of behavior. Consequently, humors and soul-substance do not qualify as abstractions. But weight, size, and shape do; these are analytic abstractions of a physical order. Norms and culture are comparable abstractions of a sociocultural order. An abstraction exists in the mind of the observer where it can be manipulated and used as a check against new observations. The abstraction must correspond to something "in" the the concrete action itself, otherwise it cannot have analytic utility, since it cannot have any bearing on the action, just as humors and soul-substance do not. Hence norms and culture are aspects of action abstracted for certain analytic purposes.

Culture, which I have define here as a system of symbols and meanings, I consider to be one important determinant of action, and I hold that social action is a *meaningful* activity of human beings. Social action requires commonality of understandings; it implies common codes of communication; it entails generalized relationships among its parts mediated by human understanding. That one act can have consequences for another is not only a function of the effects of that act; it is also a function of the meaning which that act has for the persons involved. The difference between raising one's hand to help and to threaten may be very difficult for the proverbial Martian to distinguish, but for Americans, the meanings of these acts are significantly different. The

198

study of culture is concerned, then, with the study of social action as a *meaningful* system of action, and it is therefore, by definition, concerned with the question of "meaning-in-action."

Any observed act or series of acts can be abstracted in two different ways. To establish norms, the observer asks of the action, "What are the rules which specify that kind of action's proper occurrence?" This question implies that the observed act is an instance of a kind, class, or category of acts and, as such, is not a wholly unique event. An abstraction defines the norm for that class of acts; it is a specification for how instances of that class of acts should proceed from the point of view of the pattern for action. In the words of that very old limerick, as amended, "Who has the right to do what, and with which, and to whom," when, where, and how.

Norms are patterns for action which apply to some culturally defined unit. There are two important clauses here. One concerns "patterns for action," the other "cultural units."

The action may be that of a person, if that is the cultural unit so defined in the particular culture being studied, or it may be for a status such as 'the father' in American culture, or in Yap the *thagith* ('ancestral ghost'), or it may be for a set of actors (statuses) in a culturally defined unit such as marriage, or family relations in America, or *mil e mit* ('exchange') in Yap culture.

It is possible for the anthropologist to define analytic units as he sees fit, and then to ask if norms are provided for such units. But this—in the nature of the case—cuts across cultural units or ignores their existence altogether. For example, one may ask, "What is the role of the father in the family?" and define 'father' and 'family' according to certain criteria but without reference to any particular culture, thereby ignoring the possibility that no such unit as the 'father' or 'family' exists in the culture being studied. Indeed, far too often in my view, ethnographic reports provide the norms for units which the anthropologist invents, ignoring the units which are designated in the particular culture. Such analyses are invariably faulty in some degree.

Such externally defined cross-culturally comparable units may ultimately be necessary and important tools of analysis. They depend, however, on the prior demonstration of some etic scheme or set of significant universals. There is no need to debate whether such a scheme is presently available; that is not the issue here.

What is important is that we distinguish sharply between norms which are defined in terms of a particular culture's units and norms which are defined in terms of some other analytic scheme. I propose that this distinction is an important one for the purposes of our work at this time, because "norms," as I use this abstraction, are properties of cultural units and not of analytic units with possible or presumed cross-cultural applicability.

Norms as "patterns for action" are sometimes associated with "templates." *Pattern* and *template* are precisely the images that are intended here. *Pattern* is used in the sense of a dress pattern which guides a sewer in cutting and stitching the panels of cloth. The details that are relevant (by cultural definition) to the dress or garment being made are precisely specified in the pattern; the size, the shape, the lines along which the sewing should proceed, and so forth. So, too, the *template*, which is practically synonymous with the term *pattern*. I leave it as an interesting question whether norms can be considered to be iconic signs in Peirce's and Silverstein's schemes (see Silverstein's chapter in this volume).

The point about norms being like patterns and templates is that they are more or less complete, detailed, and specific instructions for how the culturally significant parts of the act are to be performed, as well as the contexts in which they are proper. They specify certain dimensions of action that are to be reproduced, though they omit other parts which are at the option of the actor.

Kroeber and Kluckhohn have stated that "culture consists of patterns . . . of and for behavior" (1952: 181). By my definition, the first term should be "norms," for on both grounds—that it is *patterns* and that it is *for* (but not of) *behavior*—it is closer to what I have defined here as norms and tried to distinguish from culture.

The phrase "for action" in my definition of norms is meant to imply that norms entail the clear mandate of legitimacy, propriety, appropriateness, moral authority. Some norms may be obligatory, some preferential, some allowable, some acceptable, but none can be morally wrong in any absolute and unqualified sense. Yet this does not mean that the wrong, improper, illegal, evil are not patterned and are not themselves normatively regulated. There is a right way to be wrong; there is a proper way to be improper; there are clearly correct forms for illegal action, as any thief, critical of another thief, will readily make clear. That deviance is as normatively regulated as is conformity has been known for a long time now. For the embodiments of valued aspects of cultural premises in norms are precisely the objects toward which deviant behavior is oriented. One way or another, morality is an inalienable aspect of norms; there is a right way to do things, and there is a right way to do the wrong things as well as a right way of doing things wrongly. Otherwise the act would be meaningless, and this is a fundamental point about norms.

Finally we should note that norms are not organized in some random order along the lines of the Tylorian definition of culture. Instead, norms cluster and form structures so that certain bundles of norms make a distinct culturally designated entity. Such an entity is a cultural unit of some kind, and it is culturally defined as a unit, but since it is a unit of a normative order its cultural definition does not exhaust its definition by any means. In American culture we have institutions such as 'the family', 'the market', 'church', 'the city', and so on. These are all clusters of interrelated norms in that they contain all the rules and regulations for how action should be conducted by family members, church members, and so on. And indeed, the cultural definition of who is and who is not a member of the family, and how each differs from the other, should not conceal the fact that each member so defined must have a role to play, and that the role he plays is but another word for the normative aspect. This is an important point in the development of this paper since, as we will see, those clusters of normative elements called institutions are, in one limited sense, cognate with those clusters of symbolic elements which I will call galaxies. But institutions and galaxies are otherwise in no way isomorphic.

The question is sometimes raised as to how widely norms are shared in a society, but this proves to be an unproductive and confusing question, or, at least, a poorly posed one. One source of difficulty may arise from mistaking the cultural aspect of norms for the norms themselves. A norm is a pattern for behavior attached to a cultural unit. Culture is, by definition here, a system of symbols and meanings. The definition of the unit, the premises in terms of which it is defined and distinguished from other units—in short, the meaning of that unit—is thus embedded in the norm (just as it is embedded in the action from which the norm is abstracted). It is not possible to abstract the norm without abstracting its cultural aspects at the same time. What is widely shared and what has a high level of generality may not be the norm so much as the cultural aspects of the norm. This becomes especially true when the norm is misstated in very general terms rather than in its full detail, as for instance, when one says that the role of the mother in the American family should be nurturant. Such a statement does not specify how to be nurturant, how the mother should act when she is being nurturant, what 'to be nurturant' entails. It is insufficient to define the norm for the mother in the American family in such terms. How a rich mother should be nurturant is normatively different from how a poor mother should be nurturant; it is different for middle-class and lower-class mothers, for devout Catholic and devout Jewish mothers, for Italian and for Anglo-Saxon mothers, toward a first child or a last child, and so on. Hence the term 'nurturant' is more a cultural than a normative designation, and it is widely understandable because a variety of somewhat different normative prescriptions may be attached to it. What is widely shared is likely to be the cultural meaning of the unit, while the norm, fully and properly described, is very much more specific, at a narrower degree of generality, more restricted in scope and context, and not widely shared outside of a particular social field.

Norms differ from culture, then, in their generality, the range of different social contexts to which they apply. Norms are relatively limited, comprising detailed descriptions for how to act in relatively specific situations, whereas culture has wider and more general applicability across a range of norms in a range of social situations.

I have avoided using the phrase "level of abstraction" here. I have also avoided saying that one is at a "higher or more general level of abstraction" and that the other is at a "lower level of abstraction," because this would introduce confusion. Norms and culture are both abstractions. Each abstracts somewhat different things with reference to different questions, but neither is "more abstract" than the other. Culture is far more widely and generally applicable with respect to the range of social contexts and situations; norms are highly restricted and less generally applicable to the range of contexts and situations.

Culture is, by definition here, a system of symbols and meanings. Every norm, as I have indicated, has cultural aspects embedded in it, and therefore an important methodological procedure for studying culture is to separate the cultural aspects from the norms themselves.[2]

Culture contrasts with norms in that norms are oriented to patterns *for action*, whereas culture constitutes a body of definitions, premises, statements, postulates, presumptions, propositions, and perceptions about the nature of the universe and man's place in it. Where norms tell the actor how to play the scene, culture tells the actor how the scene is set and what it all means. Where norms tell the actor how to behave in the presence of ghosts, gods, and human beings, culture tells the actors what ghosts, gods, and human beings are and what they are all about. Obviously, how to behave toward gods, ghosts, and human beings is not unrelated to how these are defined or conceived to be, or in what they are believed to consist, regardless of whether such beliefs can be shown to be scientifically right or wrong.

At this point it may be helpful to indicate what culture, as I see it, is *not*. Culture is not that Tylorian inventory of pots, pans, rocks, and crocks which must of necessity end with the phrase "et cetera," thereby constituting a list of all those things with which man is not born but which he somehow creates or learns. Culture is, partially, patterns of learned behavior, but it is also much more. Definitions which distinguish what is learned from what is instinctive or existential in man exist in abundance. But such definitions provide no ground for distinguishing psychology from sociology or anthropology or any of the other social sciences, except as subdivisions of the study of culture. By Tylorian definition, a belief in God, in the patterns of peristalsis and of hunger, and in what the eyes tell the brain are all on a par, for they are all, to a greater or lesser extent, learned behaviors. Culture is man's adaptation to nature, too, but it is more. Nature, as a wholly independent "thing" does not exist, except as man formulates it.

All such definitions of culture lead to a difficulty that may be called "naïve cultural determinism," the sort where when one asks, "Why do the Nuer practice the levirate?" and the answer is given, "Because it is their culture; their culture tells them to." Or when one asks why some people use lots of chili peppers in their food and the answer comes back that that is a part of their culture heritage.

Whatever other defects these definitions of culture have, they all fail to distinguish norms from culture and they fail to define culture rigorously and with respect to some wider, more comprehensive theory of social action. But most important, they omit any concern for meaning, which is such a crucial component of social action.

A point which I made earlier and briefly requires yet another word of explication. The world at large, nature, the facts of life, whatever they may be, are always parts of man's perception of them as that perception is formulated through his culture. The world at large is not, indeed it cannot be, independent of the way in which his culture formulates his vision of what he is seeing. There are only cultural constructions of reality, and these cultural constructions of realities are decisive in what is perceived, what is experienced, what is understood. In this sense, then, 'nature' and the 'facts of life' are always a special case of the cultural definition of things; they have no independent existence apart from how they are defined by the culture.

One special case of this is what science determines the facts of nature to be. Science is, of course, a cultural system of a very special sort, but it is no less a part of culture. But just because science determines that a particular construction of reality is also real makes it no less a cultural construction of reality. We know this for many reasons, not the least of which is that the scientific reality of today is not the scientific reality of yesterday nor will it be the scientific reality of tomorrow. Meaning is thus not simply attributed to reality. Reality is itself constructed by the beliefs, understandings, and comprehensions entailed in cultural meanings.

There are two fundamental functions of culture. The first is that special integrative function which Parsons calls "pattern maintenance." Culture places disparate parts of the social system together into a meaningful whole. Put another way, it forms the unifying principle(s) for the total normative system by providing a single set of symbols and meanings to which each differentiated part of that normative system is related, thus relating each part of the normative system to all other parts more or less directly through their meanings. I have called this culture's *regnant* function.

The second function of culture might be called *generative*. Here the emphasis shifts from a "given" or synchronic view of a total system to one in which alternations, changes, innovations, and losses from the normative system are the subject of attention. A very loose analogy which may be helpful is with the function of Greek and Latin in the coining of new names for items of technology or species and genera of plants and animals. When a new insect or new animal is found, it is not given a wholly unique name, but usually one derived from the Greek or Latin root consistent with the extant taxonomy and with the hypothesized place of the new organism in that taxonomy. So, too, with items of technology. In much the same way, new roles do not appear out of the sky like bolts from the blue but are generated instead from whatever their previous conditions were, and in important part from "first principles." *These first principles are cultural.* This is a very rough and superficial version of what I mean by "culture" being "generative." Social life is meaningful; new meanings are established with reference to old meanings and grow out of them and must be made, in some degree, congruent with them; and exchange, whenever and wherever it occurs, must be articulated with the existing system of meanings.

Since the meaningful aspects of norms are, by definition, the cultural aspects, one important constraint on changes in norms is their meaning(s). Hence the regnant and generative functions of culture are neither more nor less than the process of maintaining continuity and some degree of coherence between the aspects of the total action system in terms of the meanings of its parts. I certainly do not intend to reify culture so that it stands up on its hind legs and howls when an unacceptable change is considered or wags its tail in approval when the change "makes sense." The use of the terms *regnant* and *generative*, then, should not be construed as a form of "cultural determinism."

In discussing the functions of culture I purposely did not invoke the common, and perhaps generally expected, point that culture provides the actor with a way of organizing his experience and his perception of the world into some sort of meaningful form, perhaps a meaningful "whole." My reason for this is simple. From the point of view of culture as a system, it provides the basis for the construction of reality—for the actor, of course; who else is there? From the point of view of the human being, the actor in the sociocultural system of action, a decisively large and important part of his definition of the situation of action is his internalized version of both the normative and cultural systems. This does not exhaust the orientation of the actor to the situation of action. He has drives, he has had experiences, he has learned lessons both large and small, he has, to put it briefly, a system of motives. His motivational system consists very largely, but not entirely, in his internalization of the cultural aspects of the norms of the community to which he belongs. But the organization of his motives, the organization of the cultural aspects which he has internalized, interacts with his psychobiological states, his personal history or life experiences, with the specifics of the situation in which he finds himself. Hence it goes without saying that one function of culture is to provide the actor with an important part of the material—but by no means all the material—from which he constructs reality. For if culture is not internalized by actors, where can it be, except in the heads of observers?

I have defined culture as a system of symbols and meanings. Social action requires commonality of understanding, implies common codes of communication, and entails generalized relationships among its parts mediated by human understanding. These are also the meanings of the term "collective" in Durkheim's concept "collective representations" (see below). The "collective" part thus refers to the sharedness of the symbols and meanings. The "representations" are another way of stating what is meant by "symbols." These are perhaps best understood as vehicles for conceptions, or more precisely the vehicles *and* their conceptions. These are the units, the elements which are defined and differentiated in a particular society as representing reality—not simply social reality, but the total reality of life within which human beings live and die. Man constructs the reality within which he lives. It is constructed as a body of definitions, premises, statements, postulates, presumptions, perceptions, feelings, understandings, units, images, categories about what we Westerners call "the nature of the universe" and man's place in it. And so it consists in the units or representations or symbols such as family, community, reality, the sacred, and so forth in American culture. Different cultures are constructed of different units. Such units, as they are conceptualized, are the vehicles for conceptions. The distinction between "vehicle" and "conception" is possible but should not be overemphasized, for the two are in some degree inseparable. Hence the definition of culture as "symbols *and* meanings."

II

The study of culture symbols and the very separate and different study of culture as a system of symbols and meanings (a difference I shall discuss later) have centered largely on religion, ritual, magic, and myth, and occasionally art.

The fact that the study of cultural symbols and the study of culture as a system of symbols and meanings originated in these areas is a statement of their historical development; the fact that such studies continue to flourish almost exclusively in these fields is a comment about some serious misconceptions embedded in these studies.

Durkheim was not solely responsible for this. Weber had a hand in it too. Durkheim set part of the stage by the problem he posed in *The Elementary Forms of the Religious Life*. He asked how the content of the beliefs and practices of totemism and other ritual and religious systems could be accounted for. Obviously the beliefs about gods, ghosts, and ghouls could not be based on the real, existential nature of gods, ghosts, and ghouls because they did not exist; hence, these beliefs and practices were not based on *that* objective reality. But, Durkheim argued, they must be based on some objective reality and in the end he affirmed that the objective reality on which all religious belief is based is "society." There is no need to debate this. The points for our purposes are two. First, Durkheim saw the religious system as a complex symbolic system that embodied the values and beliefs of a society as a set of postulates and propositions which were treated as given, taken as truth. Many of these beliefs and postulates were cast in concrete images —symbols—and this complex of idea and image he called a "collective representation." Second, the collective representations were determined by and served to mark diacritically the social structure, the social forms. "Society" in the sense of the system of social relations, or the social structure, was the objective reality which the collective representations reflected.

But the reverse was not true. Institutions such as kinship, economics, and politics were seen by Durkheim to have their bases in objective reality. The gods, ghosts, and ghouls problem in reverse is that if the content of religious belief cannot be referred to real gods, ghosts, or ghouls, the content of kinship *can* be referred to real relations of consanguinity and affinity and the content of economics can be referred to real problems of production, distribution, and consumption of real goods and services. Without blaming it all on Durkheim, the fact remains that since his time, anthropologists have held pretty consistently to this premise. Where institutions are related to real, existential facts it is presumed that they must somehow be "based on" or "related to" them, but where no such facts can be shown to exist, then the institution tends to be treated as primarily symbolic and expressive.

There are two misconceptions here. The first is that institutions which appear to be "based on" objective realities (such as property, goods, and services; birth, copulation, and death; or the exchange of women) need not be examined for symbolic, meaningful, or expressive aspects because the objective realities of consanguinity, affinity, and property are directly expressed in the institutions themselves. And so kinship has been studied as a system of social relations built around the facts of consanguinity and affinity, and the exchange of women. Most kinship studies have focused on the problem of how norms organize activity to get jobs done. But the symbolic and meaningful aspects of these activities have seldom been studied carefully. In other words, they have been studied primarily as social or normative systems, only rarely as cultural systems.

The second misconception follows from the Durkheimian view, shared by Weber among others, that religion is concerned with ultimate meanings and values of a society, that the collective representations of the religious system embody the society's symbols and meanings in terms of which life is experienced and understood.

Here we must stop to realize that it does not follow from this that religion *alone* has the monopoly on the ultimate symbols and meanings of a society, or even that these symbols and meanings are best expressed and most easily studied through the religious system and its rituals. The fact is that the ultimate values, the collective representations, what I call the system of symbols and meanings, permeate the total society and its institutions and are not confined to religion, to ritual, to magic, or to myth alone. The system of symbols and meanings intertwines every other system in a society, be it kinship or political or technological or economic, or whatever.

I have distinguished here between the study of cultural symbols and the study of culture as a system of symbols and meanings; the preceding points are underlined by this distinction. The analysis of cultural symbols is not the same thing as the study of culture as a total system of symbols and meanings. These are not unrelated endeavors, but they are not identical. The problem of deciphering religious symbols, for example, is not the same thing as the problem of analyzing the total culture as a system of symbols and meanings. The one simply analyzes certain symbolic sets for their meanings. The other is based on a total social theory in which the concept of culture plays a significant part.

Max Weber was concerned with the development of capitalism. His argument was that social action could only be understood if the meaning of the situation of action for the actor was understood, for subjective meaning was one important determinant of the choice among possible courses of action. To state it very briefly, Weber held that the system of meanings embedded in the symbols and beliefs of Calvinism played a role in the development of capitalism through the effect those meanings had on the actors' selection among different courses of action. Capitalism, viewed as a system of social norms for how economic and related action should proceed, was in part motivated by the meanings and symbols of the religious setting within which it developed. Similarly, Weber's studies of religion focused on the way elements of meaning related to the structure of norms and the patterns for action. There was no study of meaning per se, only the question of how meaning affected norms.

Herein lies another misconception. Whether there is an objective base to religious beliefs and practices is quite beside the point. The point is that each part of an act has both normative and cultural aspects, the former oriented toward the organization of action, the latter symbolic-meaningful in orientation. Both norms and culture are analytic categories, abstractable aspects of every act.

There are, therefore, four different questions that can be asked rather than just the traditional two. First, there is the question of how norms are structured, how they are constituted, how they are organized as patterns for action. Second, there is the question of how a culture is constituted, how its symbols and meanings are structured. The third question is that of the relationship between culture and norms from the point of view of the normative system; that is, the problem is of the relationship of symbols and meanings to norms from the point of view of the normative system. The fourth question is just the reverse of the third, that is, the relationship of norms to the symbols and meanings from the point of view of the cultural system.

Another misconception is the assumption of the Durkheimian and Weberian traditions that there is some kind of isomorphism between the aggregate or structure of norms called an institution and a comparable aggregate or structure of symbols and meanings. It is revealing that the latter has not been blessed with a traditional name like "institution," a fact which suggests that it is not often considered as a problem.

For convenience, I will call such an aggregate or structure of symbols and meanings a *galaxy*. The misconception, then, is the assumption that each institution is isomorphic with a particular galaxy. It is easy to see how such a misconception could have developed. Since the traditional question has always been one of asking (after Weber) about the symbolic-meaningful aspects of an institution, the search for those symbolic-meaningful elements has tended to stop at the boundary of the institution. The question was how meaning affected action, not how meanings were structured apart from any particular system of action.

But the closer one looks, the more apparent it is that there is not only no such isomorphism, but that there is every reason to believe that such an isomorphism is not possible. This is because the system of symbols and meanings cuts across the system of norms, or, stated differently, a given galaxy is dispersed among a number of different institutions. Further, any given institution is intersected by a series of galaxies just as any given galaxy is intersected by a series of institutions. Put in very old-fashioned and not quite precise terms, logico-meaningful integration crosscuts functional integration, and vice versa.

Still another misconception consists in the fact that the traditional rubrics, such as religion, myth, ritual, kinship, economics, and so forth, are all defined either in terms of our own ethnocentric (mis)interpretations of our own social system, or in the functional terms which have dominated anthropological work during the last seventy-five years or so. There the chief concern has been with how things are organized, how the social order is constructed, and how roles are defined to get things done. Problems of symbol and meaning have never been and are not now a primary concern. Since the problems are not constructed with such concerns in mind, it should be no surprise that they are hardly suitable for answering questions of meaning.

A difficulty with my book *American Kinship* is that I did not fully appreciate this point when I began it. After the book was too far along to go back and begin again, it became perfectly clear that kinship was not the right unit of study since kinship, nationality, religion, education, and the whole sex-role system were all parts of the same cultural galaxy. I should have followed where the symbols and meanings led instead of following anthropological tradition and stopping arbitrarily at the boundary of the institution called "kinship." When I did move across that boundary, I found (not surprisingly) that my analysis of certain symbols and meanings was not quite right because it was limited to, and limited by, the study of the traditional institutional unit, kinship. Put another way, starting with "kinship," as I defined it in traditional ethnocentric and functional terms, I only came to realize late in the analysis that the system of symbols and meanings was not isomorphic with any such category, but instead spread far beyond its boundaries.

I have used the term *ethnocentric* here and I should make it clear that ethnocentric categories are not wrong in themselves. What is wrong is to compare things that are not comparable and to analyze things by categories that do not apply. Indeed, the whole enterprise in cultural analysis starts with our own society as a point of departure, not only because we know it (or can know it) in both accuracy and depth, but because it is precisely our own society which is problematic in our lives. But when a category is defined in terms of How-Does-It-Organize-People-To-Do-Jobs? it simply does not compare very well with a category which is defined in terms of What-Does-It-Mean? except in that limiting case where meaning equals function. There is nothing wrong, for example, with comparing the American family with a comparable unit in another system, but we must either compare the two as forms of social organization or else as cultural, meaningful units.

If we start with the question of meaning and how it is symbolized, we must first ask how each culture slices the pie of what is defined as its reality, its experience. I would insist that this is no less an analytic scheme, a theoretical statement, than any other. I am not arguing for a return to "natural categories" or for the use of common sense. I am arguing as forcefully as I can in favor of a particular theoretical scheme, the central feature of which is the premise that different cultures have different structures of meaning and that these structures are carried by symbols which are likely to be different. I do not rule out the possibility that there may be universals. But I do rule out the attempt to state them a priori and the attempt to infer them from common sense and the so-called facts of life. Examples would be the various culture-nature distinctions, or right-left, or head-feet, or up-down, or we-they. These may very well be universal symbols in cultural codes. But until that is established, we must *not* ask, "How do the Bongo Bongo handle the culture-nature distinction?"; rather we must ask, "Do the Bongo Bongo have one of the culture-nature distinctions, and if so, in what form?"

I turn now to the relationship between culture and norms, first from the point of view of the normative system and second from the point of view of the cultural system. If we take a particular cultural unit and consider its normative aspects we can see immediately that it is structured by a number of different kinds of cultural components. The American "father," for instance, has a "kinship" component, an age component, a sex-role component, a class component, a religious component, and so forth. None of the components spells out any specific form of action, although each is closely associated with an action component. Yet each of the cultural components is a part of the definition of the "father" as a cultural unit.

The different cultural components of units such as "father" come from different cultural domains or subsystems of symbols. I have called this the "conglomerate" level because there is a conglomeration of elements from a variety of different cultural domains which come together to form a cultural unit, and this cultural unit has a norm or pattern for action attached to it. The word *level* should not be misunderstood. I do not mean higher or lower level of abstraction, but simply, a differently defined abstraction. By *conglomerate*, I simply mean the operation of taking a cultural unit which has a clear norm attached to it and analyzing the cultural components of that unit for the light such analysis sheds on understanding the normative definition of that unit. Thus, in analyzing the unit "father," we do not have to trace the age or sex-role components far beyond the boundary of "father" in order to analyze their places in the structure of the unit "father." It is unnecessary, in other words, to exhaust the entire domain of sex role as a symbol and meaning system.

If we reverse our perspective and ask the same question about the relationship between norms and culture from the point of view of the culture, a different picture emerges. It is culture, a very different analytic objective, that is our problem.

An important methodological issue arises at this point. As I have said, pure cultural domains crosscut different institutional structures. Since symbols and meanings are the object of our study, and since the only way to establish meaning is by studying all its occurrences in context, it is only from a survey of all possible kinds of contexts that the full array of different meanings associated with any given symbol, or cluster of symbols, is possible. It is not possible simply to say "What is the meaning of sex as a symbol?" Rather, one must inspect every normative usage of sex as a symbol in the widest array of possible contexts. Only then can the full cluster of meanings be established. Equally important, only then can the associations of different symbols and different clusters of meanings be shown. And further, only then can the variations, permutations, transmutations, inversions, and transformations of meaning from one context to another be located.

As an example, consider the relationship between the substantive nature of blood and the spiritual nature of kinship in American culture. Common sense might suggest that spirit and substance are inimical, opposed, and incompatible categories. Quite the contrary, for there is in Western European kinship a close association between the spiritual and the substantive, and in certain contexts the spiritual is defined as substantial rather than as part of the order of law or the code for conduct.

It is the way in which symbol and meaning are dispersed throughout the normative system that defines the meanings of a symbol, that demonstrates which symbols are clustered into galaxies, and that reveals how meanings are ordered and reordered in relation to each other. It is also in this way that we can understand the conditions under which one meaning is primary or encompassing in one normative context, and is connotative, secondary, encompassed, or suppressed in other normative contexts.

At this point the question of how the cultural system itself is structured becomes methodologically relevant. After we have derived the symbols and meanings from the array of contexts defined by the normative system, after we have inspected the different symbols and meanings in the full range of their contextual locations, then we can consider them apart from the normative set and examine them in terms of how the cultural system itself is ordered. It is in this sense that I have argued that culture needs to be studied on its own, in its own terms, as a system apart from and not reducible to other systems. The culture must be looked at as a whole and not in bits and pieces, each tied to a normative chunk with loose ends hanging about, precisely because the institutions are not isomorphic with galaxies and precisely because different cultural galaxies crosscut and intersect different institutional structures so that no one institutional structure yields more than a peculiarly biased sample of the culture.

Here then is the heart of a theory of culture, and it is here that we know tidbits, odds and ends, but, in fact, know the least. One may hope that this condition has been the result of more time having been spent with the Weberian and Durkheimian formulations (where social action and social structure are the basic problem) than with the question of culture itself. But whatever the reason, the fact remains.

III

I have postulated that anthropologists should deal with culture as a system of symbols and meanings in its own right and with reference to its own structure. (It should be unnecessary to add that every symbol can have a number of different meanings and that every meaning can have a number of different symbols.)

In this section, the problem I will deal with is how the different meanings of a symbol relate to each other. I have called a cluster of symbols and their meanings a galaxy. This does not specify what kind of relationship symbols and their meanings have to each other, but only that they form a larger unit of some kind and have some relationship to each other. The galaxy is an abstraction which asks whether it can be demonstrated that a significant cluster can be distinguished from an aggregate of loosely related symbols and meanings. As I have indicated, the concept of a galaxy is based on the development of a concept which is symmetrical with, and comparable structurally to, the relationship between institution and norm.

If a cluster of symbols and their meanings can be shown to have some features which distinguish it from other clusters, then the probability arises that a total system may be discerned which is distinct from other total systems. This is to say that a total cultural system is an analytic possibility, and that a total cultural system is composed of a structure of galaxies just as a total social system is composed of a structure of institutions. Whether the cultural system can be distinguished as an entity is a problem. How to do so is another. And how that total cultural system is structured is a third.

I have offered the hypothesis in *American Kinship* that each galaxy has its central, core, key, master, unifying, dominant, or epitomizing symbol. I use this array of words on purpose, and I am careful to avoid becoming committed to any one of them. This wariness springs from the fact that I am convinced that all meaning is to some degree context-

214

defined or context-determined (within the framework of norms), and that it remains an empirical question to show whether two meanings are related to each other as extensions, as derivations, as denotations or connotations, metaphors or metonyms, and so forth; in other words, just what relationship two (or more) meanings do bear to each other.

My hypothesis is that each galaxy has its epitomizing symbol; this epitomizing symbol is only one form of the possibly very few epitomizing symbols that characterize the total culture. It is a plausible hypothesis that two different total cultural systems could exist, with each composed of exactly the same inventory or set of symbols, but that the members of each set are differently related to each other. Thus, for example, if Louis Dumont is correct (as I think he is) then the difference between Indian culture and American culture is only in a reversal of the way an identical symbol-set is related; in the former, *homo hierarchicus* is encompassing, in the other *homo equalis* is encompassing (Dumont 1970). Yet with equal justification one may see each of these societies equally well in terms of an epitomizing symbol; hierarchy in the Indian example, equality in the American culture, each symbol subordinating the other symbol, but each necessarily entailing the other.

Another example of the interrelationship of symbol sets may further clarify my meaning. The family and relatives in American culture are defined in terms of the symbols "blood" and "marriage." Blood is sometimes associated with flesh as in the phrase "flesh and blood." This in turn means what family means, 'kind', 'sort', so that "kin" are one "kind" of people. Their "kind-ness" is located in the fact that they are of one blood. A number of other meanings attach to blood, but I will not list them all here. Suffice it to say that blood means both oneness and unity of substance, as well as a unity which is marked by common solidarity. That is, the roles or the code for conduct of blood relatives is supposed to be (normatively, it should be) governed by a common claim on the diffuse, enduring solidarity of all others. This is qualified by substantive or blood distance so that the claim is strongest for those who share most blood, weakest for those who share the least. This is not an exhaustive account but is intended only as an illustration. (For further detail see Schneider 1968, 1972; and Schneider and Smith 1974.)

But blood is only one form of substance, and only one form of substance which is symbolized as natural substance. And the code for conduct that enjoins diffuse and enduring solidarity is in turn only one kind of code for conduct and one kind of "law." We see that the institutional setting called "family" and "relatives" in America uses one variant of the symbol of substance, and that is the natural substance, plus one of the meanings of law, and that is the code for the conduct which enjoins diffuse and enduring solidarity. And this same set of symbols and meanings is found in the institutions of religion, nationality, education, and perhaps elsewhere (Schneider 1969a, 1972).

There is one interesting transformation in the area of nationality. Here the particular symbol is land, locality, locus, place. At first glance, place and blood do not seem to be related as symbols, yet a moment's consideration will convince many (if not all) Americans that what they mean by land and place is very close to what they mean by blood. Both are substantive, both are natural, and both are symbols which define a person's identity—as a member of a family or a member of a nation. The symbol of birth is closely interwoven with those of blood and place too, because whether in Gilbert and Sullivan's formulation "For he is an Englishman" or in the Naturalization and Immigration Service, which asks for Place of Birth, land and place are linked to birth and blood in such a way that they can be seen as variant formulations or transformations of each other.

If one ignores the institutional context and simply follows out the symbols themselves, it seems clear that the symbol of coitus epitomizes a series of symbols and meanings in a single figure. There is the difference between the two opposite sexes; their union as a married pair; the creativity which follows that unity, in the form of conception; and the child as a consequence of that union. As a mode of diffuse and enduring solidarity, coitus presents both long-term and short-term solidarity, for as the physical union is a form of solidarity with a short time span, the consequence, the child, creates a solidarity over a longer time span, a solidarity that extends into the future. Again, the two large domains of nature and law are united in the figure of coitus.

I am now dealing with a galaxy in which coitus is the epitomizing symbol. In different specialized contexts at the normative level, the various changes on that epitomizing symbol and the galaxy it coordinates are rung: blood for the family; land and birth for nationality; common faith, belonging, and the unqualified or diffuse and enduring solidarity of those so bound with god, for religion. Education adds a time dimension, moving people through "classes" to the "birth" of graduation.

If coitus is the epitomizing symbol of one such galaxy, it is certainly only one. A more inclusive symbol of which coitus can be seen as only one element is what, in American culture, may be called "sex." "Sex" has two distinct aspects: the conjunctive and the disjunctive. The conjunctive aspect is, of course, coitus. The disjunctive aspect is what can be called its "sex-role" aspect. Here the two sexes are defined in opposition to each other and the system centers on making and maintaining the opposing distinctions. One may ask whether coitus is a part of sex or whether sex is a part of coitus. The answer, I would suggest, is both. If so, then why do I say that sex is the more general of the two? The answer is simple. Although coitus entails the playing out of different sex roles, it does so because there is a presumption already established in the symbol of coitus that the sexes are different. It is that meaning of coitus, that the different be unified, which gives coitus its more specific meaning; it is the disjunctive aspects of sex role in the symbol of sex that give sex its generalized meaning. Sex as sex role is the epitome of differentiation and manifests itself through almost everything, from electrical junctions to personal pronouns.

Where does "love" fit into this galaxy? How does love relate to sex? Love cannot relate merely as another statement of coitus; although love comprehends coitus, love is, at the same time, the bridge between the spiritual and the substantive. Perhaps love is best understood as that variant of the symbol, coitus, which stresses the conduct aspect of coitus—the aspect of law before the aspect of nature, the aspect of spirituality and emotion—all of which are unstressed in the symbol of coitus. Symbolically, love is not so general as sex. Love is one of many elements in the total galaxy epitomized by the symbol of coitus. Other symbols within this galaxy include nationality and government, marriage and parenthood, and friendship.

It is at this point that the work of Lévi-Strauss, Dumont, V. Turner, and others becomes directly relevant, for they have worked out in some detail some of the difficult kinds of relationships of symbols and meanings to each other. They have shown how certain symbols can exist in a simple relationship of duality, or in a matrix-metamatrix relationship so that they are $+/-$ with respect to each other, or $+/$not-plus to each other. They may exist in contradiction to each other as opposites or as opponents, dominant and subordinate, marked and unmarked, stressed and unstressed, encompassing and encompassed, and so on. This is perhaps one of the most important areas in which there is already a constructive base for a theory of culture. It should be stressed that these concepts rest on the premise that any symbol has many meanings, on the premise that symbols and meanings can be clustered into galaxies, and on the premise that galaxies seem to have core or epitomizing symbols as their foci.

Synchronic analysis, including the kinds of transformation(s) of cultural elements, of symbols and meanings, which are detailed in the Lévi-Straussian or Dumontian manner, shows the ways in which symbols and meanings are interrelated. As I have said earlier, diachronic analyses are also possible. Culture change (not social change, but cultural change) does not seem to take place by the instant total replacement of one system by another, but rather by precisely such shifts and transformations as Lévi-Strauss and Dumont have suggested. What is at one time encompassed becomes encompassing, what is at one time in a +/not-plus relationship shifts to a +/− relationship. Matriliny is embedded in patriliny as patriliny is embedded in matriliny, and each implies the other, as Lévi-Strauss has argued. What may appear over time as a radical sea change may, on closer examination, be just a shift from the implicit to the explicit. Norms become more important in the analysis of diachronic shifts because norms, unlike culture, are concerned with patterns for action and are thus directly tied to specific situations of action. Situational pressures for change on the one hand and pressures for maintenance of the *status quo* on the other are differently distributed between norms and culture. Norms must be responsive to situations of action in a way that culture need not be. Yet the situational changes with consequent changes in norms that can take place are clearly bounded, if not precisely defined, by the symbols and meanings of a particular situation of action. It is in this sense that culture has the regnant role I ascribed to it earlier in this paper. Culture therefore has a longevity, an inertia, a stability which, though not absolute, are greater than those of norms and the institutions into which norms cluster.

The last problem I want to consider is that of integration. If galaxies are ordered, so too is the total cultural universe, and the order of the cultural universe is simply another way of stating its integration—*not*, I must stress, as a functional mechanism but as a system of symbols and meanings. A culture is a total system; it does not have loose ends and unintegrated pieces and parts that do not articulate with other parts. It holds together as a meaningful system.

To say that culture is a meaningful system is not to say that if one looks at the total cultural system, one cannot say, "Aha! Over here it says that 'Love Is The Greatest' and over there, it says that 'Money Is In First Place And Whatever It Is That Is In Second Place Is Way Behind.'" It is obvious to anyone who has tried to analyze American culture that love and money are definitely related to each other. That actors can read the meaning of situations in more than one way derives from the fact that meanings are polysemic. And the ability that actors have to read meanings so as to create impasses in their own activity is hardly news to anyone who has lived through his own or his child's toilet training. But that is not to say that conflict is built into culture. Rather, it is a statement about conflict being the human condition because, at least in part, actors must always choose from a multiplicity of meanings.

If one looks at culture as a system of symbols and meanings, then culture is perfectly integrated in the special and narrow sense that these symbols and meanings articulate into a total system with a "culturalogic" of its own. It is only on the assumption that there are primary meanings or absolute meanings that it is necessary to regard culture as a conflict-ridden system. And it is only on the assumption that there is a one-to-one correlation between culture and action that conflict must be seen as a part and parcel of culture; obviously conflict is part and parcel of action.

But when the system of symbols and meanings is seen to be structured of contradictions and oppositions which are in turn mediated by articulating mechanisms, as coitus articulates both the natural and the lawful aspects of relatedness, then the idea of "culture conflict" is obviously a misnomer. It is a misnomer, as I have suggested, that derives from a definition of culture very different from the one I have used here, a definition that treats culture as indistinguishable from other aspects of action, that conceives of it as patterns for action instead of as the symbols and meanings out of which those patterns are constituted.

In conclusion, I want to reiterate one of the first and most fundamental points of this paper. It is natives' cultures we are studying, not our own theory. It is the natives' multiple conceptions, the natives' various views, the natives' definitions, the many native meanings that are at issue. That is the problem. How do the natives conceive of the world? How do they formulate the givens of this life, and life's meanings? What units do the natives define and how do *they* define them? What symbols and what meanings do they attach to these units? The fundamental methodological maneuver is to ask the natives—not once or even twice but in many different ways and therefore at many different times, with every possible eliciting device. Only when this has been done can we begin to say what the cultural symbols are and what they mean.

Every people has its explicit ideology, its own sort of social theory. This is an important datum and must not be brushed aside. But it is not the same as the analyst's theoretically constructed view of the native culture, nor should the analysis of culture be confused with the culture being analyzed. The native views must be derived by an outside observer or by an observer who places himself on the outside as best he can. Since parts of the native views are unconscious to the native, both in the sense that he is not aware of something and in the sense that he represses knowledge of something, the end product must necessarily be the observer's description of the native views. The fundamental error is in premature closure, the careful selection of material from arbitrarily or functionally circumscribed areas which do not accord with any native cultural units or any native definition of those units. Or to put it in more familiar terms, it is the imposition of an etic grid which is procrustean.

NOTES

1. I am particularly indebted to Steve Barnett, James Boon, Paul Friedrich, John Kirkpatrick, and Keith Basso for a close and careful reading of the last draft of this paper and for suggestions which have substantially improved it. My thanks are also due to John Kirkpatrick and David Kemnitzer for a close reading of the first draft, to conversations with Marshall Sahlins and Michael Silverstein for clarification of a number of points, and to the members of the Seminar for their discussion, which led to the serious rethinking of the first draft of this paper. For its faults, I alone must bear responsibility.

2. There may be important methodological problems depending on whether the cultural aspects are abstracted directly from observed behavior or from the normative system, but I will not go into that problem here.

9

"From the Native's Point of View": On the Nature of Anthropological Understanding

CLIFFORD GEERTZ
The Institute for Advanced Study

Several years ago a minor scandal erupted in anthropology: one of its ancestral figures told the truth in a public place. As befits an ancestor, he did it posthumously, and through his widow's decision rather than his own, with the result that a number of the sort of right-thinking types who are with us always immediately rose to cry that she, an in-marrier anyway, had betrayed clan secrets, profaned an idol, and let down the side. What will the children think, to say nothing of the layman? But the disturbance was not much lessened by such ceremonial wringing of the hands; the damn thing was, after all, already printed. In much the same fashion as James Watson's *The Double Helix* (1968) exposed the way in which biophysics in fact gets done, Bronislaw Malinowski's *A Diary in the Strict Sense of the Term* (1967) rendered established accounts of how anthropologists work fairly well

---

Reprinted by permission of the American Academy of Arts and Sciences, Boston, Massachusetts. Bulletin of the American Academy of Arts and Sciences, Vol. 28, No. 1, 1974.

implausible. The myth of the chameleon fieldworker, perfectly self-tuned to his exotic surroundings, a walking miracle of empathy, tact, patience, and cosmopolitanism, was demolished by the man who had perhaps done most to create it.

The squabble that arose around the publication of the *Diary* concentrated, naturally, on inessentials and missed, as was only to be expected, the point. Most of the shock seems to have arisen from the mere discovery that Malinowski was not, to put it delicately, an unmitigated nice guy. He had rude things to say about the natives he was living with, and rude words to say it in. He spent a great deal of his time wishing he were elsewhere. And he projected an image of a man about as little complaisant as the world has seen. (He also projected an image of a man consecrated to a strange vocation to the point of self-immolation, but that was less noted.) The discussion was made to come down to Malinowski's moral character or lack of it, and the genuinely profound question his book raised was ignored; namely, if it isn't, as we had been taught to believe, through some sort of extraordinary sensibility, an almost preternatural capacity to think, feel, and perceive like a native (a word, I should hurry to say, I use here "in the strict sense of the term"), how is anthropological knowledge of the way natives think, feel, and perceive possible? The issue the *Diary* presents, with a force perhaps only a working ethnographer can fully appreciate, is not moral. (The moral idealization of fieldworkers is a mere sentimentality in the first place, when it isn't self-congratulation or a guild pretense.) The issue is epistemological. If we are going to cling—as, in my opinion, we must—to the injunction to see things from the native's point of view, where are we when we can no longer claim some unique form of psychological closeness, a sort of transcultural identification, with our subjects? What happens to *verstehen* when *einfühlen* disappears?

As a matter of fact, this general problem has been exercising methodological discussion in anthropology for the last ten or fifteen years; Malinowski's voice from the grave merely dramatizes it as a human dilemma over and above a professional one. The formulations have been various: "inside" versus "outside," or "first person" versus "third person" descriptions; "phenomenological" versus "objectivist," or "cognitive" versus "behavioral" theories; or, perhaps most commonly "emic" versus "etic" analyses, this last deriving from the distinction in linguistics between phonemics and phonetics, phonemics classifying sounds according to their internal function in language, phonetics classifying them according to their acoustic properties as such. But perhaps the simplest and most directly appreciable way to put the matter is in terms of a distinction formulated, for his own purposes, by the psychoanalyst Heinz Kohut (1971), between what he calls "experience-near" and "experience-distant" concepts.

An experience-near concept is, roughly, one which someone—a patient, a subject, in our case an informant—might himself naturally and effortlessly use to define what he or his fellows see, feel, think, imagine, and so on, and which he would readily understand when similarly applied by others. An experience-distant concept is one which specialists of one sort or another—an analyst, an experimenter, an ethnographer, even a priest or an ideologist—employ to forward their scientific, philosophical, or practical aims. "Love" is an experience-near concept, "object cathexis" is an experience-distant one. "Social stratification," or perhaps for most peoples in the world even "religion" (and certainly "religious system"), are experience-distant; "caste" or "nirvana" are experience-near, at least for Hindus and Buddhists.

Clearly, the matter is one of degree, not polar opposition—"fear" is experience-nearer than "phobia," and "phobia" experience-nearer than "ego dyssyntonic." And the difference is not, at least so far as anthropology is concerned (the matter is otherwise in poetry and physics), a normative one, in the sense that one sort of concept is to be preferred as such over the other. Confinement to experience-near concepts leaves an ethnographer awash in immediacies, as well as entangled in vernacular. Confinement to experience-distant ones leaves him stranded in abstractions and smothered in jargon. The real question, and the one Malinowski raised by demonstrating that, in the case of "natives," you don't have to be one to know one, is what roles the two sorts of concepts play in anthropological analysis. Or, more exactly, how, in each case, ought one to deploy them so as to produce an interpretation of the way a people lives which is neither imprisoned within their mental horizons, an ethnography of witchcraft as written by a witch, nor systematically deaf to the distinctive tonalities of their existence, an ethnography of witchcraft as written by a geometer.

Putting the matter this way—in terms of how anthropological analysis is to be conducted and its results framed, rather than what psychic constitution anthropologists need to have—reduces the mystery of what

223

"seeing things from the native's point of view" means. But it does not make it any easier, nor does it lessen the demand for perceptiveness on the part of the fieldworker. To grasp concepts which, for another people, are experience-near, and to do so well enough to place them in illuminating connection with experience-distant concepts theorists have fashioned to capture the general features of social life, is clearly a task at least as delicate, if a bit less magical, as putting oneself into someone else's skin. The trick is not to get yourself into some inner correspondence of spirit with your informants. Preferring, like the rest of us, to call their souls their own, they are not going to be altogether keen about such an effort anyhow. The trick is to figure out what the devil they think they are up to.

In one sense, of course, no one knows this better than they do themselves; hence the passion to swim in the stream of their experience, and the illusion afterward that one somehow has. But in another sense, that simple truism is simply not true. People use experience-near concepts spontaneously, unselfconsciously, as it were colloquially; they do not, except fleetingly and on occasion, recognize that there are any "concepts" involved at all. That is what experience-near means—that ideas and the realities they inform are naturally and indissolubly bound up together. What else could you call a hippopotamus? Of course the gods are powerful, why else would we fear them? The ethnographer does not, and, in my opinion, largely cannot, perceive what his informants perceive. What he perceives, and that uncertainly enough, is what they perceive "with"—or "by means of," or "through" . . . or whatever the word should be. In the country of the blind, who are not as unobservant as they look, the one-eyed is not king, he is spectator.

Now, to make all this a bit more concrete, I want to turn for a moment to my own work, which, whatever its other faults, has at least the virtue of being mine—in discussions of this sort a distinct advantage. In all three of the societies I have studied intensively, Javanese, Balinese, and Moroccan, I have been concerned, among other things, with attempting to determine how the people who live there define themselves as persons, what goes into the idea they have (but, as I say, only half-realize they have) of what a self, Javanese, Balinese, or Moroccan style, is. And in each case, I have tried to get at this most intimate of notions not by imagining myself someone else, a rice peasant or a tribal sheikh, and then seeing what I thought, but by searching out and analyzing the symbolic forms—words, images, institutions, behaviors—in terms of which, in each place, people actually represented themselves to themselves and to one another.

The concept of person is, in fact, an excellent vehicle by means of which to examine this whole question of how to go about poking into another people's turn of mind. In the first place, some sort of concept of this kind, one feels reasonably safe in saying, exists in recognizable form among all social groups. The notions of what persons are may be, from our point of view, sometimes more than a little odd. They may be conceived to dart about nervously at night shaped like fireflies. Essential elements of their psyche, like hatred, may be thought to be lodged in granular black bodies within their livers, discoverable upon autopsy. They may share their fates with *doppelganger* beasts, so that when the beast sickens or dies they sicken or die too. But at least some conception of what a human individual is, as opposed to a rock, an animal, a rainstorm, or a god, is, so far as I can see, universal. Yet, at the same time, as these offhand examples suggest, the actual conceptions involved vary from one group to the next, and often quite sharply. The Western conception of the person as a bounded, unique, more or less integrated motivational and cognitive universe, a dynamic center of awareness, emotion, judgment, and action organized into a distinctive whole and set contrastively both against other such wholes and against its social and natural background, is, however incorrigible it may seem to us, a rather peculiar idea within the context of the world's cultures. Rather than attempting to place the experience of others within the framework of such a conception, which is what the extolled "empathy" in fact usually comes down to, understanding them demands setting that conception aside and seeing their experiences within the framework of their own idea of what selfhood is. And for Java, Bali, and Morocco, at least, that idea differs markedly not only from our own but, no less dramatically and no less instructively, from one to the other.

In Java, where I worked in the fifties, I studied a small, shabby inland county-seat sort of place; two shadeless streets of whitewashed wooden shops and offices, and even less substantial bamboo shacks crammed in helter-skelter behind them, the whole surrounded by a great half-circle of densely packed rice-bowl villages.[1] Land was short, jobs were scarce, politics was unstable, health was poor, prices were rising, and life was altogether far from promising, a kind of agitated stagnancy in which, as I once put it, thinking of the curious mixture of borrowed fragments of modernity and exhausted relics of tradition that characterized the place, the future seemed about as remote as the past. Yet in the midst of this depressing scene there was an absolutely astonishing intellectual vitality, a philosophical passion really, and a popular one besides, to track the riddles of existence right down to the ground. Destitute peasants would discuss questions of freedom of the will, illiterate tradesmen discoursed on the properties of God, common laborers had theories about the relations between reason and passion, the nature of time, or the reliability of the senses. And, perhaps most importantly, the problem of the self—its nature, function, and mode of operation—was pursued with the sort of reflective intensity one could find among ourselves in only the most recherché settings indeed.

The central ideas in terms of which this reflection proceeded, and which thus defined its boundaries and the Javanese sense of what a person is, were arranged into two sets of contrasts, at base religious, one between 'inside' and 'outside', and one between 'refined' and 'vulgar'.[2] These glosses are, of course, crude and imprecise; determining exactly what the terms involved signified, sorting out their shades of meaning, was what all the discussion was about. But together they formed a distinctive conception of the self which, far from being merely theoretical, was the one in terms of which Javanese in fact perceived one another and, of course, themselves.

The "inside"/"outside" words, *lair* and *batin* (terms borrowed, as a matter of fact, from the Sufi tradition of Muslim mysticism, but locally reworked) refer on the one hand to the felt realm of human experience and on the other to the observed realm of human behavior. These have, one hastens to say, nothing to do with "soul" and "body" in our sense, for which there are in fact quite other words with quite other implications. *Batin*, the "inside" word, does not refer to a separate seat of encapsulated spirituality detached or detachable from the body, or indeed to a bounded unit at all, but to the emotional life of human beings taken generally. It consists of the fuzzy, shifting flow of subjective feeling perceived directly in all its phenomenological immediacy but considered to be, at its roots at least, identical across all individuals, whose individuality it thus effaces. And similarly, *lair*, the "outside" word, has nothing to do with the body as an object, even an experienced object.

Rather, it refers to that part of human life which, in our culture, strict behaviorists limit themselves to studying—external actions, movements, postures, speech—again conceived as in its essence invariant from one individual to the next. These two sets of phenomena—inward feelings and outward actions—are then regarded not as functions of one another but as independent realms of being to be put in proper order independently.

It is in connection with this "proper ordering" that the contrast between *alus*, the word meaning "pure," "refined," "polished," "exquisite," "ethereal," "subtle," "civilized," "smooth," and *kasar*, the word meaning "impolite," "rough," "uncivilized," "coarse," "insensitive," "vulgar," comes into play. The goal is to be *alus* in both the separated realms of the self. In the inner realm this is to be achieved through religious discipline, much but not all of it mystical. In the outer realm, it is to be achieved through etiquette, the rules of which here are not only extraordinarily elaborate but have something of the force of law. Through meditation the civilized man thins out his emotional life to a kind of constant hum; through etiquette, he both shields that life from external disruptions and regularizes his outer behavior in such a way that it appears to others as a predictable, undisturbing, elegant, and rather vacant set of choreographed motions and settled forms of speech.

There is much more to all this, because it connects up to both an ontology and an aesthetic. But so far as our problem is concerned, the result is a bifurcate conception of the self, half ungestured feeling and half unfelt gesture. An inner world of stilled emotion and an outer world of shaped behavior confront one another as sharply distinguished realms unto themselves, any particular person being but the momentary locus, so to speak, of that confrontation, a passing expression of their permanent existence, their permanent separation, and their permanent need to be kept in their own order. Only when you have seen, as I have, a young man whose wife—a woman he had in fact raised from childhood and who had been the center of his life—has suddenly and inexplicably died, greeting everyone with a set smile and formal apologies for his wife's absence and trying, by mystical techniques, to flatten out, as he himself put it, the hills and valleys of his emotion into an even, level plain ("That is what you have to do," he said to me, "be smooth inside and out") can you come, in the face of our own notions of the intrinsic

227

honesty of deep feeling and the moral importance of personal sincerity, to take the possibility of such a conception of selfhood seriously and appreciate, however inaccessible it is to you, its own sort of force.

Bali, where I worked both in another small provincial town, though one rather less drifting and dispirited, and, later, in an upland village of highly skilled musical instruments makers, is of course in many ways similar to Java, with which it shared a common culture to the fifteenth century.[3] But at a deeper level, having continued Hindu while Java was, nominally at least, Islamized, it is quite different. The intricate, obsessive ritual life, Hindu, Buddhist, and Polynesian in about equal proportions, whose development was more or less cut off in Java, leaving its Indic spirit to turn reflective and phenomenological, even quietistic, in the way I have just described, flourished in Bali to reach levels of scale and flamboyance that have startled the world and made the Balinese a much more dramaturgical people with a self to match. What is philosophy in Java is theater in Bali.

As a result, there is in Bali a persistent and systematic attempt to stylize all aspects of personal expression to the point where anything idiosyncratic, anything characteristic of the individual merely because he is who he is physically, psychologically, or biographically, is muted in favor of his assigned place in the continuing and, so it is thought, never-changing pageant that is Balinese life. It is dramatis personae, not actors, that endure; indeed, it is dramatis personae, not actors, that in the proper sense really exist. Physically men come and go, mere incidents in a happenstance history, of no genuine importance even to themselves. But the masks they wear, the stage they occupy, the parts they play, and, most important, the spectacle they mount remain, and comprise not the facade but the substance of things, not least the self. Shakespeare's old-trouper view of the vanity of action in the face of mortality—all the world's a stage and we but poor players, content to strut our hour, and so on—makes no sense here. There is no make believe; of course players perish, but the play doesn't, and it is the latter, the performed rather than the performer, that really matters.

Again, all this is realized not in terms of some general mood the anthropologist in his spiritual versatility somehow captures, but through a set of readily observable symbolic forms: an elaborate repertoire of designations and titles.[4] The Balinese have at least a half-dozen major sorts of labels, ascriptive, fixed, and absolute, which one person can apply to another (or, of course, to himself) to place him among his fellows. There are birth-order markers, kinship terms, caste titles, sex indicators, teknonyms, and so on and so forth, each of which consists not of a mere collection of useful tags but a distinct and bounded, internally very complex, terminological system. When one applies one of these designations or titles (or, as is more common, several at once) to someone, one therefore defines him as a determinate point in a fixed pattern, as the temporary occupant of a particular, quite untemporary, cultural locus. To identify someone, yourself or somebody else, in Bali is thus to locate him within the familiar cast of characters—"king," "grandmother," "thirdborn," "Brahman"—of which the social drama is, like some stock company roadshow piece—*Charley's Aunt* or *Springtime for Henry*—inevitably composed.

The drama is of course not farce, and especially not transvestite farce, though there are such elements in it. It is an enactment of hierarchy, a theater of status. But that, though critical, is unpursuable here. The immediate point is that, in both their structure and their mode of operation, the terminological systems conduce to a view of the human person as an appropriate representative of a generic type, not a unique creature with a private fate. To see how they do this, how they tend to obscure the mere materialities—biological, psychological, historical—of individual existence in favor of standardized status qualities would involve an extended analysis. But perhaps a single example, the simplest further simplified, will suffice to suggest the pattern.

All Balinese receive what might be called birth-order names. There are four of these, "firstborn," "secondborn," "thirdborn," "fourthborn," after which they recycle, so that fifthborn child is called again "first-born," the sixth "secondborn," and so on. Further, these names are bestowed independently of the fates of the children. Dead children, even stillborn ones, count, so that in fact, in this still high-birthrate, high-mortality society, the names don't really tell you anything very reliable about the birth-order relations of concrete individuals. Within a set of living siblings, someone called "firstborn" may actually be first, fifth, or ninth born, or, if somebody is missing, almost anything in between, and someone called "secondborn" may in fact be older. The birth-order naming system does not identify individuals as individuals, nor is it intended to; what it does is to suggest that, for all procreating couples, births form a circular succession of "firsts," "seconds," "thirds," and "fourths," an endless four-stage replication of an imperishable form. Physically men appear and disappear as the ephemerae they are, but socially the acting figures remain eternally the same as new "firsts," "seconds," and so on emerge from the timeless world of the gods to replace those who, dying, dissolve once more into it. All the designation and title systems, so I would argue, function in the same way: they represent the most time-saturated aspects of the human condition as but ingredients in an eternal, footlight present.

Nor is this sense the Balinese have of always being on stage a vague and ineffable one either. It is, in fact, exactly summed up in what is surely one of their experience-nearest concepts: *lek*. Lek has been variously translated or mistranslated ('shame' is the most common attempt); but what it really means is close to what we call stage fright. Stage fright consists, of course, in the fear that, for want of skill or self-control, or perhaps by mere accident, an aesthetic illusion will not be maintained, that the actor will show through his part. Aesthetic distance collapses, the audience (and the actor) lose sight of Hamlet and gain it, uncomfortable for all concerned, of bumbling John Smith painfully miscast as the Prince of Denmark. In Bali, the case is the same: what is feared is that the public performance to which one's cultural location commits one will be botched and that the personality— as we would call it but the Balinese, of course, not believing in such a thing, would not—of the individual will break through to dissolve his standardized public identity. When this occurs, as it sometimes does, the immediacy of the moment is felt with excruciating intensity and men become suddenly and unwillingly creatural, locked in mutual embarrassment, as though they had happened upon each other's nakedness. It is the fear of faux pas, rendered only that much more probable by the extraordinary ritualization of daily life, that keeps social intercourse on its deliberately narrowed rails and protects the dramatistical sense of self against the disruptive threat implicit in the immediacy and spontaneity even the most passionate ceremoniousness cannot fully eradicate from face-to-face encounters.

Morocco, Middle Eastern and dry rather than East Asian and wet, extrovert, fluid, activist, masculine, informal to a fault, a Wild West sort of place without the barrooms and the cattle drives, is another kettle of selves altogether.[5] My work there, which began in the mid sixties, has been centered around a moderately large town or small city in the foothills of the Middle Atlas, about twenty miles south of Fez. It's an old place, probably founded in the tenth century, conceivably even earlier. It has the walls, the gates, the narrow minarets rising to prayer-call platforms of a classical Muslim town, and, from a distance anyway, it is a rather pretty place, an irregular oval of blinding white set in the deep-sea-green of an olive grove oasis, the mountains, bronze and stony here, slanting up immediately behind it. Close up, it is less prepossessing, though more exciting: a labyrinth of passages and alleyways, three-quarters of them blind, pressed in by wall-like buildings and curbside shops and filled with a simply astounding variety of very emphatic human beings. Arabs, Berbers, and Jews; tailors, herdsmen, and soldiers; people out of offices, people out of markets, people out of tribes; rich, superrich, poor, superpoor; locals, immigrants, mimic Frenchmen, unbending medievalists, and somewhere, according to the official government census for 1960, an unemployed Jewish airplane pilot—the town houses one of the finest collections of rugged individuals I, at least, have ever come up against. Next to Sefrou (the name of the place), Manhattan seems almost monotonous.

Yet no society consists of anonymous eccentrics bouncing off one another like billiard balls, and Moroccans, too, have symbolic means by which to sort people out from one another and form an idea of what it is to be a person. The main such means—not the only one, but I think the most important and the one I want to talk about particularly here—is a peculiar linguistic form called in Arabic the *nisba*. The word derives from the triliteral root, *n-s-b*, for "ascription," "attribution," "imputation," "relationship," "affinity," "correlation," "connection," "kinship." *Nsīb* means "in-law"; *nsab* means "to attribute or impute to"; *munāsaba* means "a relation," "an analogy," "a correspondence"; *mansūb* means "belonging to," "pertaining to"; and so on to at least a dozen derivatives, from *nassāb* ("genealogist") to *nīsbīya*, ("[physical] relativity").

Nisba itself, then, refers to a combination morphological, grammatical, and semantic process which consists in transforming a noun into what we would call a relative adjective but what for Arabs is just another sort of noun by adding *ī* (f., *īya*): Ṣefrū/Sefrou—Ṣefrūwī/native son of Sefrou; Sūs/region of southwestern Morocco—Sūsī/ man coming

231

from that region; *Beni Yazḡa*/a tribe near Sefrou—*Yazḡī*/a member of that tribe; *Yahūd*/the Jews as a people, Jewry—*Yahūdī*/a Jew; 'Adlun/ surname of a prominent Sefrou family—'*Adlūnī*/a member of that family. Nor is the procedure confined to this more or less straightforward "ethnicizing" use, but is employed in a wide range of domains to attribute relational properties to persons. For example, occupation (*hrār*/silk—*hrārī*/silk merchant); religious sect (*Darqāwā*/a mystical brotherhood—*Darqāwī*/an adept of that brotherhood or spiritual status) (Ali/The Prophet's son-in-law—'*Alawī*/descendant of the Prophet's son-in-law, and thus of The Prophet).

Now, as once formed, nisbas tend to be incorporated into personal names—Umar Al-Buhadiwi/Umar of the Buhadu Tribe; Muhammed Al-Sussi/Muhammed from the Sus Region—this sort of adjectival attributive classification is quite publicly stamped onto an individual's identity. I was unable to find a single case where an individual was generally known, or known about, but his or her nisba was not. Indeed, Sefrouis are far more likely to be ignorant of how well-off a man is, how long he has been around, what his personal character is, or where exactly he lives, than they are of what his nisba is—Sussi or Sefroui, Bhuadiwi or Adluni, Harari or Darqawi. (Of women to whom he is not related that is very likely to be all that he knows—or, more exactly, is permitted to know.) The selves that bump and jostle each other in the alleys of Sefrou gain their definition from associative relations they are imputed to have with the society that surrounds them. They are contextualized persons.

But the situation is even more radical than this; nisbas render men relative to their contexts, but as contexts themselves are relative, so too are nisbas, and the whole thing rises, so to speak, to the second power: relativism squared. Thus, at one level, everyone in Sefrou has the same nisba, or at least the potential of it—namely, Sefroui. However, within Sefrou such a nisba, precisely because it does not discriminate, will never be heard as part of an individual designation. It is only outside of Sefrou that the relationship to that particular context becomes identifying. Inside it, he is an Adluni, Alawi, Meghrawi, Ngadi, or whatever. And similarly within these categories: there are, for example, twelve different nisbas (Shakibis, Zuinis, etc.) by means of which, among themselves, Sefrou Alawis distinguish one another.

The whole matter is far from regular: what level or sort of nisba is used and seems relevant and appropriate (to the users, that is) depends heavily on the situation. A man I knew who lived in Sefrou and worked in Fez but came from the Beni Yazgha tribe settled nearby—and from the Hima lineage of the Taghut subfraction of the Wulad Ben Ydir fraction within it—was known as a Sefroui to his work fellows in Fez, a Yazghi to all of us non-Yazghis in Sefrou, an Ydiri to other Beni Yazghas around, except for those who were themselves of the Wulad Ben Ydir fraction, who called him a Taghuti. As for the few other Taghutis, they called him a Himiwi. That's as far as things went here, but not as far as they can go, in either direction. Should, by chance, our friend journey to Egypt, he would become a Maghrebi, the nisba formed from the Arabic word for North Africa. The social contextualization of persons is pervasive and, in its curiously unmethodical way, systematic. Men do not float as bounded psychic entities, detached from their backgrounds and singularly named. As individualistic, even willful, as the Moroccans in fact are, their identity is an attribute they borrow from their setting.

Now as with the Javanese inside/outside, smooth/rough phenomenological sort of reality dividing, and the absolutizing Balinese title systems, the nisba way of looking at persons—as though they were outlines waiting to be filled in—is not an isolated custom, but part of a total pattern of social life. This pattern is, like the others, difficult to characterize succinctly, but surely one of its outstanding features is a promiscuous tumbling in public settings of varieties of men kept carefully segregated in private ones—all-out cosmopolitanism in the streets, strict communalism (of which the famous secluded woman is only the most striking index) in the home. This is indeed, the so-called mosaic system of social organization so often held to be characteristic of the Middle East generally: differently shaped and colored chips jammed in irregularly together to generate an intricate overall design within which their individual distinctiveness remains nonetheless intact. Nothing if not diverse, Moroccan society does not cope with its diversity by sealing it into castes, isolating it into tribes, dividing it into ethnic groups, or covering it over with some common-denominator concept of nationality, though, fitfully, all have now and then been tried. It copes with it by distinguishing, with elaborate precision, the contexts—marriage, worship, and to an extent diet, law, and education—within which men are separated by their dissimilitudes, and those—work, friendship, politics, trade—where, however warily and however conditionally, they are connected by them.

To such a social pattern, a concept of selfhood which marks public identity contextually and relativistically, but yet does so in terms— tribal, territorial, linguistic, religious, familial—which grow out of the more private and settled arenas of life and have a deep and permanent resonance there, would seem particularly appropriate. Indeed, the social pattern would seem virtually to create this concept of selfhood, for it produces a situation where people interact with one another in terms of categories whose meaning is almost purely positional, location in the general mosaic, leaving the substantive content of the categories, what they mean subjectively as experienced forms of life, aside as something properly concealed in apartments, temples, and tents. Nisba discriminations can be more specific or less, indicate location within the mosaic roughly or finely, and they can be adapted to almost any changes in circumstance. But they cannot carry with them more than the most sketchy, outline implications concerning what men so named as a rule are like. Calling a man a Sefroui is like calling him a San Franciscan: it classifies him, but it doesn't type him; it places him without portraying him.

It is the nisba system's capacity to do this—to create a framework within which persons can be identified in terms of supposedly immanent characteristics (speech, blood, faith, provenance, and the rest)—and yet to minimize the impact of those characteristics in determining the practical relations among such persons in markets, shops, bureaus, fields, cafés, baths, and roadways that makes it so central to the Moroccan idea of the self. Nisba-type categorization leads, paradoxically, to a hyperindividualism in public relationships, because by providing only a vacant sketch, and that shifting, of who the actors are—Yazghis, Adlunis, Buhadiwis, or whatever—it leaves the rest, that is, almost everything, to be filled in by the process of interaction itself. What makes the mosaic work is the confidence that one can be as totally pragmatic, adaptive, opportunistic, and generally *ad hoc* in one's relations with others—a fox among foxes, a crocodile among crocodiles—as one wants without any risk of losing one's sense of who one is. Selfhood is never in danger because, outside the immediacies of procreation and prayer, only its coordinates are asserted.

Now, without trying to tie up the dozens of loose ends I have not only left dangling in these rather breathless accounts of the senses of selfhood of nearly ninety million people but have doubtless frazzled even more, let us return to the question of what all this can tell us, or could if it were done adequately, about "the native point of view" in Java, Bali, and Morocco. Are we, in describing symbol uses, describing perceptions, sentiments, outlooks, experiences? And in what sense? What do we claim when we claim that we understand the semiotic means by which, in this case, persons are defined to one another? That we know words or that we know minds?

In answering this question, it is necessary, I think, first to notice the characteristic intellectual movement, the inward conceptual rhythm, in each of these analyses, and indeed in all similar analyses, including those of Malinowski—namely, a continuous dialectical tacking between the most local of local detail and the most global of global structure in such a way as to bring them into simultaneous view. In seeking to uncover the Javanese, Balinese, or Moroccan sense of self, one oscillates restlessly between the sort of exotic minutiae (lexical antitheses, categorical schemes, morphophonemic transformations) that make even the best ethnographies a trial to read and the sort of sweeping characterizations ("quietism," "dramatism," "contextualism") that make all but the most pedestrian of them somewhat implausible. Hopping back and forth between the whole conceived through the parts that actualize it and the parts conceived through the whole that motivates them, we seek to turn them, by a sort of intellectual perpetual motion, into explications of one another.

All this is, of course, but the now familiar trajectory of what Dilthey called the hermeneutic circle, and my argument here is merely that it is as central to ethnographic interpretation, and thus to the penetration of other people's modes of thought, as it is to literary, historical, philological, psychoanalytic, biblical, or for that matter to the informal annotation of everyday experience we call common sense. In order to follow a baseball game one must understand what a bat, a hit, an inning, a left fielder, a squeeze play, a hanging curve, or a tightened infield are, and what the game in which these "things" are elements is all about. When an *explication de texte* critic like Leo Spitzer (1962) attempts to interpret Keats's "Ode on a Grecian Urn," he does so by repetitively asking himself the alternating question "What is the whole poem about?" and "What exactly has Keats seen (or chosen to show us) depicted on the urn he is describing?," emerging at the end of an advancing spiral of general observations and specific remarks with a reading of the poem as an assertion of the triumph of the aesthetic mode of perception over the historical. In the same way, when a meanings-and-symbols ethnographer like myself attempts to find out what some pack of natives conceive a person to be, he moves back and forth between asking himself, "What is the general form of their life?," and "What exactly are the vehicles in which that form is embodied?," emerging in the end of a similar sort of spiral with the notion that they see the self as a composite, a persona, or a point in a pattern. You can no more know what *lek* is if you don't know what Balinese dramatism is than you can know what a catcher's mitt is if you don't know what baseball is. And you can no more know what mosaic social organization is if you don't know what a nisba is than you can know what Keats's Platonism is if you are unable to grasp, to use Spitzer's own formulation, the "intellectual thread of thought" captured in such fragment phrases as "Attic shape," "silent form," "bride of quietness," "cold pastoral," "silence and slow time," "peaceful citadel," or "ditties of no tone."

In short, accounts of other peoples' subjectivities can be built up without recourse to pretensions to more-than-normal capacities for ego effacement and fellow feeling. Normal capacities in these respects are, of course, essential, as is their cultivation, if we expect people to tolerate our intrusions into their life at all and accept us as persons worth talking to. I am certainly not arguing for insensitivity here, and hope I have not demonstrated it. But whatever accurate or half-accurate sense one gets of what one's informants are, as the phrase goes, really like does not come from the experience of that acceptance as such, which is part of one's own biography, not of theirs. It comes from the ability to construe their modes of expression, what I would call their symbol systems, that such an acceptance allows one to work toward developing. Understanding the form and pressure of, to use the dangerous word one more time, natives' inner lives is more like grasping a proverb, catching an illusion, seeing a joke—or, as I have suggested, reading a poem—than it is like achieving communion.

NOTES

1. For a full description of the town, see Geertz (1965).
2. For a fuller discussion of these concepts, see Geertz (1960).
3. For the town, see Geertz (1963); for the village, Geertz (1966).
4. For these see Geertz (1973). A few sentences in following paragraphs have been taken verbatim from that essay.
5. The Moroccan work is in process of completion. For a general characterization of the country, see Geertz (1968).

References

AGAR, MICHAEL
1973   *Ripping and Running: A Formal Ethnography of Urban Heroin Addicts* (New York: Academic Press).

AKSU, AYHAN
1973   "The Development of Request Forms in Turkish Children," term paper for Rhetoric 260, University of California, Berkeley.

ALSTON, WILLIAM P.
1964   *Philosophy of Language* (Englewood Cliffs, N.J.: Prentice-Hall).

ARGYLE, MICHAEL AND R. INGHAM
1972   "Gaze, Mutual Gaze, and Proximity," *Semiotica* 6:32–49.

ATKINS, JOHN AND L. CURTIS
1969   "Games Rules and Rules of Culture," in *Game Theory in the Behavioral Sciences*, ed. Ira R. Buchler and Hugo G. Nutini (Pittsburgh: University of Pittsburgh Press), pp. 213–34.

BASSO, KEITH H.
1967   "Semantic Aspects of Linguistic Acculturation," *American Anthropologist* 69: 471–77.

BENVENISTE, EMILE
1966a "Structure des relations de personne dans le verbe," in *Problèmes de linguistique générale* (Paris: Librairie Gallimard), pp. 225–36.
1966b "Les relations de temps dans le verbe français," in *Problèmes de linguistique générale* (Paris: Librairie Gallimard), pp. 237–50.

BEVER, THOMAS G. AND PETER S. ROSENBAUM
1971   "Some Lexical Structures and Their Empirical Validity," in *Semantics*, ed. Danny D. Steinberg and Leon Jakobovits (Cambridge: Cambridge University Press), pp. 586–99.

BLACK, MAX
1962   *Models and Metaphors* (Ithaca, N.Y.: Cornell University Press).

BLOM, JAN-PETTER AND JOHN J. GUMPERZ
1971   "Social Meaning in Linguistic Structure: Code-Switching in Norway," in *Language in Social Groups: Essays by John J. Gumperz*, ed. Anwar S. Dil (Stanford, Calif.: Stanford University Press), pp. 274–310.

239

BLOOMFIELD, LEONARD
1933   *Language* (New York: Henry Holt & Co.)

BODINE, ANN
1974   "Further Investigations of English Third Person Singular Pronouns," paper presented at the Seventy-Third Annual Meeting of the American Anthropological Asssociation, Mexico City.

BREAL, MICHEL
1964   *Semantics: Studies in the Science of Meaning* (New York: Dover Publications). (First published in 1900 by Henry Holt & Co.)

BROWN, ROGER
1958   *Words and Things* (Glencoe, Ill.: Free Press).
1965   *Social Psychology* (Glencoe, Ill.: Free Press).

BROWN, ROGER AND ALBERT GILMAN
1960   "The Pronouns of Power and Solidarity," in *Style in Language*, ed. Thomas A. Sebeok (Cambridge, Mass.: M.I.T. Press), pp. 253–76.

CARNAP, RUDOLF
1955   *Philosophy and Logical Syntax* (London: Routledge and Kegan Paul).
1958   *Symbolic Logic* (New York: Dover Publications).

CASAGRANDE, JOSEPH B. AND KENNETH H. HALE
1967   "Semantic Relations in Papago Folk-Definitions," in *Studies in Southwestern Ethnolinguistics*, ed. Dell H. Hymes and William E. Bittle (The Hague: Mouton and Co.), pp. 165–96.

CHAFE, WALLACE L.
1970   *Meaning and the Structure of Language* (Chicago: University of Chicago Press).

CHOMSKY, NOAM
1965   *Aspects of the Theory of Syntax* (Cambridge, Mass.: M.I.T. Press).

COOKE, J. R.
1970   *The Pronominal Systems of Thai, Burmese and Vietnamese*, University of California Publications in Linguistics, no. 52 (Berkeley and Los Angeles: University of California Press).

D'ANDRADE, ROY G., NAOMI R. QUINN, SARA BETH NERLOVE, AND A. KIMBALL ROMNEY
1972   "Categories of Disease in American-English and Mexican-Spanish," in *Multidimensional Scaling*, ed. A. Kimball Romney, Roger N. Shapard, and Sara Beth Nerlove (New York: Seminar Press), 2:9–54.

DAY, DAVID
1968   "Address Terms in a Classroom," paper for Rhetoric 152, University of California, Berkeley.

DIXON, R. M. W.
1971   "A Method of Semantic Description," in *Semantics*, ed. Danny D. Steinberg and Leon A. Jakobovits (Cambridge: Cambridge University Press), pp. 436–71.
1972   *The Dyirbal Language of North Queensland*, Cambridge Studies in Linguistics, no. 9 (Cambridge: Cambridge University Press).

DUMONT, LOUIS
1970   *Homo Hierarchicus* (Chicago: University of Chicago Press).

References

EL GUINDI, FADWA
1972 "The Nature of Belief Systems," Ph.D. diss., University of Texas, Austin.
1973 "The Internal Structure of the Zapotec Conceptual Stem," *Journal of Symbolic Anthropology* 1:15–34.
1974 "Structure and Natives' Knowledge of Culture," paper presented at the Seventy-Third Annual Meeting of the American Anthropological Association, Mexico City.

ERVIN, SUSAN
1962 "The Connotations of Gender," *Word* 18:249–61.

ERVIN-TRIPP, SUSAN
1971 "Sociolinguistics," in *Advances in the Sociology of Language*, ed. J. Fishman (The Hague: Mouton and Co.), 1:15–91.
1973 *Language Acquisition and Communicative Choice* (Stanford, Calif.: Stanford University Press).

FERNANDEZ, JAMES W.
1972 "Persuasions and Performances: Of the Beast in Every Body . . . and the Metaphors in Every Man," *Daedalus* 101(1):39–60.
1974 "The Mission of Metaphor in Expressive Culture," *Current Anthropology* 15(2):119–46.

FLAVELL, J. H. AND D. J. STEDMAN.
1961 "A Developmental Study of Judgments of Semantic Similarity," *Journal of Genetic Psychology* 98:279–93.

FORTES, MEYER
1969 *Kinship and the Social Order* (Chicago: Aldine Publishing Co.).

FRAKE, CHARLES O.
1962 "The Ethnographic Study of Cognitive Systems," in *Anthropology and Human Behavior*, ed. Thomas A. Gladwin and William C. Sturteveant (Washington, D.C.: Anthropological Society of Washington), pp. 72–85.
1964 "Notes on Queries in Ethnography," *American Anthropologist* 66:132–45.

FRIEDRICH, PAUL
1966 "Structural Implication of Russian Pronominal Usage," in *Sociolinguistics*, ed. William Bright (The Hague: Mouton and Co.), pp. 214–59.
1972 "Social Context and Semantic Feature: The Russian Pronominal Usage," in *Directions in Sociolinguistics*, ed. John J. Gumperz and Dell Hymes (New York: Holt, Rinehart and Winston), pp. 270–300.

GARDNER, CAROL
1968 "A Scale of Politeness of Request Forms in English," term paper for Speech 164a, University of California, Berkeley.

GEERTZ, CLIFFORD
1960 *The Religion of Java* (Glencoe, Ill.: Free Press).
1963 *Peddlers and Princes* (Chicago: University of Chicago Press).
1964 "Ideology as a Cultural System," in *Ideology and Discontent*, ed. David E. Apter (Glencoe, Ill.: Free Press), pp. 47–76.
1965 *The Social History of an Indonesian Town* (Cambridge, Mass.: M.I.T. Press).
1966 "Tihingan: A Balinese Village," in *Village Communities in Indonesia*, ed. Koentjarahingrat (Ithaca, N.Y.: Cornell University Press).
1968 *Islam Observed* (New Haven, Conn.: Yale University Press).
1972 "Deep Play: Notes on the Balinese Cockfight," *Daedalus* 101:1–37.

1973 "Person, Time and Conduct in Bali," in *The Interpretation of Cultures* (New York: Basic Books).

GEOGHEGAN, WILLIAM
1973 *Natural Information Processing Rules: Formal Theory and Application to Ethnography*, Language Behavior Research Laboratory Monograph 3 (Berkeley: University of California).

GOODENOUGH, WARD
1965 "Yankee Kinship Terminology: A Problem in Componential Analysis," *American Anthropologist* 67(5,2):259–87.
1970 *Description and Comparison in Cultural Anthropology* (Chicago: Aldine Publishing Co.).

GORDON, DAVID AND GEORGE LAKOFF
1971 "Conversational Postulates," in *Papers from the Seventh Regional Meeting of the Chicago Linguistic Society*, pp. 63–84.

GREENBERG, JOSEPH
1966 "Language Universals," in *Current Trends in Linguistics*, ed. Thomas A. Sebeok, vol. 3, *Theoretical Foundations* (The Hague: Mouton and Co.), pp. 61–113.

GUMPERZ, JOHN J.
in press "The Semantics of Code-Switching in Conversation," in *Social Action in Conversational Practice*, ed. John J. Gumperz and Jenny Cook Gumperz (New York: Academic Press).

GUMPERZ, JOHN J. AND ELEANOR HERASIMCHUK
1972 "The Conversational Analysis of Social Meaning: A Study of Classroom Interaction," in *Sociolinguistics: Current Trends and Prospects*, Georgetown Monograph Series on Language and Linguistics, no. 25. (Washington, D.C.), pp. 99–134.

GUMPERZ, JOHN J. AND EDUARDO HERNANDEZ-CHAVEZ
1971 "Bilingualism, Bidialectalism, and Classroom Interaction," in *Language in Social Groups: Essays by John J. Gumperz*, ed. Anwar S. Dil (Stanford, Calif.: Stanford University Press), pp. 311–39.

HAAS, MARY R.
1944 "Men's and Women's Speech in Koasati," *Language* 20:142–49.

HALE, KENNETH
1971 "A Note on a Walbiri Tradition of Antonymy," in *Semantics*, ed. Danny D. Steinberg and Leon A. Jakobovits (Cambridge: Cambridge University Press), pp. 472–82.

HALLIDAY, MICHAEL A. K.
1975 "Learning How to Mean," in *Foundations of Language Development: A Multidisciplinary Approach*, ed. Eric and Elizabeth Lenneberg (New York: UNESCO).

HATCH, EVELYN
1973 "Studies in Language Switching and Mixing," paper presented at the Ninth International Congress of Anthropological and Ethnological Sciences, Chicago.

HAUGEN, EINAR
1953 *The Norwegian Language in America* (Philadelphia: University of Pennsylvania Press).

242

References

HENLE, PAUL (editor)
1962 *Language, Thought and Culture* (Ann Arbor: University of Michigan Press).

HENLEY, NANCY M.
1973 "Status and Sex: Some Touching Observations," *Bulletin of the Psychonomic Society* 2:91–93.

HORNE, ELINOR C.
1967 *Beginning Javanese* (New Haven, Conn.: Yale University Press).
1973 *Javanese Dictionary* (New Haven, Conn.: Yale University Press).

HOUSH, JACQUELYN
1972 "When Is an Imperative an Imperative: A Study of Requests Made by Teachers in Preschool Classrooms," term paper for Linguistics 120, University of California, Berkeley.

HOWELL, RICHARD W.
1967 "Linguistic Choice as an Index to Social Change," Ph.D. diss., University of California, Berkeley.

HYMES, DELL
1964 "Introduction: Toward Ethnographies of Communication," *The Ethnography of Communication, American Anthropologist* 66(6:2):1–34.
1967 "Models of the Interaction of Language and Social Setting," *Social Forces* 23(2):8–28.
1971 "Sociolinguistics and the Ethnography of Speaking," in *Social Anthropology and Language*, ed. Edwin Ardener (London: Tavistock Publications), pp. 47–93.
1972 "Models of the Interaction of Language and Social Life," in *Directions in Sociolinguistics*, ed. John J. Gumperz and Dell Hymes (New York: Holt, Rinehart and Winston), pp. 35–71.
1973 "Toward Linguistic Competence," *Texas Working Papers in Sociolinguistics* 16.

JAKOBSON, ROMAN
1957 *Shifters, Verbal Categories, and the Russian Verb* (Cambridge, Mass.: Harvard University Russian Language Project).
1959 "On Linguistic Aspects of Translation," in *On Translation*, ed. Reuben A. Brower (Oxford: Oxford University Press).
1971 "Results of a Joint Conference of Anthropologists and Linguists," in *Selected Writings by Roman Jakobson* (The Hague: Mouton and Co.), 2:554–68.

JOHNSON, S.
1967 "Hierarchical Clustering Schemes," *Psychometrika* 32:241–53.

KATZ, JERROLD
1972 *Semantic Theory* (New York: Harper and Row, Publishers).

KATZ, JERROLD AND JERRY A. FODOR
1963 "The Structure of a Semantic Theory," *Language* 39:170–210.

KOHUT, HEINZ
1971 *Analysis of Self: A Systematic Approach to the Psychoanalytic Treatment of Narcissistic Personality Disorders* (New York: International Universities Press).

KROEBER, ALFRED L. AND CLYDE KLUCKHOHN
1952 *Culture: A Critical Review of Concepts and Definitions*, Papers of the Peabody Museum of Harvard University, vol. 47, no. 1.

KRUSKAL, J. B.
1964 "Multidimensional Scaling by Optimizing Goodness of Fit to a Non-Metric Hypothesis," *Psychometrika* 29:1–27, 115–219.

LAKOFF, GEORGE
1971 "Presupposition and Relative Well-formedness," in *Semantics*, ed. Danny D. Steinberg and Leon A. Jakobovits (Cambridge: Cambridge University Press), pp. 329–44.
1972 "Hedges: A Study in Meaning Criteria and the Logic of Fuzzy Concepts," in *Papers from the Eighth Regional Meeting of the Chicago Linguistic Society*, pp. 183–228.

LAKOFF, ROBIN
1972 "Language in Context," *Language* 48:907–27.

LAWSON, CRAIG
1967 "Request Patterns in a Two Year Old," term paper for Speech 164a, University of California, Berkeley.

LEECH, GEOFFREY N.
1970 *Towards a Semantic Description of English* (Bloomington: Indiana University Press).

LEVI-STRAUSS, CLAUDE
1963 *Totemism* (Boston: Beacon Press).
1966 *The Savage Mind* (Chicago: University of Chicago Press).

LOUNSBURY, FLOYD G.
1956 "A Semantic Analysis of Pawnee Kinship Usage," *Language* 32:158–94.

LOWIE, ROBERT
1917 *Culture and Ethnology* (New York).

MALINOWSKI, BRONISLAW
1930 "Kinship," *Man* 30:19–29.
1967 *A Diary in the Strict Sense of the Term* (New York: Harcourt, Brace & World).

MARKEL, NORMAN N., L. D. PREBOR, AND J. F. BRANDT
1972 "Bio-Social Factors in Dyadic Communication: Sex and Speaking Intensity," *Journal of Personality and Social Psychology* 23:11–13.

MEHRABIAN, ALBERT AND J. T. FRIAR
1969 "Encoding of Attitude by a Seated Communicator via Posture and Position Cues," *Journal of Consulting Clinical Psychology* 33:330–36.

METZGER, DUANE AND G. WILLIAMS
1963 "Tenejapa Medicine 1: The Curer," *Southwestern Journal of Anthropology* 19:216–34.
1966 "Procedures and Results in the Study of Native Cognitive Systems: Tzeltal Firewood," *American Anthropologist* 68:398–407.

MILLER, G. A., E. GALANTER, AND R. PRIBRAM
1960 *Plans and the Structure of Behavior* (New York: Holt, Rinehart and Winston).

MORRIS, CHARLES
1964 *Signification and Significance* (Cambridge, Mass.: M.I.T. Press).

NEEDHAM, RODNEY
1972 *Belief, Language, and Experience* (Chicago: University of Chicago Press).

References

NEWMAN, STANLEY
1944 *Yokuts Language of California,* Viking Fund Publications in Anthropology, vol. 2 (New York: Wenner-Gren Foundation).

O'GRADY, GEOFFREY N.
1964 *Nyangumata Grammar,* Oceanic Linguistic Monographs, no. 9 (Sydney: University of Sydney).

PEIRCE, CHARLES S.
1932 *Collected Papers of C. S. Peirce,* ed. Charles Hartshorne and Paul Weiss, vol. 2 (Cambridge, Mass.: Harvard University Press).

PERCY, WALKER
1958 "Metaphor as Mistake," *Sewanee Review* 66:79–99.

POST, EMILY
1922 *Etiquette* (New York: Funk and Wagnalls).

READ, HERBERT
1952 *English Prose Style* (London: G. Bell and Sons).

REDDY, MICHAEL J.
1969 "A Semantic Approach to Metaphor," in *Papers of the Fifth Regional Meeting of the Chicago Linguistic Society,* pp. 240–51.

RICHARDS, I. A.
1938 *Interpretation in Teaching* (London: Routledge and Kegan Paul).
1948 *The Philosophy of Rhetoric* (Oxford: Oxford University Press).

RICOEUR, PAUL
1963 "Structure et hermeneutique," *Esprit* 31:596–627.

ROGERS, ELAINE
1967a "Work- versus Person-Oriented Requests," paper for Speech 164a, University of California, Berkeley.
1967b "Formality of Request and Forms of Address," paper for Speech 164a, University of California, Berkeley.

SAPIR, EDWARD
1929 "Male and Female Forms of Speech in Yana," in *Donum Natalicium Schrijnen,* ed. St. W. J. Teeuwen (Nijmegen-Utrecht: Dekker and Van de Vegt), pp. 79–85.

SCHEFFLER, HAROLD W.
1972 "Kinship Semantics," in *Annual Review of Anthropology,* ed. Bernard J. Siegel (Palo Alto, Calif.: Annual Reviews), 1:309–28.

SCHEFFLER, HAROLD W. AND FLOYD G. LOUNSBURY
1971 *A Study in Structural Semantics: The Siriono Kinship System* (Englewood Cliffs, N.J.: Prentice-Hall).

SCHNEIDER, DAVID M.
1953 "Yap Kinship Terminology and Kin Groups," *American Anthropologist* 55:215–36.
1965 "American Kin Terms and Terms for Kinsmen: A Critique of Goodenough's Componential Analysis of Yankee Kinship Terminology," *Formal Semantic Analysis, American Anthropologist* 67(5:2):288–308.
1968 *American Kinship: A Cultural Account* (Englewood Cliffs, N.J.: Prentice-Hall).

1969a "Kinship, Nationality and Religion in American Culture: Toward a Definition of Kinship," in *Forms of Symbolic Action, Proceedings of the 1969 Annual Spring Meeting of the American Ethnological Society*, pp. 116–25.

1969b "Componential Analysis: A State-of-the-Art Review," paper presented at the Wenner-Gren Symposium on Cognitive Studies and Artificial Intelligence Research, University of Chicago Center for Continuing Education, Chicago.

1970a "What Should Be Included in a Vocabulary of Kinship Terms?," *Proceedings of the Eighth International Congress of Anthropological and Ethnological Sciences*, 2:88–90.

1970b "American Kin Categories," in *Echanges et communications*, ed. J. Pouillon and P. Maranda (The Hague: Mouton and Co.), pp. 370–81.

1972 "What is Kinship All About?" in *Kinship Studies in the Morgan Centennial Year*, ed. Priscilla Reining (Washington, D.C.: Anthropological Society of Washington), pp. 32–63.

SCHNEIDER, DAVID M. AND RAYMOND T. SMITH
1973 *Class Differences and Sex Roles in American Kinship and Family Structure* (Englewood Cliffs, N.J.: Prentice-Hall).

SEARLE, JOHN R.
1969 *Speeech Acts: An Essay in the Philosophy of Language* (Cambridge: Cambridge University Press).

SELBY, HENRY A.
1974 *Zapotec Deviance: The Convergence of Folk and Modern Sociology* (Austin: University of Texas Press).

SHATZ, MARILYN AND R. GELMAN
1973 *The Development of Communication Skills: Modifications in the Speech of Young Children as a Function of Listener*, Monographs in Social Research and Child Development, vol. 38, no. 5.

SHIBLES, WARREN A.
1971a *An Analysis of Metaphor in Light of W. A. Urban's Theories* (The Hague: Mouton and Co.).

1971b *Metaphor: An Annotated Bibliography and History* (Whitewater, Wis.: Language Press).

SILVERSTEIN, MICHAEL
1972 "Linguistic Theory: Syntax, Semantics, Pragmatics," in *Annual Review of Anthropology*, ed. Bernard J. Siegel (Palo Alto, Calif.: Annual Reviews), 1:349–82.

SINCLAIR, JOHN McH. AND R. M. COULTHARD
1974 *Towards an Analysis of Discourse* (London: Oxford University Press).

SLOBIN, DANIEL I.
1973 "Cognitive Prerequisites for the Development of Grammar," in *Studies of Child Language Development*, ed. Charles A. Ferguson and Daniel Slobin (New York: Holt, Rinehart and Winston), pp. 175–208.

SPIRO, MELFORD E.
n.d. "Family and Kinship in Village Burma," unpublished manuscript.

SPITZER, LEO
1962 *Essays on English and American Literature* (Princeton: Princeton University Press).

References

SPRADLEY, JAMES P.
1971 *You Owe Yourself a Drunk: An Ethnography of Urban Nomads* (Boston: Little, Brown & Co.).

TANNER, NANCY
1972 "Speech and Society among the Indonesian Elite: A Case Study of a Multilingual Community," in *Sociolinguistics*, ed. J. B. Pride and J. Holmes (Middlesex, Eng.: Penguin Books), pp. 125–41.

TEETER, KARL V.
1970 "Review of Leonard Bloomfield's *The Menominee Language*," *Language* 46:524–33.

TRIANDIS, HARRY C.
1972 *The Analysis of Subjective Culture* (New York: John Wiley & Sons).

UHLENBECK, E. M.
1970 "The Use of Respect Forms in Javanese," in *Pacific Linguistic Studies in Honour of Arthur Capell*, ed. S. A. Wurm and D. C. Laycock (Canberra: Linguistic Circle of Canberra), pp. 441–66.

ULLMAN, STEPHEN
1962 *Semantics: An Introduction to the Science of Meaning* (New York: Barnes and Noble).

URBAN, WILBUR MARSHALL
1939 *Language and Reality* (London: George Allen and Unwin).

WALDRON, R. A.
1967 *Sense and Sense Development* (London: André Deutsch, the Language Library).

WATSON, JAMES
1968 *The Double Helix* (New York: Atheneum).

WEINREICH, URIEL
1964 *Languages in Contact: Findings and Problems* (The Hague: Mouton and Co.).
1966 "Explorations in Semantic Theory," in *Current Trends in Linguistics*, ed. Thomas A. Sebeok (The Hague: Mouton and Co.), 3:395–477.

WERNER, OSWALD
1970 "Cultural Knowledge, Language, and World View," in *Cognition: A Multiple View*, ed. Paul L. Garvin (New York: Spartan Press), pp. 155–76.
1972 "Ethnoscience 1972," in *Annual Review of Anthropology*, ed. Bernard J. Siegel (Palo Alto, Calif.: Annual Reviews), 1:271–308.

WHORF, BENJAMIN L.
1956 *Language, Thought and Reality: Selected Writings of Benjamin Lee Whorf*, ed. J. B. Carroll (Cambridge, Mass.: M.I.T. Press).

WITTGENSTEIN, LUDWIG
1963 *Philosophical Investigations*, 2d ed. (Oxford: Oxford University Press).

ZIMMERMAN, DON H. AND CANDY WEST
1973 "Conversational Order and Sexism: A Convergence of Theoretical and Substantive Problems," paper presented at the Linguistics Conference, California Polytechnic Institute, San Luis Obispo.

Index